Presidential Power
Theories and Dilemmas

Presidential Power
Theories and Dilemmas

JOHN P. BURKE
University of Vermont

**WESTVIEW
PRESS**

A Member of the Perseus Books Group

Westview Press was founded in 1975 in Boulder, Colorado, by notable publisher and intellectual Fred Praeger. Westview Press continues to publish scholarly titles and high-quality undergraduate- and graduate-level textbooks in core social science disciplines. With books developed, written, and edited with the needs of serious nonfiction readers, professors, and students in mind, Westview Press honors its long history of publishing books that matter.

Published by Westview Press,
A Member of the Perseus Books Group
2465 Central Avenue
Boulder, CO 80301
www.westviewpress.com

Every effort has been made to secure required permissions for all text, images, maps, and other art reprinted in this volume.

Westview Press books are available at special discounts for bulk purchases in the United States by corporations, institutions, and other organizations. For more information, please contact the Special Markets Department at the Perseus Books Group, 2300 Chestnut Street, Suite 200, Philadelphia, PA 19103, or call (800) 810-4145, ext. 5000, or e-mail special.markets@perseusbooks.com.

Set in 10.5-point Adobe Garamond Pro

Library of Congress Cataloging-in-Publication Data

Names: Burke, John P., 1953– author.
Title: Presidential power : theories and dilemmas / John P. Burke.
Description: Boulder, Colorado : Westview Press, 2016. | Includes
    bibliographical references and index.
Identifiers: LCCN 2015047728| ISBN 9780813349671 (paperback) | ISBN
    9780813350097 (e-book)
Subjects: LCSH: Presidents—United States. | Executive power—United States.
    | United States—Politics and government. | BISAC: POLITICAL SCIENCE /
    Government / Executive Branch. | POLITICAL SCIENCE / Government /
    General. | POLITICAL SCIENCE / Political Process / Leadership.
Classification: LCC JK516 .B788 2016 | DDC 352.23/50973—dc23
LC record available at http://lccn.loc.gov/2015047728

10 9 8 7 6 5 4 3 2 1

Contents

Illustrations

Preface

Understanding presidential power is central to understanding the American presidency and its place in politics. The nation looks to the president for direction on an ever-growing number of domestic and foreign policy issues and expects him or her to achieve results and make progress. Right or wrong, this is the political reality, and one that is unlikely to change in the near future. Given this, how can presidents effectively exercise power to achieve their goals while still remaining within the rightful bounds and limits of the office? This major dilemma has been—and will continue to be—one that presidents have grappled with, and it forms the heart of this book.

This book brings together in one volume what I believe are the major theories and dilemmas of presidential power. It interlaces a number of strands of my scholarly interests and my research that has spanned more than three decades. As a graduate student at Princeton, I had the good fortune to work with Fred I. Greenstein. His pursuit, on the basis of new archival evidence, of constructing a different understanding of Dwight D. Eisenhower's presidency fascinated me. Greenstein's research revealed a more nuanced leadership style, and it was a game changer: not only did it suggest a more successful Eisenhower presidency but it also differed markedly from conventional wisdom that assumed a president needed to be a hands-on, direct bargainer.

I was inspired to delve in, and one of my earliest publications examined Eisenhower's battle with Democrats in Congress over the federal budget in 1957. Leading presidential scholars of the period, such as Richard E. Neustadt, as well as contemporary observers often use the budget battle of 1957 as an example of Ike at his worst. My research not only depicted a more engaged Eisenhower but also demonstrated that he deployed a varied and more complex set of strategies to attain his policy goals.

My inquiry into the presidency and budget politics continued with the early Reagan presidency. Reagan enjoyed remarkable success during his first year in office, achieving significant budget cuts and tax reform, but he encountered resistance from Congress in subsequent years. In my view, the latter resulted from Reagan's lack of flexibility during the remainder of his first term. But at the time I noted two other factors. One was his successful deployment of direct public appeals to pressure Congress to follow his policy lead. Reagan was not the first president to use this tactic, but his communication skills and his ability to build public support served him very well in 1981. The second factor was Reagan's changing political fortunes after his first year. At the time, I had only a glimmer of understanding of the shifting political opportunities and challenges presidents face as they advance through their term or terms in office. Since then, I have developed a longtime interest in this area and have focused much of my research on presidents' transition to office, its effects on early presidential efforts, as well as the dynamics of the second term.

Political history has always fascinated me. In the early 1990s, I greatly benefited from working with Herbert Brownell in writing his memoirs. Brownell was Eisenhower's first attorney general and, before that, presidential candidate Thomas E. Dewey's chief political adviser. Herb was not only a delight to work with but also significantly enhanced my understanding of the politics of the time. Of all my scholarly efforts over the years, this one I most enjoyed and fondly recollect.

Writing this book has enabled me to bring together my scholarly work and gave me the opportunity to share with my colleagues how I have structured my presidency courses over the years. Many deserve thanks for making this book possible, but first and foremost I am indebted to students at the University of Vermont who took my courses on the American presidency: they provided me with continuous dialogue and feedback. I want to thank Craig Rimmerman for inviting me to submit a proposal for his Dilemmas in American Politics series for Westview Press. Initially, I did not think I had the time to write it, but he persevered. I especially want to thank Ada Fung, senior editor at Westview Press, for her astute guidance. Dear reader, she has saved you from much unneeded professorial verbiage. Well done, Ada! Sincere gratitude to the Westview Press team: Acquisitions Director Grace Fujimoto, Sales and Marketing Director Renee Malis, Senior Marketing Manager Victoria Henson, my project editor Carolyn Sobczak, and my copyeditor Christina Yeager.

I would also like to thank the many reviewers whose feedback helped make this book better, including Christopher Banks (Kent State University), Samuel Bassett (Lake Forest College), Meena Bose (Hofstra University), Matthew Dickinson (Middlebury College), Victoria Farrar-Myers (Southern Methodist University), Phillip Henderson (Catholic University), James Josefson (Bridgewater College), James Pfiffner (George Mason University), Adam Warber (Clemson University), and others who wish to remain anonymous. A special thanks also to my "aides-de-camp" in the Dean's office: Sally Bartlett, Lise Larose, and Molly Nilan.

Last, but certainly not least, I want to thank R. Stafford Johnson, my spouse, for putting up with me as I wrote this book. Stafford was ever patient and encouraging as I worked on it, all the while as I put in long hours serving as an associate dean of our College of Arts and Sciences.

John P. Burke

Introduction

Presidential Power and Its Dilemmas

This book examines the issues and theories of *presidential power,* that is, the ability of a president to attain political and policy goals. Examining presidential power is central to understanding the presidency, which is important because for better or worse, intentional or not, the American presidency has emerged as the central focus of our system of government. Starting in the twentieth century, especially since Franklin D. Roosevelt's presidency and his efforts to grapple with the Great Depression and World War II, we have turned to the presidency to solve national and international problems. What traditionally might have been regarded as largely local or state-level problems—or even matters of personal choice and responsibility—are seen today as presidential issues, calling for executive response and action. A few examples include the quality of education in local public schools, the costs of college and university education, gun violence and gun control, racial tensions in communities, health care, and environmental quality and conservation issues. If you are surprised that these were not always regarded as matters of clear presidential response and action, then that is all the more telling.

Policies that we take for granted today were not seen as presidential issues, much less the responsibility of the federal government, in eras past. Housing for the poor and the indigent? Until federal housing projects began in the 1930s under Roosevelt, the local "poorhouse" was the only option for those without housing. Financial support for retired seniors? Social Security started during FDR's second term, but before that retirement income was entirely the responsibility of individuals. This was the same case for medical care, though local charity hospitals were sometimes available to those who could not pay. For seniors, government-assisted medical care started to be seriously discussed only after World War II, during Harry Truman's presidency, and it took until 1965, during Lyndon Johnson's administration, for Medicare to become law. And before Dwight D. Eisenhower's successful effort in 1956 to create interstate highways, states and locales created their own turnpikes, parkways, or freeways, but often they were not connected. In each of these cases, the president took the initiative to bring these issues under federal jurisdiction.

Of course, not all public policy originates with the president; much can percolate through Congress on its own and become law. Although this book focuses on how presidents secure their policy ends and goals, Congress is still obviously central to attaining presidential initiatives, especially if legislation is required, and the president must convince Congress to take action. How do presidents influence Congress? Is it just through traditional, direct bargaining? What about alternative strategies such as approaching Congress indirectly through third parties or using presidential appeals to the public to exert pressure on their congressional representatives? Presidents also often attempt to achieve their ends acting on their own through a variety of executive actions such as executive orders, proclamations, and declarations. This invites certain questions of power: Does the president legitimately possess those powers? Is the president powerful enough to successfully assert these claims? Congress plays a role here as well in recognizing, and often legislatively authorizing, presidential claims to power but also sometimes denying them. Given this, presidents often exercise caution with executive actions when Congress is assertive and act bolder when it is not.

And as we shall explore in Chapter 3, the Supreme Court has had final say on a number of important constitutional issues in this area. Sometimes the president wins, and at other times the president loses. These tactics are all part of the presidential power toolkit, and as we shall explore throughout this book, presidents often need to employ some combination of these methods to achieve their goals. Depending on the situation and the context, some work better than others.

A DIGRESSION BACK IN TIME:
EARLY AND ENDURING DILEMMAS

To begin framing our analysis of the issues and challenges concerning presidential power and its dilemmas, let us go back in time to a president of a different era,

Rutherford B. Hayes. He served as the nineteenth president from 1877 to early 1881, and he kept extensive diaries of his life. On March 18, 1878, he records a typical day as president:

> I rise at about 7 a.m.; write until breakfast, about 8:30 a.m. After breakfast, prayers—i.e., the reading of a chapter in the Bible, each one present reading a verse in turn, and all kneeling repeat the Lord's Prayer; then, usually, [I] write and arrange business until 10 a.m. From 10 to 12 in the Cabinet Room, the Members of Congress having the preference of all visitors except Cabinet ministers. Callers "to pay respects" are usually permitted to come in to shake hands whenever the number reaches about a half dozen waiting. Twelve to 2 p.m., on Tuesdays and Fridays, are Cabinet hours. On other days that time is given to miscellaneous business callers. At 2 p.m., lunch. I commonly invite to that— cup of tea and biscuit and butter with cold meat—any gentleman I wish to have more conference with than is practicable in hours given to miscellaneous business. After lunch the correspondence of the day, well briefed, and each letter in an envelope, is examined. By this time it is 3:30 p.m., and I then drive an hour and a half. Returning I glance over the business and correspondence again, take a fifteen or twenty minutes' nap, and get ready to dine at 6 p.m.[1]

There are a number of revealing items here. The president's cabinet mattered more than it does today, and Hayes met with them regularly as a group. Members of Congress might stop by to visit, but these calls were not necessarily scheduled. The White House at the time was an open, public building. As Hayes notes, "presentable" folks could actually enter and "pay respects" to the president. Most notably, the president's day ended at three thirty in the afternoon, much earlier than it does today, and dinner followed promptly at six o'clock. (No alcohol was served, by the way, in the Hayes White House. A popular nickname for his wife was "Lemonade Lucy," and the joke at the time was that at a Hayes White House formal dinner water flowed like wine.) Hayes was hardly overburdened by his official duties. Sunday was even more leisurely: "I have gone to church at least once every Sunday since I became President. Sunday after lunch I ride regularly with Secretary [of Treasury John] Sherman two to three hours. We talk over affairs and visit the finest drives and scenes near Washington."[2]

The most important takeaway is that things have changed considerably since Hayes's day. The contemporary presidency looks much different. For example, today's Congress members do not simply "drop by" or visit unless scheduled. Meetings of the full cabinet are rare, and good luck to citizens who want to enter the White House and pay their respects to the president. There is no mention in Hayes's diary of the press, of presidential speeches and travel, or of the White House staff. In fact the latter was quite small, fewer than ten in number. Hayes's long-time friend William King Rogers and then the president's own son, Webb Hayes, each served as personal secretary to the president (what was then the chief of staff position). But it was a vastly different job compared to that of the president's chief aides today. Neither was a substantive policy or strategic political adviser. They provided familiar comfort to Hayes, organized his letters and correspondence, took notes at meetings, and arranged his schedule. Today, the White House staff numbers over twenty-five hundred (and this is a conservative estimate).

However—and this is a very important point—Hayes still had to reckon with a core dilemma of presidential power: how to exert influence and work with the other two branches of government to achieve his legislative agenda. High on his list were returning the former states of the Confederacy to home rule while preserving the rights of African Americans and encouraging civil service reform. He often vetoed legislation, especially attempts to weaken the gold standard, to curtail federal monitoring of elections in the South, and to remove the federal government's power to deal with the Ku Klux Klan. Hayes used his executive powers to send troops to stop a national railroad strike and to pursue Mexican bandits across the border. He also issued an executive order that prevented federal employees from being required to make campaign contributions. Although not the broad agenda of a contemporary president, Hayes still needed to exert power and influence to achieve his goals. In this, Hayes struggled: his civil rights policies and efforts at civil service reform met with great resistance.

Hayes also serves as an example of the impact of political and historical context on a president's power, an issue we explore in this book. In Hayes's case, as a Republican, he had to deal with a Democratic majority in the House. This was not the progressive Democratic Party of today. Rather, it was a party that gained control of the House as southern states returned to home rule and white southerners, opposed to post–Civil War Reconstruction and civil rights for African Americans, rose to political power once again. Hayes did not always have an easy time with his own party either. The Republican Party's old guard, the "Stalwart" wing, clung to political patronage and fought against Hayes's efforts for civil service reform. In addition, Hayes was president during an era of congressional dominance, and his position was somewhat weakened because of this. Moreover, it was an era when party leaders and political bosses essentially determined the party's candidate for the presidency.

Hayes's presidency also helps illustrate the issue I refer to as the "internal time" of the presidency. What are the opportunities and constraints on power in each year of a president's first term? And what about the remaining four if there is a second term? Hayes became president in 1876 after a contested election, one in which he lost the popular vote but won the Electoral College by one vote after an improvised commission awarded him electoral votes in several southern states. It was not unlike the Bush-Gore election in 2000 but more weakening to the president in the way that it was resolved. Hayes's opponents quickly labeled him "President Rutherfraud" and "His Fraudulency." He also pledged not to run for reelection. Neither was helpful to Hayes's attempts to exercise presidential power during his time in office.

GREATER EXPECTATIONS MAGNIFY
THE DILEMMAS OF PRESIDENTIAL POWER

If Hayes encountered difficulty and often considerable opposition in achieving his goals, think about the situation contemporary presidents face. The presidency has more of an impact on policy; the reach of policy initiatives is substantially broader; the daily activity of the White House is much more frenetic; and the twenty-four-hour media cycle (and Internet) is ever watchful. The role of the president and our expectations of the presidency have grown and heightened over time.

We now expect the president to be the chief proposer of domestic policies in response to the issues of the day. This ranges across a number of policy domains that would have been unfathomable not only to Hayes but also to a later president such as Franklin D. Roosevelt, including mandated health care, immigration reform, gay and lesbian rights, climate change, abortion policy, and gun control regulations, to list but a few. We also expect the president to be the guardian of our economic well-being. If there is a recession, if inflation and unemployment rates rise, or if stock markets drift downward, we turn to the White House for action.

In terms of foreign affairs, we expect the president to immediately have a strategy for dealing with any international crisis that develops. Should American force be needed, we expect the president to be a skilled commander in chief who is knowledgeable about military affairs and adept at crafting a successful response (hopefully one with a quick resolution). We expect the president to also manage crises in the domestic arena. If a school shooting occurs, we expect the president to address it and to propose remedies to minimize chances of it happening again. If a hurricane or a flood strikes, we expect an appropriate presidential response and immediate action. We expect the president to always be a skilled public communicator, one who is never caught off guard, always reassuring at times of crisis but also able to contextualize the issues and put forth the right policy initiatives. We shall explore the demands of this "public presidency" also in this book.

Finally, in the aftermath of September 11 and during the continuing war on terror, we expect the president to be ever vigilant in protecting homeland security and to take steps against those who threaten it. This is a relatively new presidential assignment and perhaps the most difficult of all. There is some history here in terms of presidents claiming inherent national security powers, and as we shall explore, the Supreme Court has ruled in a number of cases that presidents can go only so far with those claims. And as recent presidents have also experienced, excessive claims to power and the actions stemming from such claims can sometimes boomerang and hurt them.

All of these expectations can be summed up as our desire for the president to be a successful head of government. But there is an added major assignment. We also expect the president to be a successful head of state, respected by other world leaders, and the symbol and spokesperson of America's role in world affairs. In many political systems, these two roles are separated: the latter is represented by a monarch or a president, and the former by a prime minister or chancellor. This is how it is done in most of Europe, Russia, Japan, India, Israel, and Iraq, to name but a few. In the United States, both roles are filled by one person. Pardon the pun, but this is surely a "heady"—and difficult—assignment. In short, for contemporary presidents, the scope of power is vastly different and more challenging than ever. Thus, the enduring dilemmas of presidential power even from the days of Rutherford B. Hayes, including how to work with the other two branches to achieve presidential goals and how to contend with the specific challenges presented by political and historical context, are magnified for contemporary presidents. With ever-growing expectations for leadership in a greater number of areas, it is imperative for contemporary presidents to utilize every tool of presidential power available to them, from bargaining and public appeals to executive actions, to achieve a successful presidency.

PLAN OF THE BOOK

So, what should presidents do to manage and resolve the public's expectations and the power they must wield to accomplish their goals? There are no easy, simple answers. However, broad lessons and conclusions about presidential power, based upon practical, presidential experience as well as scholarly insight, can be drawn. The job description for contemporary presidents has expanded significantly since the days of the Framers of our Constitution, but presidents are still constrained by the blueprint of "separate but shared powers" as laid out in the Constitution. In this book, I examine the various tools of power available to presidents and the historical and political circumstances in which they must exercise power, hopefully in an understandable way for readers who are learning about the presidency.

Chapter 1 begins with the creation of the presidency during the Constitutional Convention of 1787, laying the foundation for the book's discussions of why the issue of presidential power is so crucial. The chapter is called "The Madisonian Dilemma" to reflect James Madison's key role at the convention, which earned him the title of "architect of the Constitution." Madison believed that although a national executive was needed, "checks" on too much executive power were also required. His solution was that each branch of the federal government should share in some of the powers of the others, contesting for power and thus preventing any one branch from becoming too dominant. Unfortunately, there was little guidance in how that contest might be properly resolved. Nor, I might add, was there much anticipation that, in future times, we might expect more leadership on the president's part and thus more empowerment, not less. Control rather than empowerment is embedded in Madison's constitutional legacy, and that is the crux of the major dilemma of presidential power. This chapter also explores how George Washington immediately had to create a new presidency when he took office but with imperfect guidance in Article II (which directly addresses the presidency) to rely upon. It also explores the quick rise of political parties, and how that put a major wrench in the Framers' ideas on how selection of a president should work and how Congress and the presidency should operate and interact.

Chapter 2, "Neustadt and the Modern Conception of Presidential Power," moves us forward into the modern presidency and introduces what remains one of the most important works on this topic: Richard E. Neustadt's classic,

Presidential Power: The Politics of Leadership. The first edition was published in 1960, followed by several others and with the final one covering the Reagan presidency. This chapter explicates and unpacks Neustadt's work and explores some of its difficulties and challenges. However, we also begin to examine alternatives to Neustadt's theory. Although his point about recognizing that power is at stake and exercising influence through bargaining remains important, the process of attaining presidential goals is a complex one. And as we shall see, there are other paths to attaining presidential ends beyond what Neustadt lays out.

In Chapter 3, "The Executive's Prerogative: Inherent Constitutional Powers," we explore why the exercise of constitutional powers remains important to presidents. Neustadt argues that use of constitutional "commands" does not do a president much good and that presidents who just stick to the Constitution are mere "clerks." However, the issue is more complex: because much is left unstated in the Constitution, it requires interpretation. In particular, this chapter focuses on what has been termed the exercise of a president's inherent and prerogative powers—those not clearly given to the president, but those that might be interpreted as present in the office based on several clauses in Article II. Such powers were anticipated but left broadly undetermined by the Framers of the Constitution, and today they have become a key part of post-9/11 executive action. Using presidential prerogative, Neustadt's "clerks" can still claim great power, depending on the circumstances. At the same time, we must bear in mind that this is contested terrain. Although the Supreme Court is often reluctant to intervene in cases involving the powers of the other two branches, it does so on occasion. We shall explore the major patterns in the court's reasoning, in its jurisprudence, in these cases, because this is important to understanding the dilemmas in the exercise of the president's prerogative. Finally, we shall examine how claims—and often the exercise—of inherent powers became increasingly important for both Presidents George W. Bush and Barack Obama in the post-9/11 era.

Chapter 4, "Going Public and Presidential Power," focuses on public appeals and public support as a source of power. For Neustadt, what he calls "public prestige" is an ancillary resource, something that is only useful in bolstering bargaining power. However, though Neustadt may be correct about its impact on bargaining, his conception of the impact of public appeals may be too limited. In this chapter, we explore the idea that direct appeals to the public for support are often seen by presidents as a tool of power in its own right. A number of scholars, Samuel Kernell most notably, have argued that going public is now a central component of presidential power. Others, such as George C. Edwards III, have argued that it is overrated: little public opinion is actually moved and politically activated by presidential appeals. Presidents may not positively profit as much as they might think from going public. Finally, this chapter looks at how the ever-changing media pose significant challenges to presidents. In short, presidents must go public in ways that recognize the media technology of the times—they suffer when they don't.

In Chapter 5, "Presidential Power and Historical Time, Variously Interpreted," we discuss the historical factors that might affect the exercise and analysis of presidential power. The point in time a president occupies office may present both challenges and opportunities that are different had he or she become president earlier or later. As we shall see, scholars differ on the historical factors that most affect the successes or failures of a presidency. Is it the broader political regime or political coalition in which presidents finds themselves located, as Stephen Skowronek argues? Others argue that the interjection of new policy ideas, shifts in political ideology, or swings in public mood are of greater significance, and we consider all of these forms of historical change in this chapter. Furthermore, we examine whether and how presidents are able to understand the historical place they occupy. Can they understand the specific opportunities and challenges facing them and take appropriate steps during their time in office? Or is historical context simply something that helps us form a fuller understanding of a president's exercise of power as we study it in hindsight?

In Chapter 6, we turn inward and consider the internal rhythms of a president's first (and sometimes only) term. In short, we consider how the individual years of a term matter in different ways, and the different challenges presidents face in each year. This chapter begins with what we have learned as presidential scholars about the changing power situation within a presidential term—for example, that successful transitions greatly matter. It is crucial for presidents to use their transition periods to get personnel in place, organize the White House staff, and develop an early set of policy initiatives. Failure here likely proves problematic, whereas success bolsters presidential power. The remainder of the first term presents other challenges. Almost every president is dealt a blow when the first midterm congressional elections occur. After that, opportunities to secure proposals might surface in the pipeline, but they are often diminished by a decline in congressional support. And not long after the midterms, attention shifts to reelection.

Chapter 7 focuses on the internal rhythms of the second term, when presidents often seem to be especially bedeviled and politically weakened. This chapter explores some of those dynamics and how they differ from aspects of the first term. Recent reelections have been largely won based on the challenger's shortcomings, not the positive presentation of a prospective agenda. Given this, how do presidents build support for a second-term agenda? Most presidents suffer from a "sixth-year itch" on the part of the electorate, and party support in Congress suffers; thus, many have turned to foreign policy to secure their legacy in the second term. Has this worked? The question of presidential power in the second term is further complicated by the almost certain loss of congressional seats in the midterm and by waning focus on the president's agenda during the final two years of the second term as attention quickly turns to the election of a successor.

It is clear, even from this introduction, that contemporary presidents face a great number of tasks and challenges and that there are no easy answers or simple theories on how to best exercise presidential power. Given all they face, presidents today cannot rely on a single method of exercising power, nor can they ignore how historical context and the internal rhythms of their first and second terms can influence their presidencies. In the book's conclusion, I attempt to deduce broad lessons based on what we have learned of the benefits and limitations of each tool of power as well as what we have come to understand about the opportunities and challenges of historical time and internal time. I lay out a blueprint for how contemporary presidents might exercise power to address problems and achieve their goals.

NOTES

1. Charles R. Williams, ed., *The Diary and Letters of Rutherford B. Hayes, Nineteenth President of the United States,* vol. 3 (Columbus: Ohio State Archeological and Historical Society, 1922), 469, http://apps.ohiohistory.org/hayes/browse/chapterxxxvi.html.
2. Ibid.

1

The Madisonian Dilemma

The major challenges and questions of presidential power, including the core dilemma of how presidents might negotiate with the legislative branch of government to achieve their goals, are sewn into the constitutional history and design of the American republic. One simple contributing factor is the long historical existence of the US Constitution. Although amended from time to time, it has been in effect for over 225 years, arguably making it the oldest national constitution (some claim that the Republic of San Marino's *Statuti* of 1600 predates it). To put this in perspective, one study found that the median life of other national constitutions was a mere nineteen years.[1]

Back in 1787, the *Framers,* the group of delegates who drafted the Constitution, could anticipate neither the scope of power that the federal government would exercise over time nor the role that the president would assume within the American political system. They were clearly bound by the historical period within which they deliberated. How could they have known what American government and politics might be like in a hundred, two hundred, or two hundred fifty years? That there would be a constitutional, much less political, debate over government-mandated health care would have been foreign to them. Constitutional concerns about laws prohibiting marriage of same-sex couples would have been incomprehensible to the Framers. These concerns are more recent, but earlier questions regarding such issues as the federal government's ability to establish a national bank to stabilize economic transactions or its power to desegregate local public schools would have also been beyond the Framers' scope.

Explicit questions about presidential powers have also cropped up such as whether the president has the power to prevent corporations from selling arms abroad to nations involved in military conflict and whether the president possesses the power to appoint officials when the Senate is in recess. As for war powers, the Framers thought they had solved that issue by granting Congress the power to declare war. However, on only five occasions have these constitutional provisions been clearly followed: the War of 1812 against Britain, the Mexican-American War of 1846, the Spanish-American War at the end of the nineteenth century, World War I, and World War II. Korea, Vietnam, Afghanistan, and Iraq were not formally "declared wars." Other presidential powers, legislative actions, and national commitments were invoked to justify those wars—and they were wars.

After September 11, 2001, the nature of war changed. We are now engaged in an ongoing war on terror with an enemy that is not clearly another nation-state. What is proper conduct in this war? What rights do enemy combatants possess? Is it permissible for the federal government to engage in broad surveillance of *domestic* telephone traffic, in the name of protecting homeland security? These are vexing questions that we have little past experience to draw upon, and they are surely ones that the Framers did not anticipate. However, although the work of the Framers in crafting *Article II* of the Constitution, which focuses on the presidency, has created dilemmas and questions, it has not failed to provide a working framework for the exercise of presidential power—emphasis on "working." Article II has been reinterpreted and amended, pointing to the complicated nature of presidential power. It is not a static blueprint for presidential success, nor should it be.

Another major source of the dilemmas of presidential power stems from the way our Constitution structures power at the national level. The United States operates within a republican form of government in which executive power is counterbalanced with legislative power and judicial influence (if not, at times, intervention). This is not unusual. What is more unique to our experience are the particular ways in which each branch is not the exclusive master of its own domain of power. Each branch, to varying degrees, participates in the exercise of the powers and authority of the other branches. This system of *separate but shared powers* is part of James Madison's genius in our constitutional design. All national executives—whether prime ministers, premiers, or presidents—struggle for power with their respective national legislatures. But because shared power is constitutionally mandated under the American system, that struggle can often be more complex and challenging.

A final factor is the length of the US Constitution. It is, to date, one of the shortest at about 4,400 words. India's, by contrast, is one of the longest with over 117,000 words. This is not just an interesting factoid; it has implications for power. The longer a constitution, the more governmental power is delineated and made clear. Questions regarding executive power still exist, but likely there are fewer of them. The brevity of the American constitution means that much remains subject to interpretation, and that, by extension, means presidential power is more contestable and, of course, more problematic.

We begin the chapter by examining the Constitutional Convention of 1787, during which the delegates engaged in their lengthy deliberations about the composition, powers, and selection process for a new national executive. We also explore the debates about the merits of the new Constitution, especially focusing on the presidency, during its ratification. Both the discussions during the convention and during the Constitution's ratification are crucial to understanding why the dilemmas and challenges of presidential power are deeply imbedded in the American political system. They are also useful in examining the issue of whether a broader set of shared intentions among the Framers can be discerned, intentions that could be useful in guiding proper constitutional interpretation of the office and its powers today. We then take a look at George Washington's efforts to put the words of Article II into practice, which had a major impact on the office. Finally, we examine the quick emergence of political parties and changes in the election process that were in marked contrast to what the Framers envisioned, developments that further deepened the dilemmas of power for American presidents.

LESSONS LEARNED FROM THE
ARTICLES OF CONFEDERATION

We must turn to history to understand why examining and establishing guidelines for the exercise of governmental power, and thus presidential power, figured so substantially in the Framers' deliberations during the Constitutional Convention and the ratification of the Constitution. Colonial government under Britain provided one set of lessons on power, especially the tensions that resulted from the strong authority of royal governors. However, the lessons of national government under the Articles of Confederation had an especially strong impact on the Framers—its weaknesses set the stage for issues they needed to address.

After the Revolutionary War against Britain, the United States did not immediately adopt our present Constitution. Instead, the states adopted a loose confederation from 1781 until 1789, when the Constitution was fully ratified. The *Articles of Confederation* established a "perpetual union" of the states, but it was a weak confederacy at best and more of a "firm league of friendship" among the states, as its own Article II states. Distrust of national power was strong: it took from November 1777, when it first passed Congress, until March 1781, when it achieved final ratification by the states, for even this weak national government to be formally adopted.

One of the primary defects of the Articles of Confederation was that it lacked a chief executive. The "president" was simply the presiding officer of the Congress (of which there were eleven; the first was Samuel Huntington of Connecticut, and the last was Cyrus Griffin of Virginia). However, the absence of an executive or executive branch was not the only defect. Although a unicameral Congress existed, it was weak. Members did not vote as individuals but by state bloc. Each state was allotted one vote, regardless of differences in population. Members were annually appointed by their state legislature and were subject to immediate recall should their home state deem it appropriate. In addition, no member could serve for more than three years over a six-year period (term limits are not a new idea). Congress's structure under the Articles channeled the members toward state rather than national interest.

Legislation was difficult to enact because passage required 9 of 13 votes. This was a steep barrier—a supermajority that far surpasses the 60 votes needed to avoid filibuster and gain approval in the Senate today. Had the same rules remained in effect, a bill today would need 70 votes in the Senate and 301 votes in the House to pass. Even when passage was secured, Congress had little power of direct enforcement. Carrying out legislation depended on the good graces of each individual state to enforce Congress's will.

By deliberate design, political power under the Articles almost exclusively rested in the individual states. Per the Articles of Confederation, "Each state retains its sovereignty, freedom, and independence, and every power, jurisdiction, and right, which is not by this Confederation expressly delegated to the United States in Congress assembled." What little political power present at the national level was further constrained by the federal government established by the Articles, which yielded a weakened nation. Congress had no direct power to levy taxes, although it could make "requests" for funds from the states. As a result, revenue was hard to come by and there was little financial ability to pursue broader national projects. The federal government could not regulate interstate commerce, which led to disastrous results such as tariff wars between states. The absence of an executive weakened national unity and undermined our effectiveness in foreign affairs. Imagine if today there was no president to take immediate charge of national security but just the presiding officer of Congress. In addition, there was no real bureaucracy. Committees of the Continental Congress directly superintended the limited programmatic powers at the national level. The one major exception to this pattern occurred in 1781 when a very small Department of Foreign Affairs was established.[2]

Concern over the effectiveness of the Articles began to mount. By 1785, James Madison and George Washington were exchanging letters regarding problems with the Articles and the need for a stronger national government. In September 1786, James Monroe wrote to Madison that the lack of sufficient revenue "endangers the govt" and "will most probably induce a change of some kind."[3] That same month, twelve delegates (including Madison and Alexander Hamilton) from five states met in Annapolis, Maryland, to discuss the ongoing problems of trade and commerce and the inability of the federal government to raise sufficient revenue. This "Meeting of the Commissioners to Remedy Defects of the Federal Government" made no immediate proposals for reform; too few states were represented. However, under Hamilton's leadership, it did propose to Congress a further meeting to be held the next year in Philadelphia. On February 21, 1787, Congress voted in favor of a meeting to consider revising the Articles.

However, the idea of implementing even limited revisions to the Articles raised concerns in some quarters. In August 1786, Congress rejected a plan to give the federal government better means of collecting revenue from the states and enhanced powers in the areas of trade and commerce. The less populated states, favored under the Articles because they were equal to more populous states, had reservations about any changes that might alter the balance of political power among the states. Rhode Island refused to send delegates to the Philadelphia meeting. Delaware sent delegates but explicitly prohibited them from making any revisions in the Articles that would lessen the voting equality among the states.

THE CONSTITUTIONAL CONVENTION: CRAFTING A NEW NATIONAL EXECUTIVE

Determining what transpired during the convention over the summer of 1787 is not an easy task. One of the early actions of the delegates was to pass a motion binding them to secrecy: members were explicitly instructed that "Nothing spoken in the House be printed, or otherwise published or communicated without leave."[4] William Jackson was appointed secretary to the convention and was charged with keeping a journal of the proceedings. Congress ordered its publication in 1818, but the journal's content proves disappointing. It largely consists of records of votes on various resolutions, with little narrative about debate among the members. A better source, and certainly the most authoritative, is the notes that James Madison carefully kept of the proceedings. Although they are meticulous and present a flavor of the debate, they are not by any means a transcript of the proceedings and were revised by him over many decades.[5] Moreover, Madison did not publish them during his lifetime; they appeared in print only in 1840, four years after his death. He was the last surviving member of the convention; no one else was alive to question what he had recorded. Other delegates also kept notes, although none as extensive as Madison's.[6] It is important to explore the delegates' deliberations and discussions in depth, because they have contributed much to our understanding of the meaning and the importance of the constitutional document.

Monday, May 14, 1787, was the official first day of the convention, but it actually took until May 25 for seven states to be represented and for official business to commence. The first order of business was to select a presiding officer. Robert Morris of Pennsylvania proposed George Washington for that esteemed position, and Washington was then selected without opposition or even debate. A committee was also appointed to come up with rules of procedure, which were presented and debated the next day. One rule is of particular interest for our purposes: "When the House shall adjourn, every member shall stand in his place, until the President pass him."[7] Another important rule governed how the delegates would cast votes. They did not vote as individuals; rather, each state delegation was given one vote, and the delegates of each state would vote individually to determine how their state's one vote might be cast. In many instances over the summer of 1787, state delegations were evenly divided.

The Virginia Plan: Shared Powers, Veto, and Impeachment

On Tuesday, May 29, 1787, during the first full week of deliberations, Virginia's governor, Edmund Randolph, presented what came to be known as the *Virginia Plan*. It made clear that significant change in the Articles, if not a wholesale departure from them, was in the mind of at least some delegates. The plan, which had been crafted by Madison, proposed a stronger federal structure rather than a loose confederacy of the states. Madison was its architect, but the job of introducing it to the convention fell to the more senior Randolph. That Madison apparently had a high-pitched voice and was short in stature (five-foot-three by some accounts) may also have been factors.

The plan was not fully fleshed out. It envisioned a National Legislature that would consist of two deliberative bodies but did not specify the length of term for its members. This was also the case for the plan's National Executive, although it did specify that members would be ineligible for a second term. More importantly, the plan did not answer the crucial question of how the executive was to be constituted: Was this one individual or a committee of persons? Madison's notes of the convention refer to the executive as "it," not he or they. But an executive was clearly envisioned: it would possess "general authority to execute the National law" and "ought to enjoy the Executive rights vested in Congress by the Confederation."[8] This proposal was clearly a marked departure from the exclusively legislative structure of the federal government under the Articles.

Important features of the Virginia Plan differed substantially from the final version of the Constitution. For example, the plan specified that the "first branch" of Congress was to be elected by the people, while the "second branch" was to be selected by the first branch from a list of nominees produced by the state legislatures. Notably, the executive was "to be chosen by the National Legislature," presumably both branches, but further particulars are not set out. The plan envisioned a national legislature whose seats were apportioned according to "quotas of contribution, or to the number of free inhabitants."[9] This would mean that wealthier, more populated states would have advantages within Congress as well as in the selection of an executive—a departure from state equality under the Articles.

However, the core of the Virginia Plan was classic Madison, and in it we begin to see some similarities to the Constitution—and the dilemmas for presidential power that it embodies. Three branches of government were clearly delineated—an executive, a judiciary, and the existing legislative—a fundamental change from the Articles of Confederation. But, more importantly, the plan contained elements of Madison's theory of separate but shared powers. Madison felt that this idea was central to a republican government and fundamental to how governmental power might be controlled and its abuses contained. For example, the Virginia Plan specified that legislative power was not vested solely in the National

Legislature but was subject to veto by a "council of revision" to consist of "the executive and a convenient number of National Judiciary."[10] Executive power was constrained by the ability of the National Judiciary (today's Supreme Court) to remove the president from office. These particular checks did not survive over the summer of 1787, but the general idea that each branch needed to check the other branches remained.

Through revisions to the Virginia Plan, the removal process for a dissolute president fell to Congress with the House voting on articles of impeachment and the Senate acting as the body of final judgment and "conviction." The role of the judicial branch in impeachment remained only to the extent that the chief justice presides over the Senate trial. In terms of the veto, that power was altered in the next stage of the convention's deliberations, when it assembled as a "Committee of the Whole on the State of the Union" (Committee of the Whole, for short) to consider the Virginia Plan and various others plans from May 30 until June 13. Veto power was vested in the president alone, but Congress had the ability to override the veto by a two-thirds majority in each house.

We can wonder how American politics might have worked out had some of these initial proposals from the Virginia Plan been adopted. The plan clearly envisioned something akin to a parliamentary system in its proposal to give the legislative branch the power to select the president. Would this have strengthened the connections between the president and Congress in ways that might have better facilitated the creation of a jointly acceptable legislative agenda and better smoothed its passage? Or would it have weakened the presidency and made it a mere creature or instrument of Congress? The prospect of the latter concerned many of the delegates. Consensus about the precise means for selecting the president and about the involvement of other branches in executive powers proved difficult to achieve.

Although no American president has been impeached by the House and then forced to leave office after conviction by the Senate, it is interesting to speculate what that removal process might have looked like had it been in the hands of the Supreme Court rather than Congress. Both Andrew Johnson and Bill Clinton were impeached by the House and faced trial by the Senate; Johnson escaped removal by just one vote, whereas Clinton avoided removal by a wider margin. In Richard Nixon's case, the Judiciary Committee of the House voted in favor of articles of impeachment. However, Nixon resigned his presidency before a vote of the full House took place. What would have been the fate of these presidents (and perhaps others) had the Supreme Court been the sole determiner concerning removal from office? We cannot be sure, but it seems likely the members of the court would more strongly hew to constitutional and legal analysis of the case. Similarly for the veto, strong participation by members of the Supreme Court would likely have made its exercise determined by constitutional standards rather than just on the basis of policy disagreement. Interestingly, the former—a veto based only on constitutional objections to legislation—was the practice among early presidents. It was not until Andrew Jackson's presidency that the veto was exercised on the basis of policy or political objections.

A Single Executive?

One of the most important issues concerning presidential power was handled quickly at the outset. On June 1, the day after the convention gathered as a Committee of the Whole to discuss the Virginia Plan, the composition of the executive came up for debate. Pennsylvania's James Wilson proposed that the National Executive should consist of a single person. Madison noted that there was "a considerable pause" after the motion was seconded.[11] This was a major moment in the constitutional history of the American presidency, and likely an important signal for the delegates that they were not simply remedying defects in the Articles but moving to a very different plan of constitutional government.

Roger Sherman of Connecticut and Randolph of Virginia raised strong objections to a single person holding the position. In Sherman's view, the executive was "nothing more than an institution for carrying the will of the Legislature into effect, that the person or persons ought to be appointed and accountable to the Legislature only."[12] He believed that because members of the legislature were best suited to determine the work done by the executive department, they should decide the number of people appointed to do it. Sherman also believed that the number in the executive should not be fixed: "the legislature should be at liberty to appoint one or more as experience might dictate."[13] Randolph was more direct: in his view, a single person holding the position was the "foetus [*sic*] of monarchy."[14] Wilson countered strongly that unity in the executive would give the "most energy, dispatch and responsibility to the office" and that a single executive would be "the best safeguard against tyranny."[15] However, no vote was taken on this issue. Instead, Madison voiced concern that it might be best to examine the powers of the executive before deciding on a single or plural executive.

On June 4, the issue returned to the floor. Wilson argued strongly in favor of a single person, emphasizing tranquility in addition to unity. With multiple executives, Wilson "foresaw nothing but uncontrouled [sic], continued, & violent animosities."[16] Sherman again raised objections, noting that in the states there were councils to provide advice to governors and restrain their actions. Wilson prevailed in the end; only New York, Delaware, and Maryland voted against a single executive. Washington and Madison, most notably, were in favor. And while Randolph was opposed, Virginia's one vote went in favor of a single executive.

The issue came up again after the *New Jersey Plan,* originated by William Paterson of New Jersey, was presented in mid-June. This plan was closer to the Articles and favored the less populated states: each state had equal representation in Congress, which remained unicameral. It also proposed a plural executive. Wilson rose once again to defend a single executive on June 16: "In order to controul [sic] the Legislative authority, you must divide it. In order to control the Executive you must unite it. One man will be more responsible than three. Three will contend among themselves till one becomes the master of his colleagues."[17]

The New Jersey Plan had several other interesting features, including assigning the responsibility of removing a president from office to state governors. Although it was in agreement with the Virginia Plan that the legislature should select the executive, its specification of equal representation for each state would have led to a different electoral dynamic. Imagine if today Vermont or Wyoming had equal say as California, New York, or Texas in determining who would become president.

Further Deliberations on the Veto

June 4 also proved an interesting day for presidential power because the convention took up discussion of the veto. Madison's notes on this are extensive, with many speakers bolstering their points with reference to historical examples, particularly the practices of various European monarchs. Speakers debated how this power might be exercised, the frequency with which it might be exercised, and especially problems in its abuse such as the possibility of suspending laws. In the end, the convention members agreed to remove the court from the equation, to permit the president to veto alone, but to give Congress the power to override a presidential veto with a two-thirds majority in both the House and the Senate.

One of Wilson's points in the debate is of particular interest. He astutely pointed out that the *possibility* of a veto (what we now call the "veto threat") could be as powerful as the exercise of the veto itself. Wilson believed that the veto would be used sparingly because "the Legislature would know that such a power existed, and would refrain from such laws, as it would be sure to defeat. Its silent operation would therefore preserve harmony and prevent mischief."[18] This was a prescient insight into future presidential strategy.

How do these developments factor into the Framers' conception of presidential power? Overall, deliberations over the veto focused more on the degree and severity of executive abuse and less on it as a check on legislative error or incompetence. This is not unexpected—historically, the executive was viewed with more suspicion than the parliament. Tension between monarchs and emerging legislative bodies in Europe was well known to the delegates. Convention delegates were particularly concerned about prerogative powers to block legislation—self-proclaimed by kings as inherent to their office. For our purposes, this slice of constitutional debate is important because it reveals what might have been a common mind-set among the Framers. For them, the lesson of recent history was one of the abuse of power by the executive or monarch, not legislative or parliamentary recalcitrance. And so, their goal was to check that executive abuse. The problem is that the historical context has changed. Abuse of power remains relevant, but as the scope of government has broadened beyond anything that the Framers could envision, lack of effective presidential power now must also be factored in.

Deliberations over Other Issues Affect the Presidency

The delegates worked earnestly until July 26. They did not proceed systematically article by article through the present Constitution; rather, they moved from one topic to another. Progress in one area would then loop back to discussion of another, especially if the former might affect the latter and vice versa.

Debate over the composition of Congress was the major topic of discussion in June and July. States differed in population, economy, and wealth—all important factors in determining the degree to which the delegates were prepared to move beyond the one state, one vote formula of the Articles of Confederation. If size and composition of the "first branch" (today's House of Representatives) reflected population, as their discussions increasingly indicated it would, then the power of the "lesser" states would decrease. Delegates' views on this question generally reflected the interests of the state they represented. Many had served in the Continental Congress, as well as their own state legislatures, so they knew that real political power was at stake. There was also considerable debate about how to calculate the relevant population of each state. Should slaves be included? What about immigrants? The notion of citizenship in the United States or in any individual state was not always clear. In a number of states only "freeholders," those owning physical land, could vote, which often excluded the merchant and commercial classes and, needless to say, the working class and the less fortunate.

These deliberations affected the presidency. Although the initial provision in the Virginia Plan for having the executive selected by the National Legislature persisted, as the definition of that body evolved over time, alternatives for selecting the executive were explored. On June 9 Elbridge Gerry of Massachusetts proposed that the state governors select the president. Each governor would cast a number of votes based on his state's representation in the Senate (that each state would have only two senators had not been settled at that point, and Gerry was from one of the more populated states).[19] Randolph responded that governors would not be sufficiently informed, "being little conversant with characters not within their own spheres."[20] His point was important and, as a governor himself, an interesting concession. But Randolph's argument also revealed an important concern among a number of the delegates: the character of the chief executive, which later figured into the defense of the presidency under the Constitution in the *Federalist Papers*. Although the amendment failed to pass, Gerry's proposal was perhaps a first step in moving the presidential selection process partially under the influence of the states rather than just that of Congress.

Gerry's views about the selection process for the presidency were endorsed by Alexander Hamilton. In his first speech before the convention, Hamilton outlined his own take. His comments are described extensively in Madison's notes. Not surprisingly, Hamilton argued for a strong federal government. Moreover, in his view, the president should be selected by electors who were independent of Congress. This was another example of an early suggestion that pointed to what would emerge as the Electoral College.

Hamilton was also a major advocate for a strong chief executive. On this, the views of his constitutional colleagues varied. In particular, the president's term of service and the president's eligibility for reelection were the subjects of much debate. This is a good example of how one topic of concern got entangled with other issues in the convention's proceedings. In this case, if the legislative branch selected the president, then eligibility for reelection might make the president too beholden to Congress in the hope of being reelected. If the president is not eligible for reelection, then a longer term might be in order and vice versa. Hamilton favored an executive of indefinite term, subject only to the constraints of good behavior.[21]

Roger Sherman, however, thought the proposed seven-year term was too long; Madison countered that seven years was not too long.[22] Butler Pierce of South Carolina proposed a three-year term, but that went nowhere. On this important point the delegates were clearly divided. Some feared that having a lengthy presidential term would be akin to monarchical independence and unbounded royal rule. Others feared the too-early termination of an executive of skill, character, and independence. The proposal that Congress select the president compounded these concerns: Would the selection of the president make him a creature of Congress, subject to its will? Would executive "energy" and "independence" be compromised?

Committee of Detail Fine-Tunes the Convention's Discussions

By July 26 the convention turned over the further fine-tuning of the convention's discussions to a "Committee of Detail." They were a very distinguished group: Randolph of Virginia, Wilson of Pennsylvania, Oliver Ellsworth of Connecticut, John Rutledge of South Carolina, and Nathaniel Gorham of Massachusetts. All had served in the Continental Congress at various points and were likely familiar with the defects of the Articles of Confederation. Gorham had even been the president of the Continental Congress in 1786. Randolph and Rutledge were state governors, and they would go on to serve the new Republic. Rutledge, Ellsworth, and Wilson later served on the Supreme Court. Randolph was the first attorney general of the United States and the second secretary of state. Ellsworth not only served on the court but also was a US senator and Washington's chief agent there, akin to today's majority leader of the Senate.

They began with what had been settled, at least so far, in the convention's debates. But they also took a broader view and made recommendations beyond what had already been discussed or agreed to. Their work played significantly into what would emerge in the final draft of the US Constitution in September—indeed, it could be considered a first draft. Unfortunately, we do not have precise records of their deliberations. The only documents that exist are a series of potential drafts of the Constitution that are in Wilson's papers at the Historical Society of Pennsylvania (although they do indicate substantive revisions by Rutledge).

Some of the committee's more interesting work is beyond our concern for the presidency but deserves some mention. Rutledge's aim was to limit the power of federal government, especially with respect to the powers of Congress. Wilson successfully countered this by introducing the "necessary and proper" clause on Congress's power, which was later incorporated into Article I of the Constitution. It proved to have significant impact on expanding Congress's lawmaking powers beyond those explicitly enumerated. Under the Constitution, Congress was empowered "To make all Laws which shall be necessary and proper for carrying into Execution the foregoing Powers, and all other Powers vested by this Constitution in the Government of the United States, or in any Department or Officer thereof." This was the reverse of the Articles of Confederation; under the latter, the federal government possessed only limited, enumerated powers, whereas the states possessed any residuum of implied or unspecified power.

As for the presidency, the committee's draft granted the executive important legislative powers—Madisonian design rearing its head again. It established the president's right to give information on the "state of the union," and it empowered the president to recommend to Congress "such measures as he shall judge necessary and expedient."[23] These additions found their way into the final draft of the Constitution and thus gave the president more of a role in the legislative process, beyond the veto power. The president was now a part of, to some extent, the lawmaking process. Presidential power was expanded, but at the same time it became more complicated.

At this point, delegates were still stuck on a term of seven years but without eligibility for reelection, with Congress still responsible for selecting the president by joint ballots. The issue of how the president was to be selected remained a matter of debate both before and after the Committee of Detail's report. The possibility of independent electors having a strong role in the selection process had been raised by Wilson on June 2 (he favored dividing up the states into districts and then holding a popular vote for the electors) and by Hamilton on June 18. Discussion of presidential selection was especially prevalent during the last two weeks in July.

Foreign affairs were originally more under legislative control: the Senate had power to "make treaties," and Congress had power to "make war." However, both of these were changed to the president's benefit before the convention ended.

In the final document, the Senate "ratified" treaties negotiated by the executive branch, while the Congress had the power to "declare" war ("ratify" and "declare" imply a more subsequent role to presidential action). Interestingly, in its report to the convention, the committee notes that the president's "title shall be, 'His Excellency.'"[24] This issue of proper title suggests that the president was regarded as something more than just the head of another branch of government. How "elevated" that office might be and how to properly address the person holding it were issues that George Washington dealt with early in his presidency.

In terms of state power, adoption of the *Connecticut Compromise,* which specified a House based upon population but a Senate with an equal number of members from each state, bridged the differences between the Virginia and New Jersey Plans. It also made clearer what the new Congress would look like and opened speculation of what the implications might be for presidential selection under this new legislative structure. It was a period of lively and often intense debate, some of it beginning to presage the Electoral College system. On July 17, Maryland's Luther Martin proposed a process in which electors would be chosen by state legislatures.[25] Two days later, Connecticut's Oliver Ellsworth made a similar proposal with the number of electors assigned to each state ranging from one to three. His motion actually passed but was then reversed on July 24. (Imagine the consequences for today's presidential elections if this had remained in the Constitution—the difference in the electoral votes of each state would be much narrower, and as a result, the electoral impact of more populated states would be considerably less.) Madison weighed in on several occasions; he was very suspicious of Congress having a role in selecting the president and preferred either national elections or some system of electors, perhaps chosen by the public.[26]

The Committee of Postponed Matters Tackles Presidential Selection

The Committee of Detail was unable to advance any new proposals regarding presidential selection, but the "Committee on Postponed Matters" tackled the thorny issue from August 31 to September 4 and came up with a very clever and attractive two-stage solution.[27] The first stage, the Electoral College, took into account the fear of congressional dominance over the presidency. Independent electors, selected by their state legislatures, would now cast two votes for possible presidential candidates. The number of electors for each state matched each state's numerical representation in both the House and the Senate, thus building on the foundation of the Connecticut Compromise. That they had two votes to cast might encourage them to look beyond a local favorite to someone of national stature. If a candidate received a majority, that person was selected.

However, if there was no majority, the next stage would move to Congress. The committee initially proposed that the Senate select the president, but subsequent debate revealed fears about its power, and the House was substituted instead. However, House members would not vote individually but by state bloc with each state's delegation having one vote (and initially required to vote for one of the top five candidates from the electoral vote). That the legislative branch would not directly select the president also resolved related issues. If the president no longer needed to curry favor with Congress to get reelected, then the president could be eligible for reelection and the length of each term could be shortened to four years. The prospect of the next electoral cycle would generate a president's sense of accountability—a dangled carrot that would hopefully curb the abuse of power.

The Committee on Postponed Matters also resolved other issues concerning presidential power. The president was given the power to make treaties subject to ratification by two-thirds of the Senate, as mentioned earlier. The president was also given the power to nominate members of the Supreme Court subject to the advice and consent of the Senate. The president's control over the executive branch was strengthened with ability to "require the Opinion, in writing, of the principal Officer in each of the executive Departments." The Committee on Style, a few days later, granted presidents the power to appoint "inferior Officers," except those that Congress may vest "in the Courts of Law, or in the Heads of Departments."

A Constitution Is Completed

On September 17, 1787, the final draft of the Constitution was presented, followed by an address by Franklin, which was read by James Wilson because Franklin was, once again, not in good health. Franklin noted that there were parts of the document that he could not at present approve, but experience had taught him the frailty of his own judgment and the need to pay more respect to that of others. In the end, he voiced his support for the Constitution, even with all its faults. He noted:

> I doubt too whether any other Convention we can obtain, may be able to make a better Constitution. For when you assemble a number of men to have

the advantage of their joint wisdom, you inevitably assemble with those men, all their prejudices, their passions, their errors of opinion, their local interests, and their selfish views. From such an assembly can a perfect product be expected?[28]

Franklin acknowledged that not all in the new Constitution suited him, a sentiment the assembled delegates shared. Nobody had won all that they had wished for—compromise was the order of the summer. Franklin confessed his astonishment that even though the delegates had varying personal interests, motives, and views, they were able to come together and achieve a "system approaching so near to perfection as it does."[29] However, Franklin's ending hope that all assembled would sign the document was not achieved. A number of delegates, including Randolph of Virginia, Gerry of Massachusetts, and Mason of Virginia, all declined to sign.[30]

THE DEBATE OVER RATIFICATION: THE *FEDERALIST PAPERS*

The successful drafting and signing of the Constitution was not the end of the battle. It needed to be accepted by Congress—the convention was, after all, established to suggest "revisions" in the Articles of Confederation. After some debate, Congress agreed to the ratification process laid out in Article VII of the Constitution: ratifying conventions were established in each state, and when nine states had finally ratified, the Constitution would take effect. The latter was an important concession—if not a bit of a fudge—on Congress's part. Under the Articles, unanimous agreement of *all* the states was necessary for *any* change in the Articles.

For many, the Constitution has a sort of reverential quality to it. I suspect that most Americans believe it to have been accepted by a grateful public and other notables without debate and with a feeling of perfect deliverance from the woes and perils of the Articles of Confederation. That was not the case. The nation was deeply divided over the Constitution's merits, and the ratification process was not an easy one. In fact, in many states it led to pitched political battles, dividing friends and family. There were several close contests. In Massachusetts, the sixth state to ratify, the vote was 187–168 in favor. In New Hampshire, the crucial ninth state that put the Constitution into effect, the vote was 57–47. Virginia (89–79) and New York (a very close 30–27) then followed. In Rhode Island, a popular referendum actually went against ratification, but on May 29, 1790, a ratification convention finally voted in favor, almost exactly three years since the initial meeting of the Constitutional Convention.[31]

The process was also a public one, with the arguments for and against ratification widely debated, and with lengthy arguments often published as letters in newspapers at the time. Writers often adopted pseudonyms, many of classic Greek and Roman origin. The opponents were dubbed the *Anti-Federalists;* those in favor were known as the *Federalists.* Most importantly among the latter group, Madison, Hamilton, and John Jay, working together as *Publius,* wrote eighty-five letters in New York City newspapers explicating and defending the Constitution. Collectively termed the *Federalist Papers,* they provide a crucial source for understanding the work and reasoning behind the Constitution, in addition to Madison's notes from the convention. Of the eighty-five letters, eleven focus specifically on the presidency and were written by Hamilton. However, the two most famous, *Federalist No. 10* and *Federalist No. 51,* were Madison's work.

Federalist No. 51 *Establishes a System of Checks and Balances*

Federalist No. 51 is of particular importance to us because it outlines the broader context within which the presidency operates. It establishes the core dilemma of presidential power: The president must compete with the other two branches of the federal government to achieve goals, even those that might be regarded as executive in nature. Madison's defense in *Federalist No. 51* of how the three branches of government operate together to control the power of government echoed his earlier work in crafting the Virginia Plan and his speeches at the convention. Although Madison believed that "a dependence on the people is, no doubt, the primary control on the government," he also knew that democratic will would not be enough and that "experience has taught mankind the necessity of auxiliary precautions."[32] For Madison, those precautions lay in the ways the internal composition of government is organized so that "its several constituent parts may, by their mutual relations, be the means of keeping each other in their proper places."[33] In other words, a system of checks and balances.

The concept of *checks and balances* is often not fully understood. It is, in part, the creation of the three branches of government—legislative, executive, and judicial. However, it is also the participation of each branch in the other branches' exercise of powers. To some extent, each branch's powers are "checked," or controlled, by the constitutional provisions giving the other two branches some say and influence on their activities. There is also another, often ignored part. Checks and balances are not a passive process or just an organizational construction. Madison noted that in these constitutional arrangements, real people occupy positions of power. Thus, we must factor in the motives, interests, and passions of those who hold federal office to make the balance of power work and ensure that checks and balances are effective.

As Madison argues, "The great security against a gradual concentration of the several powers in the same department consists in giving to those who administer each department the necessary constitutional means and *personal motives* to resist the encroachment of the others" (emphasis added).[34] By "department," Madison means the branches of government or the parts within them (i.e., the House of Representatives and the Senate), and "constitutional means" is the checks and balances part of the equation. Madison was a realist, stating that if men were angels, then government would not be needed. But we are not angels, so he notes that as a result, "Ambition must be made to counteract ambition. The interest of the man must be connected to the constitutional rights of the place."[35]

What are we to make of this? The first and perhaps most important point is that Madison's focus was on striking a delicate balance between creating an effective federal system of government and preventing it from becoming too powerful. There was a prevailing fear, and it was a reasonable one in 1787, of creating too much power at the federal level, and so Madison's objective was constraint and control. In *Federalist No. 51*, he correctly identifies two aims of constitutional government: "In framing a government which is to be administered by men over men, the great difficulty lies in this: you must first enable the government to control the governed; and in the next place oblige it control itself."[36]

However, what Madison largely misses, and this is a central point of this chapter, is that although government must be controlled, it must also be *empowered*. This is particularly the case for the president, the most unknown and feared piece of the Framers' design. Fear of power is understandable, but failure to acknowledge the enfeeblement of power is also problematic. This is particularly true for a weak president facing a strong Congress, although we could argue that this also works the other way, with a weak Congress and an overly strong executive. Madison assumed that ambition would effectively counter ambition. However, as Rakove notes, "*Federalist #51* does not so much explain how these ambitions will work as *assume* [emphasis added] that differences in election and tenure among the branches will foster the desired attachment between 'personal motives' and 'constitutional rights.'"[37]

Hamilton's Defense of Strong Executive Power in the Federalist Papers

What about Hamilton's views? Although united in the project of the *Federalist Papers,* Hamilton and Madison were not wholly of a common constitutional view. Indeed, their political paths were soon to diverge. Hamilton favored strong executive power coupled with strong national government and became a leading figure in the soon-to-emerge Federalist Party. Madison took a different course and aligned with Jefferson's Democratic-Republican Party.

In *Federalist No. 70,* Hamilton takes on the Anti-Federalists' charge that "a vigorous executive is inconsistent with the genius of republican government."[38] In Hamilton's view, "energy" of the executive is central to good government, and a "feeble executive implies a feeble execution of the government."[39] Subtle differences from Madison also emerge here. Hamilton focused on the need to *empower* rather than just control the exercise of executive power, which had been Madison's primary concern. According to Hamilton, the ingredients for proper energy included unity, duration, an adequate provision for compensation free of legislative mischief, and competent powers. However, he did caution that these should be meshed with ingredients proper to the exercise of executive energy within a republic, one that has "a due dependence on the people, and a due responsibility."[40]

Hamilton's discussion of competent powers, found in *Federalist No. 73,* does not actually tell us much about presidential power. Hamilton focused on the president's veto power, which some Anti-Federalists had criticized as too extensive to vest in one person. Hamilton countered that the veto protects the executive departments from unwise congressional encroachments and more broadly acts as a "salutary check" on bad legislation that threatens the public good. In his view, the legislative branch generally has the upper hand, and the president will face "hazard" in any "trial of strength" with that branch. Hamilton also noted that the president will likely use the veto infrequently, and with great caution.

In *Federalist Papers No. 74, No. 75, No. 76,* and *No. 77,* Hamilton delved into other powers, including the power to command the nation's military forces, the power to grant reprieves and pardons, the power to make treaties, and the power to appoint and nominate candidates for government positions. Hamilton's broad goal was to refute Anti-Federalists who challenged a president's constitutional possession of such powers as a threat to democracy. Hamilton's defense of these presidential powers was cast within his projection of how the system of checks and balances would work, coupled with his belief that the president's caution, discernment, and appreciation of his "sole and undivided responsibility" would yield not a tyrant nor a monarch but a wise leader hewing to the principles of republican government.

However, there is still something missing from Hamilton's arguments. He offered insight into *why* the president should possess these powers. However, he did not tell us *how* the president might effectively or strategically exercise them to achieve political or policy ends. Nor did he address to *what* ends or purposes these powers might be applied. The *Federalist Papers* take us only so far in understanding the issue of presidential power from the Framers' perspective. But we must remember that they were articles in New York newspapers urging ratification and offering arguments against the charges made by Anti-Federalists. Madison, Hamilton, and Jay were largely operating within that agenda. The *Federalist Papers* were not meant as a primer on the Constitution, or a textbook on the new American political system, but were simply an important "slice" of the Framers' thoughts, especially Madison's and Hamilton's.

DETERMINING AND INTERPRETING THE FRAMERS' INTENTIONS

Some have argued that the intentions of the Framers not only help us understand what occurred over that summer of 1787 but also are directly relevant to how we should properly understand governmental power today. This approach, often termed ***originalism,*** has particular bearing today on how some believe the Supreme Court should resolve difficult cases when interpretation of the Constitution is required. Originalists argue that the present-day meaning of the Constitution is best determined by what those words meant to the Framers. To them, the Constitution is like a contract, and like all contracts, to resolve any disputes about meaning we must return to those who initially created it. For the US Constitution, what the Framers thought, their intentions, at the time of its creation strongly matter.[41]

But can we accurately determine the Framers' intentions and meaning at the time the Constitution was created? To be sure, they had some shared concerns and ideas, such as concern about governmental weakness under the Articles of Confederation, recognition that a national executive was needed, and fear of too much governmental power. But also significant differences of view existed among the delegates: some feared departing radically from the Articles, while others wanted very significant change, to take just the broadest example. As we have seen, Madison's notes reveal a very rich debate with a wide array of views among the delegates on a variety of issues, most notably presidential power. Bear in mind, too, that the delegates continually voted on various provisions of the document over the summer of 1787, often with narrow majorities. Recall also that they voted by state bloc, as was the rule under the Articles of Confederation, and each state's delegation might have been further divided internally. The creation of the Constitution was as much a political process of compromise and shifting coalitions as an exercise that gives us clear guidance on their shared intent and meaning.[42]

Delegates also had different views about political leadership. To take just the most obvious and, indeed, very telling case, Madison believed that leaders are moved by passion and ambitions and that the Constitution must be constructed to channel these motives in a positive direction. For Hamilton, the electoral process yields virtue and positive judgment. They reach opposite conclusions about character, yet they were joined at the hip in defending adoption of the Constitution in the *Federalist Papers*.

Still, the supporters of originalism have a point: it is a constitution, and its meaning cannot shift constantly with changing political winds. There must be *some* degree of permanency. Imagine if referees and umpires were able to change the rules of football, baseball, or hockey on each call. They make tough judgment calls, but the basic rules are settled well beforehand. The game is played within its well-known rules.

The alternative view, often known as the *living Constitution* approach, grants more freedom of interpretation. Adherents of this approach note that the document itself invites a broader degree of interpretation, one not strictly limited by what might have been in the minds of its Framers. As Justice Stephen G. Breyer notes, "The Court should reject approaches to interpreting the Constitution that consider the document's scope and application as fixed at the moment of the framing."[43] To return to the sports analogy, sometimes the rules do change and, arguably, for the better. For example, introducing the three-point shot in basketball, overtime in college football, and instant replay in the NFL—the intent is to make the game better but still fair. The same goes for wrestling with the meaning of the Constitution.

The issue of how seriously we take the intentions of the Framers is a complicated question that cannot be resolved here. That they essentially worked in secrecy certainly complicates any efforts to fully comprehend their intentions.

However, there are hints, at least in my view, that the Framers themselves understood that future generations would need to struggle with understanding the Constitution's meaning and applicability.

The first thing to note is that the document itself invites interpretation. Although outside our study of presidential power, the meaning of the "necessary and proper" clause in Congress's powers in Article I is the most noteworthy example of this. It states that "Congress shall have Power To . . . make all Laws which shall be necessary and proper for carrying into Execution the foregoing Powers, and all others Powers vested by this Constitution in the Government of the United States." It clearly invites a range of other permissible activities that are not part of Congress's enumerated or express powers. Some legislative powers are more implicit and open to interpretation. And what is considered "necessary and proper" to carrying out those more clearly spelled-out powers? The document obviously does not tell us completely; rather, it invites reasonable interpretation and prudent application.

Similar interpretation of presidential powers is also needed. And as we shall discuss further in Chapter 3, this effort is very important to more contemporary exercises of presidential power. Much like with Congress's powers, some work rests on interpretation of words in the Constitution. For example, a recent controversy has arisen concerning the president's power to make appointments requiring confirmation by the Senate when it is "in recess." Those appointments then "expire at the End of their next Session," according to Article II. But when is the Senate in recess? Both Presidents George W. Bush and Barack Obama have taken one view (even short adjournments of the Senate count as a recess in their opinion), the Senate another (a recess occurs only at the official end of its yearly session). In 2014, the Supreme Court came in with a third (essentially, ten days in adjournment seems constitutionally reasonable). We will further explore this question in Chapter 3.

Other issues of interpreting the scope of proper presidential power stem from the *inherent* nature of executive office. Does the president possess certain "prerogative powers" not clearly set out in the Constitution but reasonably deducible from the role of chief executive? What powers are inherent in the president's role as commander in chief? The debate about prerogative is not a new one, not even to the Framers. In fact, we may trace it back as far as John Locke's *Second Treatise on Government* published in 1690, a work with which some of the Framers were familiar.

Interestingly, some of this debate about constitutional meaning and interpretation occurred during the 1787 convention itself. On July 26, James Wilson raised the issue of whether "having unsettled accounts" (i.e., debts) should disqualify someone from serving as president. According to Wilson: "We should consider that we are providing a Constitution *for future generations,* and not merely for the peculiar circumstances of the moment" (emphasis added).[44]

Governor Randolph also acknowledged the possibility of historical change and flexibility in interpretation. Reflecting on the Committee of Detail's draft of the Constitution, he states: "In the draught [draft] of a fundamental constitution, two things deserve attention: 1. To insert essential principles only; lest the operations of government should be clogged by rendering those positions *permanent and unalterable, which ought to be accommodated to times and events;* and 2. To use simple and precise language, and general propositions, according to the example of the constitutions of the several states" (emphasis added).[45] Randolph, a major player at the convention, recognized that the Constitution should set out "essential principles" but that those principles should be general in nature by intent and design and that they should be flexible and require interpretation. How that might plausibly work—while adhering to the project of constitutional design and its implicit constraints—he did not, unfortunately, further explore.

Randolph's nod to future times and events reminds us how limited the activities of the federal government were at the time of the Constitution's ratification. A quick look at Washington's cabinet is revealing. Only five positions existed during his presidency: secretary of state, secretary of war, secretary of the treasury, attorney general, and postmaster general. Given that cabinet officers are the heads of the major departments, the small number of them indicates the limited activities of the federal government early on. It was not until the twentieth century that the functions and scope of the federal government began to expand greatly. I doubt any of the Framers, even Hamilton, who was the chief advocate of a proactive and more expansive federal government, could have remotely anticipated the vast array of federal laws, policies, and regulations that exists today. The expanding scope of governmental activity magnifies the dilemmas of presidential power and presents a serious challenge for contemporary presidents in effectively exercising influence.

WASHINGTON'S PRESIDENCY: THE PROBLEMS OF POWER QUICKLY EMERGE

The challenge of exercising power effectively, however, is not just a contemporary one. Washington immediately faced it upon becoming president. He especially had to grapple with and try to define two of the main roles of his office—chief of state and head of government—and both presented challenges.

As chief of state, Washington carefully constructed the persona of the president such that it avoided the trappings of European monarchy. He embraced republican government, while still somewhat elevating the president. Some questions, such as how he should be addressed, were simple to answer. Some referred to him as "His Highness" or "His Excellency." A Senate committee favored "His Highness the President of the United States and Protector of Their Liberties" while the House of Representatives settled on "President of the United States." Washington approved of the latter. His inauguration was a solemn occasion, yet he gave the first inaugural address dressed plainly in a brown suit, not the military uniform in which he is often depicted in portraits of the period. Later during his first year in office, he reflected on the job he had undertaken: "My station is new, and, if I may use the expression, I walk on untrodden ground."[46]

Washington recognized that the president was a democratic representative. He held "levees" at his home to which select members of the public were invited. He traveled to every state in the union during the course of his presidency. But he was also a somewhat aloof figure and not a glad-handing politician. As he noted in a letter to Madison:

> The true medium, I conceive, must lie in pursuing such a course as will allow him (the President) time for all the official duties of his station. This should be the primary object. The next, to avoid as much as may be the charge of superciliousness, and seclusion from information, by too much reserve and too great a withdrawal of himself from company on the one hand, and the inconveniences, as well as a diminution of respectability, from too free an intercourse and too much familiarity on the other.[47]

Washington also understood that the president was the head of government, not a passive, symbolic figure. He established important practices not clearly set out in the Constitution. One of the most important was holding periodic meetings with his cabinet. This was something Washington had done during the Revolutionary War when he would meet with his top generals. There is no mention of a "cabinet" in the Constitution, only the vague wording that the president has the power to "require the Opinion, in writing, of the principal Officer in each of the executive Departments." Washington took those words carefully to heart and created something that served his own needs as well as those of the executive branch.

Washington also moved quickly to assert his authority over the executive branch. Although the president had the power to nominate certain federal officials, the issue of *who*—the president or Congress—had the power to remove them was not explicitly stated. On several occasions, Washington asserted that right and successfully removed officials from office. These actions ensured that the executive branch attained a degree of needed independence from Congress.

Washington generally deferred to Congress in his interactions with it, although he did assert executive leadership when he deemed it necessary. There were some initial stumbles. Early on, he personally went to the Senate to deliver a treaty and listen to its "advice and consent," as stated in Article II. The Senate was not ready to act with speed, and Washington left, apparently quite angered over the episode. Thereafter, communications between Washington and Congress were conducted in writing. However, Washington did establish the practice of personally addressing the Congress with an annual report on the state of the union. His successor, John Adams, did the same, but Jefferson ended the practice and sent only a written report. It was not until Woodrow Wilson's presidency that the custom of a personal speech by the president resumed. Washington also deferred to Congress by exercising the veto sparingly: in his view the president should do it only if he found constitutionally based objections. This practice persisted until Andrew Jackson's presidency; Jackson believed that political and policy disagreements were also bases for a veto, and his successors agreed wholeheartedly.

Washington also did not shy away from asserting what he believed were the inherent powers of the president. On his own, he issued a neutrality proclamation concerning hostilities between Britain and France. Some members of Congress expressed concern, but Washington won out in the end. Washington also took a narrow view of the Senate's involvement in any actual negotiations over a treaty. The executive branch held the constitutional right to make the treaty, whereas the Senate's role was limited to discussing and ratifying (or not) the treaty after the documents were drawn up.

Washington especially asserted the inherent power of *executive privilege,* the claim made by many presidents that Congress and the courts should be prevented access to certain information or testimony from members of the executive branch in the interests of national security or to preserve the confidentiality of executive-branch communications. In one case, regarding a congressional request that Washington turn over information concerning a military action against Native Americans (the General St. Clair expedition), he complied but only after consulting with his cabinet, especially on the constitutional rights of the president to withhold information from Congress. In another case, involving communications between the secretary of state and his ambassador to France, Washington was more selective, choosing only to release certain less-sensitive documents to Congress. The most controversial case concerned the treaty negotiated by John Jay with Britain that dealt with a number of matters still unresolved from the Revolutionary War, which was submitted to the Senate in 1795. It was unpopular in some quarters, especially with Jefferson and his supporters, who favored France; others viewed it as a bad bargain. The House of Representatives tried to enter the debate, passing a resolution requesting information on the negotiations. Washington balked at the House resolution. The Senate eventually ratified the treaty. Interestingly, Washington's moves here are not unlike those of contemporary presidents: balk at the start, assert executive privilege, but then reach a reasonable accommodation short of acquiescence.

Washington also put flesh on his role as commander in chief. On several occasions he called in the militia to suppress insurrections by several tribes of Native Americans, who were being encouraged to challenge the United States by Britain and Spain (which then controlled, soon to pass to France, the Louisiana territories and areas farther up the Mississippi River). In 1794, a new federal tax on whiskey (part of Hamilton's fiscal plans to raise federal revenue) was highly unpopular along the then frontier and led to the Whiskey Rebellion in western Pennsylvania. Washington ordered the militias from several states to respond. He traveled to Pennsylvania to oversee the military buildup and to prepare for a response, and even wore his old military uniform. The rebellion quickly collapsed. It was the first and last time an American president had personally commanded troops into battle. In none of these instances did Washington ask Congress for a declaration of war or some other formal authority. In his mind, his constitutional powers as commander in chief offered sufficient justification.

PARTISAN POLITICS INTRUDES IN PRESIDENTIAL SELECTION

The Framers' views on what politics would look like under the new Constitution were quickly derailed by two things that they had failed to anticipate: the emergence of political parties and the spread of popular elections. There were clearly differences in views at the convention of 1787, perhaps even with those holding similar views splintering off into groups or factions. However, clear partisan differences, and of an enduring character, only began to emerge in more unified form during Washington's presidency, starting within his own cabinet. His quest for talent led to political division.

On the one side, there were the Federalists, who supported a strong national government and efforts to develop commerce and manufacturing and gravitated toward Secretary of the Treasury Alexander Hamilton. On the other side were the Democratic-Republicans, aligned with Secretary of State Thomas Jefferson, who favored agrarian democracy—politics rooted in the interests of the small farmer and planter—and individual and states' rights. They differed as well on foreign policy: Hamilton's Federalists tended to favor Britain, while Jefferson's Democratic-Republicans looked toward France. The two groups were deeply divided politically, based on fundamentally different political visions of the direction of the nation. The political and policy differences between today's Democrats and Republicans pale by comparison.

As partisan coalitions began to form in Congress, the exercise of presidential power became more difficult. This is something the Framers could not have anticipated, because political parties did not enter into their calculus. Madison quickly aligned with his old friend Jefferson and led the effort in the House to oppose Hamilton's fiscal and commercial efforts. From that point on, any presidential efforts requiring legislation had to reckon with the partisan composition of the House and the Senate. By John Adams's presidency, congressional partisanship was acute; as the Jeffersonians grew in number, Adams's power and effectiveness waned. As partisanship spread, the exercise of presidential power grew more challenging and difficult.

The development of partisanship in Congress meant that by 1792, elections began to be contested on the basis of party affiliation. In the 1796 battle between Adams and Jefferson to succeed Washington, the partisan differences were clear—Adams was a Federalist, Jefferson a Democratic-Republican. Emergence of political parties affected presidential selection in another way. Recall that electors were given *two* votes; this would encourage them to cast at least one vote for someone perhaps of more national renown and not just from their home state. The House of Representatives would then select from the top five candidates. In effect, the Electoral College would act as a *nominating* body, producing a list of top candidates from which the House could make a final selection.

However, given that a two-party system had developed, it became increasingly likely that the candidate of one party would receive an Electoral College majority and thus the election would not need to be resolved by the House of Representatives. There were of course some early quirks in the process. In 1796, Adams won a majority of the electoral votes but his vice presidential running mate, Governor Thomas Pinckney of South Carolina, received fewer electoral votes than Thomas Jefferson. Under the constitutional provisions then in effect, as the runner-up, Jefferson—from the opposite party—became Adams's vice president (and, problematically for Adams, the president of the Senate). There was also a constitutional glitch in the 1800 election: Jefferson and his running mate, Aaron Burr, received the same number of electoral votes. Because neither received a majority, the election then went to the House. After thirty-six ballots in the House, Jefferson was finally elected as president. Quick ratification of the Twelfth Amendment to the Constitution in 1804 finally remedied the situation. It stipulated that the electors must cast *separate* votes for president and vice president. In addition, if no candidate achieved an Electoral College majority, the House could only vote among the top three (rather than the top five) of those garnering electoral votes. The role of the Electoral College as a *nominating* body had dropped away in light of political and partisan realities. The political parties now took on that job.

The spread of popular elections also shifted the dynamics of presidential election. Recall that the Framers had left it up to states to determine how their members of the Electoral College would be selected. In the first presidential election in 1789, four states—Delaware, Maryland, Pennsylvania, and Virginia—chose to have some form of popular vote in selecting their respective electors. By 1792, six states had moved to some form of popular vote—Kentucky, Maryland, Massachusetts, New Hampshire, Maryland, and Virginia. Legislative selection of electors further eroded with each subsequent presidential election, although some states switched back and forth. The notion that the electors would be independent evaluators of the qualifications of possible presidential candidates was clearly weakened, if not fatally so. Selection of electors increasingly became tied to party preference and popular vote.

For presidents, not only was Congress politicized along party lines but also their own election was now the product of party determination. There was now a "party nominee" for the presidency, which was good for political parties, but it made the exercise of presidential power subject to a partisan and coalitional equation that did not factor into the Framers' design, and thus even more difficult.

CONCLUSION:
IMPLICATIONS AND QUESTIONS

The Framers faced a monumental task in crafting a new constitution. Their efforts are especially notable given the limited recognition at the start of the convention that an entirely new political order would end up being created by the time the convention ended in September 1787. The creation of a national executive was an especially difficult endeavor. A legislative branch already existed, albeit different from the one that would eventually emerge. Many delegates had also served in the Continental Congress at various times, and so Congress was familiar terrain. But the presidency was a different matter. Although they did often reflect on the historical record of colonial and state governors, there were few precedents to guide them at a *national* level. The evolution of the presidency's development over that summer was remarkable; recall how it was largely undefined in the Virginia Plan. That Article II has largely endured is testimony to their efforts.

The Madisonian notion of separate but shared powers provided an answer to a central question of constitutional design: How can governmental power be controlled? But how were "shared powers" to be defined and decided? For Madison, the answer was that ambition should be pitted against ambition, that there should be a struggle for power. It was a brilliant theory, but in practice it relied too much on the personal characteristics and motives of the players. This was a calculus that Madison and the Framers did not address much, other than suggesting that the character of individuals involved and the arrangements of office and election cycle would likely remedy any issues stemming from the practice of separate but shared powers.

For the president, this became the basis of the core dilemma: How can a president effectively exercise power within this competitive arrangement? Questions relating to this dilemma cropped up immediately in Washington's presidency. What role did the president have in the legislative process? What should motivate the exercise of express powers such as exercising the veto or recommending legislation? Conversely, what role did Congress have in executive matters, beyond the impeachment, confirmation, and treaty ratification process? Some were matters of interpretation, such as negotiating the meaning of the "advice" portion of the Senate's role in "advice and consent" on treaties. Others involved debate over the even more difficult question of inherent powers. What powers of executive privilege did the president possess? What was the extent of the president's powers as commander in chief short of a formal declaration of war? What validity do presidential proclamations and executive orders have?

The Constitution provides some guidance for the broad structure of the presidency. However, the general nature of the Framers' language, somewhat intentional so as to provide flexibility for future times, also created the dilemma of how to understand and exercise presidential power. Washington's genius was in negotiating this dilemma—taking the pieces of the presidency set out in the Constitution and crafting their vagaries into a real presidency, despite the fact that he was a reluctant first president. Although Washington's presidency provided a blueprint of sorts to his successors, the challenge of answering these questions remains. Furthermore, the development of political parties and their involvement in presidential selection, also unforeseen by the Framers, created new challenges for exercising power that continue to plague presidents today. We will look at how presidents have tried to resolve these, and other, issues of presidential power in subsequent chapters.

NOTES

1. Zachary Elkins, Tom Ginsburg, and James Melton, *The Endurance of National Constitutions* (New York: Cambridge University Press, 2009), 129.

2. The secretary of the new "department" was Robert Livingston. Interestingly, Livingston retained his position as chancellor, the highest-ranking judge, of New York's state court system.

3. Letter from James Monroe to James Madison, September 12, 1786, http://founders .archives.gov/?q=%20Author%3A%22Monroe%2C%20James%22%20Recipient%3A%22 Madison%2C%20James%22&s=1111311111&r=27.

4. Gaillard Hunt, ed., *The Writings of James Madison: The Constitutional Convention* (New York: G. P. Putnam's Sons, 1902), 3:146. The Hunt edition of Madison's notes can be found online at http://oll.libertyfund.org/titles/madison-the-writings-vol-3-1787.

5. For an excellent analysis of Madison's revisions, especially the degree to which they might reflect the evolution of his political views as a Jeffersonian Democrat, see Mary Sarah Bilder, *Madison's Hand: Revising the Constitutional Convention* (Cambridge, MA: Harvard University Press, 2015).

6. These include Rufus King of Massachusetts, Robert Yates of New York (although Yates left the convention in early July), and James McHenry of Maryland (who was absent from the proceedings during June and July). More limited reflections can be found in the notes of William Pierce of Georgia, William Paterson of New Jersey, and Alexander Hamilton. The best source compiling the historical record of the convention is Max Farrand's three-volume *The Records of the Federal Convention of 1787* (New Haven, CT: Yale University Press, 1911). Farrand compiles the different sources and organizes their presentation for each daily session of the convention.

7. Hunt, *Writings of James Madison,* 3:9.

8. Ibid.,19.

9. Ibid., 41.

10. Ibid., 19.

11. Ibid., 57.

12. Ibid., 58.

13. Ibid., 58.

14. Ibid., 59.

15. Ibid., 59–60.

16. Ibid., 79.

17. Ibid., 178–179.

18. Ibid., 84.

19. Ibid., 129.

20. Ibid., 129.

21. Ibid., 195.

22. Ibid., 153.

23. Ibid., 4:110.

24. Ibid., 110.

25. Ibid., 3:454.

26. Ibid., 4:59–60, 67. See especially Madison's remarks on July 25.

27. The Committee on Postponed Matters is sometimes referred to as the Committee on Unfinished Plans, the Brearley Committee after its chair David Brearley of New Jersey, or the Committee of Eleven in Madison's notes.

28. Hunt, *Writings of James Madison,* 4:434.

29. Ibid.

30. Randolph later reversed his position and supported the Constitution at Virginia's ratifying convention. Some delegates, such as Luther Martin of Maryland, had left the convention in protest.

31. For an excellent account of the ratification process, see Pauline Maier, *Ratification: The People Debate the Constitution, 1787–1788* (New York: Simon & Schuster, 2010).

32. James Madison, "Federalist No. 51," *Federalist Papers,* Library of Congress edition, http://thomas.loc.gov/home/histdox/fedpapers.html.

33. Ibid.

34. Ibid.

35. Ibid.

36. Ibid.

37. Jack N. Rakove, *Original Meanings: Politics and Ideas in the Making of the Constitution* (New York: Alfred A. Knopf, 1996), 282.

38. Alexander Hamilton, "Federalist No. 70," *Federalist Papers,* Library of Congress edition, http://thomas.loc.gov/home/histdox/fedpapers.html.

39. Ibid.

40. Ibid.

41. In my mind, there may be a bit of error here in how this approach thinks about and applies the logic of contracts. Although the Framers "wrote up" the contract, they were not the

agents who ultimately accepted it; that role fell to the ratification conventions in each state. It is a bit like the landlord who purchases apartment lease forms at the local Staples or OfficeMax store. If a dispute between the landlord and tenant arises, it is not the "intentions" or views of the person at the Staples home office that count; rather, the intentions of the landlord and the tenant at the time the document was agreed to and signed count. The fellow at Staples only wrote up the terms and language of the lease agreement.

42. For an excellent historical analysis of the difficulties in interpreting the intent of the Framers, see Rakove, *Original Meanings*.

43. Stephen Breyer, *Making Our Democracy Work: A Judge's View* (New York: Alfred A. Knopf, 2010), 75. But also note that Breyer does not think that any new meaning or interpretation is permissible: "Rather, the Court should regard the Constitution as containing unwavering values that must be applied flexibly to ever-changing circumstances" (75).

44. Hunt, *Writings of James Madison*, 4:78.

45. These comments from Randolph come from his private notes, which Farrand includes in volume 2. Max Farrand, ed., *Records of the Federal Convention*, 2:137.

46. George Washington's letter to Catherine Macaulay Graham, January 9, 1790, http://teachingamericanhistory.org/library/document/letter-to-catherine-macaulay-graham/.

47. George Washington's letter to James Madison, May 12, 1789, http://founders.archives.gov/?q=%20From%20George%20washington%20Author%3A%22Washington%2C%20George%22&s=1511311111&r=33&sr=Madison.

Neustadt and the Modern
Conception of Presidential Power

George Washington, needless to say, was not the only American president forced to deal with the issue of presidential power within the Madisonian framework. Over time, new and shifting forces created a changing political landscape and historical context that had real impact on the executive office and the efforts of presidents to influence the political process. These historical changes produced new opportunities as well as constraints, and they generated new political, social, and economic problems that came to be viewed as the president's responsibility.

Thomas Jefferson, for example, took advantage of the development of political parties and began to tap the loyalty of his party's caucus in Congress as a way of exercising influence. Moreover, Jefferson was also not averse to broader exercises of power, even given his strong attachment to a strict interpretation of the Constitution. Most notable was the Louisiana Purchase, which doubled the geographic size of the nation in 1803. Despite having initial reservations and toying for a while with drafting a constitutional amendment that would empower him to make the purchase, as well as facing some domestic opposition (a House vote on funds for the purchase passed by the narrow margin of 59–57), a treaty was negotiated and approved, and funds for the purchase were obtained.

By the start of the twentieth century, times were especially ripe for presidential activism. The largely unregulated muscle of American industry had created conditions calling for reform and regulation. In the political landscape, the story was similar: the control of party bosses, political machines, and the power of special interests had corrupted politics in many locales. The Progressive Movement, which crossed party boundaries, developed to address these political and societal ills. Both Theodore Roosevelt and Woodrow Wilson, despite differences in party affiliation, were adherents, albeit with some political and policy differences. Both proved to be activist presidents: Roosevelt with his Square Deal, trust busting, and reliance on the office's public platform for popular support; Wilson with his New Freedoms, regulatory zeal, and similarly direct appeals to the public.

The watershed moment, though, was the presidency of Franklin D. Roosevelt (FDR). The need to deal with effects of the Great Depression clearly altered the relationship of the public and private sectors, greatly expanding the policy sphere of the federal government. And, through FDR's activism, it changed the power equation of the presidency in our politics. As a result of his efforts, the federal government took on great powers of social and economic relief, regulation, and the creation of the beginnings of a social safety net. For many scholars, FDR's administration marks the emergence of the modern presidency. FDR's efforts created a presidency that became the driving force for policy proposals: a presidency that clearly builds on the idea that it is the dominant branch of the federal government; a presidency that is center stage in media attention and a stronger force for communication to the public; and a presidency that begins the institutional development of the White House staff and its now great power.

Scholarly analysis of these events as presidential practice and politics, and their impact, from the time is slim. Perhaps the one exception is Woodrow Wilson's own writings before he became president. At first, as expressed in his 1885 book *Congressional Government,* he believed that a congressionally centered politics was the best solution. At the time, Wilson admired the British parliamentary system, but later his views changed. By 1908, in *Constitutional Government in the United States,* Wilson saw the presidency as the driving force: the presidency "will be as big as and as influential as the man who occupies it."[1]

In this chapter, we explore how the field of presidential studies began to grapple with issues of presidential power, focusing in particular on a book that proved to be a significant game changer: Richard E. Neustadt's *Presidential Power: The Politics of Leadership.* Neustadt's work was especially important in establishing why presidents need to exercise power and develop strategies, predominantly through bargaining, to achieve success. We shall also explore other forms of power presidents might exert to secure presidential goals, those that Neustadt fails to recognize, from symbolic power and loyalty power to charismatic power and dominant power. Most notably, we examine the leadership style of Dwight D. Eisenhower, a president whom Neustadt finds ineffective but who may have simply been using different means of exercising power. We also explore the later editions of Neustadt's book that touch upon aspects of presidential power that are now more central to the workings of the office for recent presidents.

RICHARD E. NEUSTADT'S *PRESIDENTIAL POWER*

A graduate of the University of California at Berkeley, Richard E. Neustadt obtained his master's degree at Harvard in 1941 before joining the US Navy during World War II. After the war, Neustadt resumed his graduate studies at Harvard and worked in the Truman White House, first as a staff member in the Bureau of the Budget (BOB), and then as a special assistant to the president.[2] This was an experience that served him well: the BOB played a major role in policy development and oversight during the Truman years, and his stint on the White House staff gave him a front-row seat on the inner workings of the Truman presidency. In early 1960, he published his remarkable book, *Presidential Power: The Politics of Leadership*. At the time of the book's publication, Neustadt was a professor of political science at Columbia University. Later that year, he became one of the two principal advisers to John F. Kennedy during his transition to the presidency.[3] Neustadt would soon return to Harvard and serve as the guiding founder in the creation of its John F. Kennedy School of Government. He retired many decades later in 1989.

Neustadt did not have an easy time in securing the initial publication of *Presidential Power*, possibly because of its new and different approach. Until its publication, scholarly work by political scientists at the time was largely bound by historical analysis of particular presidents, descriptive analysis of the office (particularly, its expanding "roles" in the American political system), or by presidential power viewed from the perspective of constitutional law. Neustadt changed that landscape. *Presidential Power*, whatever its shortcomings might be, still frames our discussion of presidential power and perhaps even serves as its foundation. Indeed, it is hard to imagine a course on the presidency that in some way does not make reference to his book.

Neustadt would return to the project over the course of his career, analyzing successive presidential administrations and then incorporating their respective lessons about power in subsequent editions of the book. The original eight chapters remained intact but eventually grew to thirteen. In 1964 and 1968, editions appeared with a new chapter on John F. Kennedy. In 1976, chapters on Lyndon Johnson and Richard Nixon were added. The 1980 edition added a chapter on Jimmy Carter, and the final edition, published in 1990, included the Ronald Reagan presidency.

In this section, I take a closer look at the major arguments in Neustadt's book and why they would prove to be very important to understanding and studying presidential power. Neustadt argues that presidents need to recognize when issues of presidential power arise and require a strategic response. He claims that constitutional and legal resources are generally not effective tools for the job and presents an alternate view that presidents must *persuade*, principally through bargaining, to attain the compliance of others. Bargaining, in turn, is enhanced by a president's reputation for past success and by his standing with the public.

Recognizing the Need for Effective Exercise of Power

In Neustadt's view, there is a huge gap between what we expect of a president and his or her ability to effectively meet those expectations, leading to potentially weak presidencies. As he notes in the preface to the 1990 edition: "Presidential weakness was the underlying theme of *Presidential Power*. . . . Weakness is still what I see."[4] Moreover, presidential expectations have increased significantly in the decades since the book was first published. What was once seen as exceptional is now a routine demand in presidential politics. Effective exercise of power is the ingredient needed to bridge that gap between expectations and the ability to achieve a commendable performance. Some presidents have been successful at this, others less so. That the path to effective power is not clearly demarcated compounds this presidential dilemma. Neustadt sets out to explore what this path entails—the resources to meet the increasing demands of the presidency must be understood and skillfully used.

To meet these ever-growing expectations, Neustadt strongly believed that the focus should be on how individual presidents *personally* conceive of power. Neustadt is not unmindful, even in the first edition, that the presidency is a large institution with a staff in the thousands. But he chose to focus on the president as an individual and his or her capacity to influence others: "Presidential on the title page means nothing but the President. Power means his influence."[5] Presidents are expected to be leaders, but the president only starts as a "clerk" in Neustadt's view, albeit an invaluable one. The president's service is in great demand, and no one else's will suffice, but the power and ability to meet those challenges are not automatically granted. In particular, the president's "formal constitutional, statutory, or customary authority"[6] is not enough. What is required, according to Neustadt, are more informal strategies of power, grounded in personal influence.

In making this claim, Neustadt takes us beyond the conception of the office that many of the Framers envisioned. Although the Framers did not say that constitutional powers alone would suffice, their views on personal influence were more subtle. As you might recall from Chapter 1, Madison believed that presidential ambition would be central, but within the context of shared powers pitting the ambitions of each branch of the federal government against each other. James Wilson favored the "energy" of the single executive. Hamilton agreed but also thought the selection process would yield presidents of character. Still, the notions of "ambition," "energy," and "character" are more than a bit vague. Neustadt suggests that effectiveness requires a more concrete and complex equation, a more developed theory of presidential power. Expectations of leadership obviously do not guarantee leadership, and presidents should recognize that they need to do more to gain influence and power.[7]

The Limits of Exercising Command

In the second chapter of his book, "Three Cases of Command," Neustadt argues for his view of effective leadership by looking at three attempts to exercise *command*, that is, exercising power through constitutional and legal means: (1) Truman's firing of General Douglas MacArthur at the height of the Korean War; (2) Truman's seizure of the nation's steel mills a year later to prevent a labor strike that might have had serious repercussions on the war effort; and (3) Eisenhower's ordering of federal troops to Little Rock, Arkansas, to quell local resistance to desegregation of its Central High School. On the surface, these three case studies seem to prove the opposite of what Neustadt is arguing: the presidents' use of formal powers in each case appears to be consequential. However, as Neustadt explores the facts and consequences of each case, he attempts to establish the limitations of formal powers and show that their deployment can have unwanted costs. Neustadt seeks to demonstrate that power as influence remains the preferred course even in situations in which constitutional and legal means seem the most logical.

Case 1: President Truman's Dismissal of General MacArthur. General Douglas MacArthur was one of the great, if not at times controversial, military figures
of the twentieth century. He had served as army chief of staff—the army's top
position—in the early 1930s and then became commander of army forces in
the Far East during World War II. After the war, he was appointed by President
Harry Truman as the Supreme Commander for Allied Powers in the Far East. In
effect, he became the military governor of Japan. When North Korea invaded
South Korea in June 1950, he immediately resumed the role of chief military
commander of United Nation forces. Truman, by the way, did not ask Congress
for any authorization of US forces to engage in combat. Rather, he relied on a
United Nations resolution—and US treaty obligations to the UN—in authorizing a military response to the North Korean invasion.

The North Koreans almost succeeded in driving US and South Korean forces
out of Korea. However, MacArthur's bold move in striking behind the battle lines
with a perilous, yet successful, land invasion at Inchon set the stage for a quick
retreat of North Korean forces almost to their border with the recently established People's Republic of China (PRC).

Yet MacArthur yearned for more: pushing the army of North Korea out of the
Korean peninsula and, perhaps, directly engaging the PRC in a military confron-
tation that would lead to its downfall. Needless to say, his aims differed from
those of the Truman administration. President Truman disliked him intensely,
but MacArthur was an immensely popular figure. The situation came to a head
in 1951. Truman finally was forced to fire him.

The immediate reason for MacArthur's dismissal was the letter that he sent in
April 1951 to Rep. Joseph Martin (R-MA), the minority leader of the House at
the time, criticizing the administration's policy in Korea. It was only the latest in
a number of public statements MacArthur had made that were at odds with administration policy, but it proved to be the final straw for Truman when the letter
was read by Rep. Martin at a House session. In my view and probably that of
most presidential scholars, Truman was correct in firing MacArthur. Neustadt,
however, takes a step back and argues that Truman's extreme measure was the
result of earlier failure. In December 1950, the White House issued a directive
requiring that any statements by military or civilian officials about war policy
obtain official clearance and approval. Although the order implicitly was directed
at MacArthur, it was framed in a general way, addressed to all departments, and
issued routinely, perhaps to spare MacArthur from personal embarrassment or to

avoid the appearance of Truman directly confronting his popular field commander. In Neustadt's view, this course of action was ill-advised. Because of this fairly subtle action, MacArthur might not have anticipated Truman's strong response to his letter, thinking that at most, there might be some mild rebuke from Truman, like before. And Truman virtually invited yet another bellicose MacArthur statement by tolerating a number of his public criticisms of the Truman administration in the past.[8]

It is clear that MacArthur's penchant for making public statements against administration policy needed to be curbed. Truman achieved this goal through command, through his use of formal power, and MacArthur was dismissed. However, this action was costly to Truman. MacArthur came home to ticker-tape parades and delivered a famous address, to thunderous applause, before a joint session of Congress. Opinion polls registered disagreement with Truman's action, and his approval rating started to plummet, declining to 22 percent approval by February 1952, the lowest recorded to date (and even lower than Nixon's on the eve of his resignation from office). Should MacArthur have been fired in this situation? Or should a more moderate course of action been pursued—which Truman thought he had done? Had Truman missed some important, earlier opportunities to resolve the situation?

Case 2: Truman's Seizure of the Steel Mills. The Korean war presented another dilemma for Truman. In 1952, Truman ordered his secretary of commerce, Charles Sawyer, to have the federal government take over steel mills across the country just hours before a labor strike was set to commence. The order was carried out, and the affected labor unions agreed that steelworkers would continue at their jobs, albeit as government employees. Truman's command appeared to work—he had seemingly averted a dangerous pause in steel production at the height of war. Unfortunately for the president, however, the steel companies took their case to federal court, which ruled that Truman did not have constitutional or statutory (law-based) authority to seize the mills. The unions then ordered a strike, but three days later, the federal court of appeals stayed the district's court decision pending an appeal to the US Supreme Court. The steelworkers returned to work and bargaining between labor and management resumed. When the Supreme Court agreed to hear the case, it ordered that no change in wages occur. Bargaining broke down, and the involved parties awaited the court's decision for a resolution.

That decision, *Youngstown Sheet & Tube Co. v. Sawyer,* often dubbed the "steel seizure case," proved to be a landmark case concerning claims of inherent presidential power. One of the chief foundations of the government's arguments in defense of Truman was that the nation was at war and, as such, the president possessed powers not clearly set out or otherwise implied by some stated clause in the Constitution to take protective action. The majority of the court disagreed. Truman complied with the court's verdict, and the steel companies resumed operation of the mills. Unsurprisingly, the unions struck. After a seven-week impasse, collective bargaining and some concessions to the steel companies on price limits resulted in a resolution. In the end, it was a costly affair for Truman. His actions led to one of the most important Supreme Court decisions ostensibly curbing presidential claims of inherent powers. The 6–3 decision was a bitter one personally for Truman. Two of Truman's appointees to the court voted against him, including Tom Clark, who had been Truman's own attorney general. We discuss the reasoning behind the court's decision in greater depth in Chapter 3.

In Neustadt's view, earlier steps could have been taken to avoid this outcome. An outgrowth of World War II, elaborate bureaucracies still existed in this period. They regulated both wages and prices to ensure economic stability, equity for labor, and fair profit for management. Had Truman more effectively utilized the wage and price-setting bureaucracy, a collective bargaining agreement might have been achieved at an earlier point, he could have avoided the seizure of the steel mills, and the Supreme Court might not have been forced to issue the *Youngstown* decision.

Case 3: Eisenhower's Ordering of Federal Troops into Little Rock. In this case, Neustadt posits that Eisenhower's command—ordering federal troops into Little Rock and federalizing the Arkansas National Guard to enforce a court mandate to desegregate its public schools—was precipitated by a series of actions by Arkansas governor Orval Faubus. Faubus, ostensibly to prevent mob violence, used the state guard to prevent African American students from starting classes at Little Rock's Central High School. The school board, which had initiated the desegregation effort, then obtained an order from the federal court mandating that integration be carried out. However, Faubus did not comply with this order; he did not insist that the state national guard accompany the students into school.

Another petition was filed instructing the governor to carry out the court's order. In the interim, Faubus met privately with Eisenhower, but the outcome was not conclusive. Days later, the federal judge commanded Faubus to stop interfering with the desegregation order, and Faubus responded by removing the state guard from patrol around the school. The next day, with the guard gone, mob violence flared. Eisenhower responded by ordering in the federal troops and by federalizing the state national guard. Central High School was finally desegregated as troops stood guard and the nine African American students were escorted inside. This was not an outcome Eisenhower wanted or anticipated. Only months before in July 1957, he told reporters that "I can't imagine any set of circumstances that would ever induce me to send Federal troops . . . into any area to enforce the orders of Federal Court. . . . I would never believe that it would be a wise thing to do in this country."[9]

In each case, Neustadt argued, although the president's command was carried out, the "decisive order was a painful last resort" and "one suggestive less of mastery than failure—the failure to gain an end by softer means."[10] Moreover, Neustadt believed that even when command is exercised it should not simply be an order. For the command to be effective, it must be carefully exercised, with appropriate planning and strategic preparation. Presidents must understand that exercising command should reside within the domain of influence, which is central to Neustadt's conception of presidential power, and that it must be sparingly used—it is "not a method suitable for everyday employment."[11]

In my view, Neustadt may be overstating his case here. He does have a point in suggesting that prior, softer steps might have been more effective before resorting to command. But both presidents did take some of those steps. Truman thought his directive to the military requiring clearance of public statements concerning war policy might curb MacArthur, and Eisenhower thought that he had Governor Faubus's agreement, following their private meeting, to assist in the integration of Little Rock's high school. Unfortunately, both presidents were mistaken and were unable to predict the fallout from their exercises of command.

Exercising Power Through Persuasion and Bargaining

So what does a president need to do to reach desired goals if command is a limited and occasional resource? For Neustadt, the core of successful leadership and the best way for presidents to attain their goals are by influencing others through *persuasion,* primarily by *bargaining* with them. Presidents' bargaining powers stem from their unique advantages, or *vantage points,* that can tilt the field in their favor if they are used well and perceived properly by others. However, presidents still need to persuade others that what the president wants is in their interest. And as a result of our Madisonian system of shared powers, those with whom presidents must deal have their own status, authority, and vantage points. As such, persuasion becomes a game of give-and-take; essentially, "the power to persuade is the power to bargain."[12] For Neustadt, bargaining's effectiveness can be enhanced by two ancillary resources that indirectly bolster the president's bargaining advantage: professional reputation and public prestige.

Professional Reputation. The first of the two ancillary resources is the president's *professional reputation,* especially as perceived within the Washington community but also by other actors in the wider political landscape, such as General MacArthur, the steel mill owners, and Governor Faubus from the case studies referenced earlier. Here, the past haunts the present: presidential weakness in the past diminishes a president's bargaining ability in the future. Likewise, past success can lead to perceptions of presidential strength and formidability. Ideally, a president would achieve the reputation of always winning, but if this is not attainable, then the president should at least make others think that it is risky to thwart or oppose presidential will. The goal is a professional reputation that enhances rather than detracts from the exercise of power.

Neustadt argues, for example, that MacArthur might not have been emboldened to make public statements challenging the administration's Korean War strategy if he had perceived Truman as a much stronger actor—a president who would fire him if he spoke out again. But because Truman had treated MacArthur delicately in the past, the general likely calculated that Truman would do so again. Likewise, the steel industry may have calculated that Truman would never take the bold step of actually seizing the mills. By April 1952, the Truman presidency was in clear trouble. The Korean War was in a stalemate, the administration was beset by a number of corruption scandals, and Truman's preferred candidate for the Democratic Party nomination, Governor Adlai Stevenson of Illinois, was rebuffing efforts to enter into the race. (Stevenson eventually relented and became the nominee, only to lose to the popular Eisenhower.) By contrast, after his inauguration in 1933, Franklin Roosevelt took Congress by storm. In its initial "Hundred Day" session, Congress speedily passed legislation the White House proposed. Roosevelt's professional reputation quickly grew; he was not the genial New York country aristocrat that some had initially thought. Rather, he was a skilled and at times cunning political operative.

Public Prestige. Those who directly deal with a president must not only consider the president's reputation as a power broker but also factor in his or her standing with the public, or *public prestige*. Like reputation, it is a game of anticipated reactions. Most of the people a president deals with, especially members of Congress, may also depend upon public support. Even if they do not depend directly on voters, public perceptions of their abilities, standing, and importance may be at stake in supporting or opposing a president: they "must take account of popular reaction to their actions."[13] Neustadt believes that presidents can appeal for public support; however—and this is a very important distinction—what he advocates is not quite the same as the contemporary strategy known as going public, coined by Samuel Kernell, which we discuss in Chapter 4. Nor is Neustadt suggesting a *plebiscitary presidency,* where presidents regularly go over the heads of members of Congress and make strong public appeals for support. Neustadt's argument is more subtle and indirect: just the *perception* of public support can positively (or negatively) affect the willingness of others to accept the presidential deal or bargain.

To return to our earlier cases, a decline in public standing also may have been a contributing factor to Truman's troubles. By early 1951, his popularity had begun to wane, which may have emboldened MacArthur to again make his views on the war known. And in 1952, the steel companies may have calculated that Truman, an unpopular lame duck, was in such a weak position that he would never do anything so bold as to seize their mills, buying time to gain a better bargain with the labor unions. In both cases, Truman acted despite his weakened position. However, Neustadt posits that had Truman's public prestige and professional reputation been stronger, he would have been in a better position earlier on to achieve the ends he desired without resorting to his ultimate powers of command.

EXERCISING INFLUENCE
BEYOND NEUSTADT'S BARGAINING

Neustadt's framing of successful presidential power as effective persuasion and bargaining is attractive, and he is undoubtedly correct in his assessment: these are tools presidents need to use. But if presidential power is the attempt to influence some person or groups of persons who are not eagerly or naturally inclined to follow the president's preferred course (and that is how Neustadt himself defines it), bargaining may not always be enough. What are the other avenues of influence open to the president? To take but one example: Lyndon B. Johnson (LBJ) is the classic case of a president who often bargained but also used other methods to achieve his goals. As president, and earlier as majority leader of Senate Democrats during six of the eight years of the Eisenhower administration, LBJ understood where each senator stood and what was needed to get him or her on his side. He was not averse to using other "inducements" if he detected weakness, whether they were political, financial, or even personal. He also was quite the physical presence, often dominating others with whom he dealt.

Other Sources of Power

When I teach about presidential power, I ask my students to ponder how we attempt to exercise some measure of power or influence in our daily lives. We constantly seek to get someone—roommate, family member, colleague, even a stranger on the street—to do something that person might otherwise be disinclined to do. What stratagems do we attempt to use? The list is always quite long, and bargaining is only one among a number of possibilities. Presidents, especially because of their exalted environs, possess an expanded menu of options for exercising influence that does not just involve bargaining. Here are but a few:

- **Symbolic power:** This power comes from the *office* of the president and the trappings associated with it, including an invitation to the presidential retreat at Camp David or an invitation to travel on Air Force One. The presidential environment and connection can be consuming and a source of awe, even for the most well-seasoned of Washingtonians. David Gergen, political commentator and former White House staff member for several presidents, has often pointed out that one of the dumber things that Jimmy Carter did was to sell the presidential yacht *Sequoia:* a nice evening cruise down the Potomac was a useful resource in dealing with members of Congress.
- **Ambition power:** This power comes from the belief that compliance with presidential preference *may* reap future rewards, even if no direct bargain is made. This type of power is particularly relevant to those seeking further advancement and favor, whether within the presidential inner circle or within Congress. It also might apply to Washington-attentive members of the media: a favorable story written today may lead to a valuable "leak" or exclusive interview in the future.

- **Loyalty power:** This type of power relies on a personal belief in the president or in his or her policy program or broader ideology. This is compliance to presidential will based upon admiration, belief, and trust without the need for the quid pro quo of a bargain. At the extreme, it can manifest as subservience, the unquestioned loyalty of the "yes man," which ultimately serves the president poorly.

- **Charismatic power:** This form of power stems from exceptional personal qualities that set a leader apart and evoke a strong sense of devotion from followers. Few if any presidents fall in this category. Perhaps FDR is an example, but he was also anathema to traditional Republicans. There were hopes for Barack Obama at the start among his most fervent followers, though those mostly disappeared as his presidency wore on.

- **Expertise and knowledge-based power:** In this case, power comes from expertise. Presidents generally defer to others' expertise, but there are some cases in which the president is the source of expertise. One largely unknown example is Gerald Ford, who exhibited mastery of the federal budget developed from his many years in Congress. On the other side, Jimmy Carter often strove to prove he was the smartest person in the room, delving deep into policy details, but his behavior often had a negative effect on deliberations.

- **Rational persuasion power:** Sometimes presidents can win simply by explaining things. As we discuss in the next section, this was a tactic that Eisenhower often employed.

- **Manipulative power:** Guilt and shame are often used to secure compliance in everyday life, and they can also be tools for presidents. So, too, presidents can be devious and shrewd in dealing with others. A more benign version of this was central to Eisenhower's "hidden-hand" exercise of power, discussed in the next section.

- **Dominant power:** Here, influence comes less from persuasion and more from domination. LBJ is the classic example, with his "Johnson treatment." One description noted that "its velocity was breathtaking, and it was all in one direction. Interjections from the target were rare. Johnson anticipated them before they could be spoken. He moved in close, his face a scant millimeter from his target, his eyes widening and narrowing, his eyebrows rising and falling. From his pockets poured clippings, memos, statistics. Mimicry, humor, and the genius of analogy made The Treatment an almost hypnotic experience and rendered the target stunned and helpless."[14] By the same token, domination can hurt a president's deliberations, as LBJ himself faced at times when he had to deal with difficult issues regarding escalation of war in Vietnam.

- **Coercive power:** In this case, power derives from the potential to penalize or punish. Or even just perception that a negative outcome might result if compliance does not occur. The Johnson treatment can also fall into this category. Richard Nixon's "enemies list" is another example, although he suffered when details of this list became public. FDR provides another cautionary tale: in the 1938 midterm congressional elections he sought to defeat several conservative Democrats who opposed his programs, but the effort largely failed and weakened Roosevelt.

- **Agenda power:** This exercise of influence is particularly important; it comes from controlling the larger context of the issue. The standard exercise of power is A (the president) trying to induce B (e.g., a powerful member of Congress) to do something he or she might not be inclined to do. But control of the broader, more encompassing agenda raises the "game" between them to a higher level. Although specific bargains within a game's broader parameters matter, in the end they may just be small potatoes. The person who wins control over framing and defining the game that is being played largely wins the war. Interestingly, George W. Bush succeeded at this in his first six months in office as he secured passage of his tax cuts. The game being played was no longer Bush's tax-cut plan versus Al Gore's "steady as she goes" plan of the 2000 campaign. Once the election was finally settled, the new agenda quickly became how much would be cut. In the end, Bush got most of what he wanted.

The bottom line here is that an array of strategies for attempting to exercise influence over others exists—bargaining is simply one of them. Influence is more complex and multistranded than what Neustadt posits. The Eisenhower presidency is especially instructive here: a presidential effort to exercise power but without bargaining as its centerpiece. Let us now look at it in more detail.

The Hidden-Hand Presidency: Eisenhower Reappraised

Eisenhower does not fare well in Neustadt's analysis of presidential power. Writing at the end of Eisenhower's presidency, Neustadt conveyed the general sentiment of many journalists and other political observers that although Ike was certainly popular, he was a passive president and certainly not a good example of a president exercising power effectively. Critiques included the following: he was too prone to delegate authority and responsibility to others, especially in foreign and national security affairs; he relied heavily on his chief of staff; and he was bogged down in weekly meetings of his cabinet and his National Security Council. It was government by committee that produced lowest-common-denominator policy advice. To top it all off, Eisenhower was an adequate speaker, but his frequent press conferences often left reporters confused about what he had in fact said. As Fred I. Greenstein observes, the conventional wisdom at the time, even among the most serious of scholars and commentators, was that he was "an aging hero who reigned more than he ruled and who lacked the energy, motivation, and political skill to have a significant impact on events."[15] This view of a passive Eisenhower especially is present in Neustadt's chapter "Men in Office," the seventh in the original book.

Not surprisingly, Neustadt praises FDR's competitive style. FDR carefully parceled out assignments, often sending one of his aides to gather information about a project or proposal without telling others who were assigned the same task. FDR kept organizations fluid and overlapping, and he liked strong and competitive personalities. All of this kept the decision-making process firmly in *his* hands. In Neustadt's opinion, Eisenhower was precisely the opposite. Eisenhower was trapped by the more organized advisory arrangements he had created, and he "seemingly preferred to let subordinates proceed upon the lowest common denominators of agreement than to have their quarrels—and issues and details—pushed up to him." Neustadt asks: "Why does one man [FDR] give himself the help he needs," and "why does the other man [Eisenhower] deny it to himself?"[16]

This commonly held view of the Eisenhower presidency began to change once the most sensitive of his presidential papers became open to researchers in the mid-1970s. Most notable of the works that took a new look at Eisenhower was Greenstein's book *The Hidden-Hand Presidency: Eisenhower as Leader*.[17] This book not only reveals him as a more activist president but outlines a leadership style and a conception of presidential power that are quite different from the one Neustadt presents as most effective. Per Greenstein, although Eisenhower did sometimes bargain, he often preferred a more indirect approach to attaining his ends. One example is his relationship to then senator Lyndon Johnson, the powerful majority leader for the Democrats for most of Eisenhower's presidency. When Eisenhower needed LBJ's cooperation, he would sometimes turn to their mutual friends in the Texas oil industry, asking them to work on Johnson. During his second term, Eisenhower used his secretary of the treasury, Robert Anderson, who was a prominent Texas lawyer and personal friend of LBJ's, "to serve as private administration conduit to and pulse taker of the mercurial Senate Democratic leader by maintaining virtually daily contact with Johnson."[18] Note that this relationship differs from that which Neustadt advocates. It is not A bargaining with B but A appealing to allied third parties, or C, who then exercise various forms of influence with B. Greenstein terms this a *hidden-hand presidency,* in which presidential activism operates through intermediaries and is often concealed from view.

One of the most interesting examples of hidden-hand leadership that Greenstein discusses is Eisenhower's efforts to deal with Senator Joseph McCarthy (R-WI) and his reckless allegations of communist influence in a wide range of public and private institutions. Unlike Truman, who challenged McCarthy head-on and with little positive effect, Eisenhower worked behind the scenes with his aides to put an end to McCarthy's demagogic activities. According to Greenstein, "The overall strategy was to avoid *direct mention* of McCarthy in the president's public statements, lest McCarthy win sympathy as a spunky David battling against the presidential Goliath. Instead Eisenhower systematically condemned the *types* of actions in which McCarthy engaged."[19] Most importantly, the White House worked extensively and in the background in the events that prompted the Senate to investigate McCarthy's conduct, which led finally to his censure in late 1954.

Eisenhower did delegate to others, but it was selective delegation not wholesale abdication. Selectivity was based on a careful assessment of his subordinates' strengths and weaknesses. If Eisenhower had a highly favorable view of a person's judgment, as was the case with Secretary of State John Foster Dulles, he permitted greater latitude. His first secretary of defense, Charles E. Wilson, was a different matter. Wilson was the president of General Motors before joining the cabinet in 1953, and Eisenhower valued him for his organizational and budgetary abilities. However, Wilson was not an expert in defense and military affairs and had little impact in these areas, which is precisely what Eisenhower wanted. Wilson's successor in 1957 was Neil McElroy, the president of Procter and Gamble—a background similar to Wilson's. Eisenhower preferred someone with strong corporate skills, but not necessarily deep expertise on defense matters.

Eisenhower deliberately made efforts to appear above the political fray because his popularity crossed party lines and he was acutely sensitive to that. Public prestige mattered to Eisenhower, but he managed it in a way that diverges from what Neustadt suggests. Eisenhower was careful to avoid being perceived as too partisan and confrontational, and so he exercised his influence behind the scenes and often indirectly. He was also willing to compromise his professional reputation to preserve his prestige, a trade-off Neustadt would see as very problematic because he believes that reputation bolsters bargaining ability. A notable example was Eisenhower's frequent and deliberate efforts to appear evasive at press conferences in order to dodge answering questions. He would sometimes say, "Well, this is the first I have heard about that," or "You cannot expect me to know the legal complexities of that issue." On one occasion, his press secretary, James Hagerty, warned him about a particularly touchy foreign policy issue that was likely to come up in a press meeting later that day. "Don't worry, Jim," Eisenhower told him, "if that question comes up, I'll just confuse them." Greenstein notes that most presidents occasionally feign ignorance, "but out-and-out denials of knowledge are far more common in Eisenhower's press conferences than in those of other modern presidents."[20] For Neustadt, expressions of ignorance, even if deliberate, threaten professional reputation. For Eisenhower, it was an expense worth paying to achieve his ends. As Greenstein observes, "There can be advantages to the lack of professional reputation as long as the actual performance of the political system and society satisfies the electorate." Moreover, Eisenhower's efforts to appear above the political fray and to not be perceived as a professional politician "can add to the store of what Neustadt properly identifies as another of the major resources for presidential influence, prestige with the general public."[21]

Eisenhower also embraced other forms of exercising influence that did not involve just bargaining; he would deal directly with others, just *not* in the way Neustadt counsels. As Greenstein notes, Eisenhower "preferred to persuade other leaders through reasoned discourse, but did so only with those of his counterparts who he thought had the capacity and motivation to be influenced by rational argument."[22] A more attentive and activist Eisenhower is also revealed in the drafting of speeches and in his private correspondence. He edited his more formal public addresses deeply and carefully. Letters to friends and associates, of which he wrote many of significant length, are models of clarity, thought, and precision. Eisenhower also valued the advice of others, whether received through formal or informal channels. He was a master of organization and understood its impact on his decision making. Although Neustadt acknowledges these resources, they are not central to his theory of presidential power in the manner of bargaining, professional reputation, and prestige. Neustadt does not have much positive to say about Eisenhower's White House and its decision-making processes. Yet, for Eisenhower, a supportive, well-functioning staff was an asset to his leadership. His most enduring contribution, which other presidents have largely followed, was the creation of the position of chief of staff and the role of the national security adviser. Although previous presidents had assigned aides the task of lobbying Congress, Eisenhower was the first to recognize that effort required better organization and staffing, so he created the Office of Congressional Affairs.

For Eisenhower, the advisory process not only was central to his decision making but also played a role in his leadership style. For example, on taking office he recognized that he needed to establish a good relationship with congressional Republicans, and so he began the practice of meeting their leaders on a regular basis through his presidency. As Eisenhower himself explained at a meeting of his soon-to-be cabinet in January 1953, shortly before he took office: "There is no Republican in Congress today who was ever there under a Republican President, with the result that anything the Executive proposes is almost automatically opposed by the Republicans in Congress."[23] In his view, "We must come at it on the basis of nurturing and carrying along these people until they understand that we . . . are their friends, that we are the guys they have to help, not kick in the teeth."[24] This is not direct influence but the establishment of positive relationships *before* efforts to influence—a type of agenda-setting activity that likely has beneficial consequences down the line.

Eisenhower's use of consultation—whether with his cabinet or the National Security Council—was part of his leadership style and a way of attaining presidential goals. Eisenhower knew that advice seeking was an effective tool for winning the willing support of those he consulted, even though he might not take their advice. Simply by being consulted, Greenstein observes, "Eisenhower's associates were encouraged to think of themselves as part of a collective enterprise rather than as individual entrepreneurs."[25] Here, A does not take the opposing interests of B as given but seeks to mold or change those interests beforehand. This strategy goes beyond Neustadt's equation, but it clearly is an important presidential tool.

Greenstein's account of the Eisenhower presidency presents a more positive depiction of Eisenhower and alerts us to the fact that presidential power needs to be more broadly understood. Power does not necessarily come from a president acting alone but involves a broader set of institutional resources upon which a president might draw and benefit. Or, if the president is particularly adept—as Eisenhower arguably was—an ability to design and mold advisory and institutional resources to serve their own needs and purposes. However, for every Eisenhower, there may be an LBJ or Nixon whose personal imprint on advisory arrangements may seem to serve personal needs, but not necessarily advance effective deliberations and ultimately sound presidential decisions.

NEUSTADT'S RELEVANCY OVER TIME: DOES BARGAINING STILL MATTER?

Readers of the first eight chapters of *Presidential Power* might come to the conclusion that, although this might have been an important work at the time it was initially published, its analysis and recommendations are now dated and largely of historical rather than contemporary interest. FDR, Truman, and Eisenhower present interesting cases in the *historical* study of presidential power, but too much has changed in our politics to make them of relevance today.

Presidential candidates are no longer selected at "brokered" conventions. This is difficult to understand today, but the national party conventions really mattered during the period that is the core of Neustadt's initial book. Presidential primaries were less important and the impact of party leaders was much greater. At the 1952 Republican Convention, for example, it was not yet clear that Eisenhower would become the nominee, but he eventually prevailed. For the Democrats in 1952, it was not until the third ballot of the convention delegates that Governor Adlai Stevenson of Illinois achieved a majority that made him his party's nominee. This was the last time that either party went beyond one ballot in selecting its respective nominee.

Other changes have occurred. The major parties are now more geographically and politically polarized. One of the foundations of FDR's "New Deal" Democratic coalition was the then solid Democratic South. That is obviously no more. The same is true for what was then-reliable Republican territory in most of New England. Members of Congress from each party were more broadly distributed across the political spectrum in the 1930s through the 1950s. That distributional band has now narrowed considerably, to say the least. Political and ideological polarization has made the president's job more difficult, especially when the opposition party controls one or both chambers of Congress (although there is considerable debate among political scientists about how much this really matters).[26]

In addition, party allegiance among voters has lessened and voters identifying themselves as independents have increased substantially since the 1950s.

Channels of communication to the public were also limited at the time of Neustadt's initial study. FDR had only radio and his fireside chats. Television started after World War II but became widespread only in the very late 1940s and into the early 1950s. The print media—newspapers and national magazines— were the dominant source of political information, but this has clearly changed significantly with the advent of cable television, the Internet, and social media.

These are all issues that we revisit in subsequent chapters as we explore the impact of historical time (the period of time in which a presidency occurs) as well as internal time (the internal rhythms within a president's first and second terms) on presidential power. Suffice it to say, they present challenges to Neustadt's theory of presidential power. In fact, Neustadt himself was cognizant of changes in the presidency and the American political system. His own shifts in narrative and perspective in the subsequent editions of his book proved that he, too, recognized the need to broaden our understanding of presidential power.

Neustadt Addresses Contemporary Presidents

Neustadt did not substantively alter the text of his original 1960 version in subsequent editions. Instead, new prefaces were written and chapters were added.[27] This is useful to us because it implicitly provides us a "test" of his original theory as time passed. Did *Presidential Power* withstand that test of time? Did the argument essentially stay the same or did it subtly change? Recognizing any revisions and additions that Neustadt made to his own argument may help us understand aspects of presidential power that have become more relevant for contemporary presidents.

Neustadt's second edition of the work included an afterword on JFK (it became Chapter 9 in subsequent editions). Although it is somewhat brief, Neustadt raises several new questions directed at appraising performance. His question on presidential purposes is particularly telling because it directs us to think not just about the *exercise* of power in a strategic or instrumental sense but also power to what *end*. Moreover, Neustadt asks whether these purposes run with or against the grain of history—were they relevant to the needs of the time? This emphasis is especially important because it introduces a focus of attention on the broader historical context of a presidency and the effect of that context on performance.

The impact of particular periods in history is not addressed in Neustadt's original theory, but he does introduce it in the second edition, and it is an important topic that we shall turn to in Chapter 5.[28]

Neustadt also draws attention to the internal time of a presidency, although this topic is not explicitly raised as a question. Neustadt noted that Kennedy's term in office was cut short, making the effects of internal time difficult to evaluate. However, in Neustadt's view, there was evidence of effectiveness in the way Kennedy took office. Presidential transitions to office and the first eighteen months in office are crucial. It is a critical learning time for a president, as Kennedy himself experienced with the Bay of Pigs fiasco in April 1961. We don't know what might have been in store after Kennedy's two years and ten months in office, but Neustadt offers some important perspective for all presidents. The fourth year is a big test, as the president prepares for reelection, while the seventh year is the beginning of the end, as attention focuses on the election of a successor. As for opportunities for accomplishment, Neustadt identifies the third, fifth, and sixth years as the most important. For our purposes, Neustadt's brief comments on the consequence of the internal rhythms of the presidential term were instructive and helped to shape future analysis of presidential power (see Chapters 6 and 7).

The third edition, published in 1976, included a new chapter on LBJ and Nixon. Neustadt acknowledges the turbulent events of the 1960s and the 1970s but concludes that the basic ingredients of presidential power have not changed very much and that power "derives from roughly the same sources as a generation ago."[29] However, he does conclude that LBJ and Nixon may have exercised too much power and that Vietnam and Watergate, respectively, became "symbols of their self-destruction." At the same time, both presidents "found their power as contingent and variable as that of others."[30]

Still, Neustadt makes some interesting new points, fine-tuning his argument to changing conditions, some of which signal important changes in his theory. For example, Neustadt cautions that extreme demands for loyalty and overeager aides striving to demonstrate loyalty could be potentially dangerous for a president and the White House—as it was for Nixon. Neustadt also raises the issue of legitimacy, or the widespread sense that a president possesses the basic right to govern. Here he points to a closer relationship between public prestige and professional reputation, especially when the president misleads the public on a large scale and a "credibility gap" develops. Legitimacy was a problem for Johnson as it became clearer, especially after the Tet offensive in early 1968, that the war in Vietnam was not going as well as the administration's public statements proclaimed. It was also an issue for Nixon once the details of the Watergate scandal and its cover-up slowly emerged in 1973 and 1974, culminating in his August 8, 1974, resignation from office. In both cases, what the president was publicly stating was met with increasing skepticism, by both the public and Washington insiders.[31]

In another new chapter (Chapter 11), Neustadt focuses on Jimmy Carter's transition to the presidency and compares it to Kennedy's transition efforts in 1960 and early 1961, in which Neustadt was a central participant. Here, Neustadt concentrates more on the institutional surroundings of the presidency and how they have changed. For example, he notes that the White House staff matters in its own right and how populating it with too many former associates in key positions—fellow Georgians in Carter's case—can lead to presidential amateur hour. Neustadt also recognizes the increasing power of the media and the public mood. Carter came across poorly on television, and the public began to sour on his presidency.

In the final edition of the work, two additional chapters were added. The first covered Ronald Reagan's presidency. Neustadt recognized that Reagan was an activist president who had strong policy convictions but believed that Reagan's biggest problem was that he lacked detailed knowledge. Not surprisingly, Neustadt takes Reagan to task for the Iran-Contra scandal—an event that might have led to Reagan's impeachment had more evidence of presidential knowledge and involvement been established. This major misstep initially involved trading military equipment to Iran in the hopes that moderate elements in the Iranian regime would put pressure on the Hezbollah militia in Syria to release American civilians that they had taken hostage. It was an ill-conceived, ill-informed, and largely fruitless effort. Both Secretary of State George Shultz and Secretary of Defense Caspar Weinberger thought the scheme foolish and believed it had ended. However, a new national security adviser, Vice Admiral John Poindexter, restarted the effort without Reagan's approval—at least by most credible accounts. Moreover, Poindexter and a White House military aide, Lt. Col. Oliver North, then came up with the even more audacious move to use the funds from the sale of arms to finance the pro-American "Contras" in Nicaragua who were waging a civil war against the leftist Sandinista regime. This was done without Reagan's knowledge or authorization. When the operation first became public, Reagan denied knowledge of the arms-for-hostages piece of it, although there was evidence to the contrary. A special committee (the Tower Commission) convened to investigate the scandal and found no presidential involvement in funding the Contras, though it did suggest reforms that the administration then put into practice. In Neustadt's view, Reagan was a good case study of his arguments on presidential power—but as a negative example. However, I believe the Iran-Contra scandal is less about the failure of presidential influence and bargaining (although the "deal" with the Iranians was a disaster) and more about the failure of Reagan to manage the machinations within the national security staff, an issue that relates to the importance of assembling and managing resources and staff (which we discuss in Chapters 6 and 7).

As with Neustadt's views on Eisenhower, evaluation of Reagan's actions as president is a matter of interpretation. Whereas Neustadt sees Reagan as a failure, other observers have applauded Reagan's efforts, valuing his economic policies and his steadfastness in strengthening the American military, with some claiming the latter had a direct effect on the decline of the Soviet Union. Still others go further and applaud Reagan's foreign policy flexibility: he initially adopted a hard line with the Soviets but became more accommodating once Gorbachev took power.

The second additional chapter in the 1990 edition, "Two Cases of Self-Help," presents two positive cases of presidential leadership. The first—Kennedy's response to the Cuban Missile Crisis in October 1962—was expected. The second was an examination of Eisenhower's deliberations in 1954 concerning US military intervention to support France in its efforts to defeat a communist insurgency in Indochina (Vietnam, Cambodia, and Laos today), then part of colonial France. This was less expected given Neustadt's earlier negative assessment of Eisenhower. By 1954, the Indochina War had been going on for eight years and French forces were seemingly set for a major defeat at an isolated fortress in northwestern Vietnam called Dien Bien Phu. The French appealed to the White House for military assistance. The stakes were high: no one wanted blame for losing more territory to the communists, but no one wanted the United States to be drawn into another Korean War. Although Eisenhower gave the possibility of military action much thought and there was extensive deliberation, he ultimately decided against intervention.

Neustadt sees a more effective Eisenhower in this episode, acknowledging that Eisenhower played an astute game. On the one hand, Eisenhower dangled the possibility of *some* assistance *if* certain conditions were met. On the other hand, he was astutely aware of the limits of American military power in the jungles of Southeast Asia. The outcome was probably the best to be hoped for at the time: partition of Vietnam into communist-controlled North and an ostensibly free South as well as the avoidance of "another Korea."[32]

The subsequent editions of *Presidential Power* do not fully square with the theory of power that Neustadt originally lays out. Although bargaining and influence remain important to the presidents covered in the later chapters, other facets of power seem equally if not more crucial in accounting for success or failure in the presidencies. Neustadt is an astute presidential observer, and he captures the central themes and issues of these presidencies. But rather than confirming his original theory, Neustadt's analysis in subsequent editions often implicitly highlights the new areas of analysis that presidential power must consider, such as making effective public appeals, understanding an administration's place in historical time, and capitalizing on the internal time of a presidency. And as we discuss throughout this book, presidents must recognize the importance of, and utilize, each facet of presidential power to successfully achieve their agendas.

Testing Neustadt's Theory Against Recent Presidencies

Let us now turn and consider the more recent presidents, those not studied by Neustadt in his book, such as Bill Clinton, George W. Bush, and Barack Obama. What would Neustadt have said about their influence and bargaining skills? Are those even the most important tools of these presidents, given how much has changed since Neustadt first wrote *Presidential Power*? Although some political scientists have cautioned us about the president's ability to have significant impact on Congress's legislative process, Neustadt remains correct in his assessment that a president's bargaining abilities do matter. Imagine the media's and political pundits' reaction if the president failed to exert influence on major pieces of legislation, particularly those central to the White House's policy agenda. Does the president *determine* the outcome? Probably not, except in extraordinary cases. But the president can and should exercise *some* influence, and key presidential achievements have been accomplished because bargaining occurs at crucial moments.

Bill Clinton secured accord on the North American Free Trade Agreement (NAFTA) in 1993 with strong Republican support by making significant bargaining concessions, including price protections for citrus and winter vegetable growers and sugar producers as well as expanded production of the C-17 cargo plane, the latter well beyond the parameters of a trade bill. However, we also need to bear in mind that free trade was part of the Republican agenda that had largely been crafted during George H. W. Bush's presidency. Whereas bargaining certainly mattered at the margins to secure sufficient congressional support, Clinton's efforts to seize control of what otherwise was part of the GOP agenda was the key to his success.

During his first year in office, George W. Bush was able to secure a major education reform bill by working closely with Sen. Edward Kennedy (D-MA) and other key Democrats in Congress to reach a compromise. Although the administration did not attain its goal of allowing students in failing public schools to use vouchers to attend private schools, other reforms such as standardized testing in public schools, annual measurement of a school's performance, and the ability of parents to transfer their children to higher-performing public schools were achieved.[33] Bargaining and compromise were key to Bush's achievement, but other factors and tactics were at play. Bush pushed for education reform early in his presidency, the most opportune moment in the internal time of a president's first term. He also carefully cultivated Kennedy and other Democrats to be in a supportive mood, inviting Kennedy and members of his family, for example, to a special White House screening of the film *Thirteen Days,* which favorably depicts JFK's handling of the Cuban Missile Crisis in 1962. As well, Bush renamed the headquarters of the Department of Justice in honor of the senator's brother Robert F. Kennedy, a former attorney general. Bush also benefited from a period of congressional goodwill in the aftermath of the 9/11 terrorist attacks—an impact of historical time.

Another success of the George W. Bush administration, the 2002 emergency spending bill that sought funds to defend the United States against foreign terrorism, could also be attributed to its timing in the aftermath of 9/11 and the widespread public concern about homeland security. Of course, it included unrelated appropriations such as $2 million to the Smithsonian Institution for constructing a new building to house its jars of biological specimens and $2.5 million to map coral reefs in Hawaii—a sign that bargaining was still necessary for the bill's passage.[34] Still, neither of Bush's successes can be wholly attributed to Neustadt's conception of presidential power as bargaining. Timing, both internal and historical, the substance of the policy initiatives, and other forms of power were also crucial to the success of these initiatives.

For Obama, the centerpiece of his first-term agenda was healthcare reform: the Patient Protection and Affordable Care Act (also known as "Obamacare"). In this case, bargaining was absolutely critical. It helped the administration secure support of key segments of the healthcare industry, especially drug manufacturers.[35] And although the administration was not successful in winning bipartisan support, it was able, through individual bargaining with key Democratic members, to secure passage in March 2010. Still, there are a couple of points to bear in mind. Perhaps the most fundamental is that healthcare reform had a long lineage within the Democratic Party's political agenda, going even as far back as the Truman presidency, so the Democrats were primed to see some form of healthcare reform pass. Equally important, Obama's administration moved on this initiative immediately after his inauguration, recognizing the importance of internal time and that they needed to act when Obama's power was at its strongest. This was in stark contrast to Clinton's unsuccessful efforts on healthcare reform—his administration's delay on this initiative was a significant contributing factor to its failure. We explore these dynamics further in Chapter 6.

And as the Obama White House learned in 2011 and 2012 when it sought a "grand bargain" with the leadership of the Republican-controlled House, sometimes bargaining is not effective. The aim was an historic agreement that combined debt reduction, revenue increases, and changes in entitlement programs. Obama and House Speaker John Boehner (R-OH) got very close to a deal, but a final White House effort to secure more tax revenue bitterly soured the process. Both sides have different accounts concerning who is to blame.[36] It would have made a fascinating case study for Neustadt to tackle. Neustadt would have likely focused on various errors in the bargaining process made by each side, such as the White House not pulling back from its quest for higher taxes on the wealthiest Americans. I think the story is more complex than that. Each side seemed eager to make a deal, but the problem was whether they could politically deliver on their concessions. Obama was worried about his electoral base going into the 2012 presidential election, whereas Boehner's hands were tied by the Republican ideological purists in the House. Bargaining today is more difficult than in the past—it is no longer just about powerful political leaders striking a deal. Today's political leaders also face the daunting task of securing support for those deals within an increasingly polarized politics. Polarization ups the ante for devising ways of exercising presidential power. Waiting until the end of his first term to strike this bargain likely did not help Obama—that point in the internal cycle of a presidency simply isn't favorable for grand efforts.

CONCLUSION: IMPLICATIONS AND QUESTIONS

Bargaining matters, that much is clear. However, deal making and brokering—whether successful or unsuccessful—are only one resource of power. The shifts in Neustadt's own narrative, as he moves from the initial account published in 1960 to the final edition in 1990, shows that even he understands the need to expand our conception of presidential power. Politics has certainly undergone change since the Reagan years: new resources for exercising influence have developed, and most notably, avenues for direct presidential communication have advanced significantly. Neustadt was initially a bit time-bound by his era, though in later editions he does allude to the importance of other factors in exercising presidential power such as historical time and internal time.

Still, Neustadt is dead right on the need for presidents to recognize their "power stakes": a president must anticipate and understand when appropriate, and decisive, action is needed. When recent presidents have failed in this, it has proven costly. George W. Bush initially bungled the response to Hurricane Katrina in 2005. There was a quick flyover of New Orleans in Air Force One, but there was no immediate action on the ground. Obama's administration failed to anticipate and monitor the implementation of their healthcare reform plan. The system of participant enrollment was plagued with failures in its rollout—the website crashed and people experienced difficulties in signing up. These problems should have been anticipated and thus could have been avoided. Another example was the scandal of the treatment of former servicemen and -women in veterans' hospitals. The system was severely mismanaged, and some veterans got preferred treatment while others experienced long delays. There had been reports for a number of years—even going back to the Bush presidency—of difficulties in veterans' hospitals, but the issue was simply not on the radar of the Obama administration.

A final question to consider is: Power to what end? This takes us beyond Neustadt's project, because he largely leaves this question untouched in his book, choosing instead to focus on influence and bargaining, but not on *what* is achieved by their use. Although Neustadt provides us no prescriptive or normative guidance on this matter, this is an important piece of presidential leadership to think about. There are two related issues to ponder here. One, which Neustadt does raise, concerns the effects when presidents become too preoccupied with power. As he observes, "Johnson and Nixon, by all accounts assiduous in thinking about power—both, indeed, preoccupied with it to the point of obsession—set themselves on disastrous courses, leading one to premature retirement and the other to forced resignation."[37] But what if they had pulled back a bit? It is likely that if they had charted a more restrained course, and set a more appropriate set of goals for their power, they could have been more successful leaders. The second issue concerns how *presidential* power, especially as we now consider the ends it seeks to achieve, squares with our system of *shared* powers. Does it create a presidency that is seen as the dominant and driving force in our political system to the exclusion of other institutions, processes, and levels of government? Perhaps the presidency is now the central focus largely because of the increasing expectations we have placed on the office and the higher bar we have set for the president's public communications. But should the presidency be so paramount? Should the presidency be the driving engine in our democracy? Should presidential policy goals—rather than Congress, an equally elected branch of our federal government—set the national agenda? Madison, I suspect, would have an answer to these questions that might differ from what our expectations are today: each branch is entitled to claim some terrain, in his view, and ambition must be pitted against ambition. But whichever the answer, there exist dilemmas in the exercise of presidential power.

NOTES

1. Woodrow Wilson, *Constitutional Government in the United States* (New York: Columbia University Press, 1908), 79.

2. The Bureau of the Budget was reorganized during the Nixon presidency into today's Office of Management and Budget (OMB).

3. Neustadt's memos to Kennedy were later published. See Charles O. Jones, ed., *Preparing to Be President: The Memos of Richard E. Neustadt* (Washington, DC: AEI Press, 2000).

4. Richard E. Neustadt, *Presidential Power and the Modern Presidents: The Politics of Leadership from Roosevelt to Reagan* (New York: Free Press, 1990), ix.

5. Ibid., 4.

6. Ibid., 321.

7. Ibid., 8.

8. Ibid., 19.

9. Quoted in Neustadt, *Presidential Power,* 25.

10. Ibid., 24.

11. Ibid., 28.

12. Ibid., 32.

13. Ibid., 73.

14. Rowland Evans and Robert Novak, *Lyndon B. Johnson: The Exercise of Power* (New York: New American Library, 1966), 104.

15. Fred I. Greenstein, "Eisenhower as an Activist President: A Look at New Evidence," *Political Science Quarterly* 94, no. 4 (Winter 1979–1980): 575–599, quote at 575.

16. Neustadt, *Presidential Power,* 135.

17. Fred I. Greenstein, *The Hidden-Hand Presidency: Eisenhower as Leader* (New York: Basic Books, 1982).

18. Ibid., 60.

19. Greenstein, "Eisenhower as an Activist President," 586. Also see Greenstein's more extensive chapter on McCarthy in *Hidden-Hand Leadership,* 155–227.

20. Greenstein, "Eisenhower as an Activist President," 588.

21. Greenstein, *Hidden-Hand Presidency,* 235.

22. Ibid., 70.

23. As quoted in ibid., 112.

24. Ibid., 112.

25. Ibid., 115.

26. Divided government was not unknown to these presidents. Truman faced a Republican-controlled Congress in 1947 and 1948, and the Democrats controlled Congress for the last six years of Eisenhower's presidency.

27. In the 1976 edition, the new material on the Johnson and Nixon presidencies appeared as an introductory chapter. In the 1980 edition, this material was moved to the end of the work and appeared as Chapter 10. The 1980 edition also included new material on Jimmy Carter that appeared as Chapter 11, "Hazards of Transition."

28. The other three questions he raises are: (1) What was the president's "feel" for power? (2) How was pressure in office handled? (3) What imprint was left of the office?

29. Neustadt, *Presidential Power,* 183.

30. Ibid., xi.

31. Neustadt is also more cognizant of the impact of the White House staff. Although he does pay greater attention to what transpires below the president than he did in the original "Men in Office" chapter, the emphasis is still on the president as an individual rather than on the broader institutional effects.

32. See Neustadt, *Presidential Power,* 300. One of the two main works that Neustadt draws upon in this partial change of heart about Ike is one that I coauthored, John P. Burke and Fred I. Greenstein (with Larry Berman and Richard Immerman), *How Presidents Test Reality: Decisions on Vietnam. 1954 and 1965* (New York: Russell Sage, 1989).

33. See John P. Burke, *Becoming President: The Bush Transition 2000–2003* (Boulder, CO: Lynne Rienner, 2004), 138–140.

34. William Welch and Jim Drinkard, "Security Bill Stuffed with Pork," *Burlington Free Press,* June 3, 2002.

35. The key deal was placing an $80 billion limit on cost savings to be imposed on manufacturers. David D. Kirkpatrick, "White House Affirms Deal on Drug Cost," *New York Times,* August 6, 2009.

36. See Bob Woodward, *The Price of Politics* (New York: Simon & Schuster, 2012); and Matt Bai, "Obama vs. Boehner: Who Killed the Debt Deal?" *New York Times Magazine,* March 26, 2012.

37. Neustadt, *Presidential Power,* xi.

3

The Executive's Prerogative: Inherent Constitutional Powers

Neustadt's discussion of command and its limitations suggests that he believed that it is not in the president's best interest to rely on, or automatically resort to, the use of formal or constitutional powers to achieve desired outcomes. Power should be pursued by other means. Yet, even from the early days of the Republic, as we saw in Washington's case, presidents have turned to these powers as a way of attaining ends, often with great success.

Washington set the foundation for exercising *express powers,* that is, those explicitly laid out in Article II. He established a presidency that was not merely a creature of the legislative branch but a reasonably independent actor within the Madisonian framework of shared powers. He also set the course for utilizing the more controversial implicit or *inherent powers*—these are not clearly stated in Article II of the Constitution but rather are derived, at least in part, from the nature of the office. Washington's claims of executive privilege against congressional requests for information, his willingness to exercise his powers as commander in chief when wars went undeclared, and his issuance of presidential proclamations and orders set important precedents. It quickly became clear that executive power was greater than that given in the simple words of the Constitution, and that it was subject to broader interpretation. Most of Washington's successors embraced that interpretative challenge, especially to the extent that it led to the expansion of their powers. Even Jefferson, a seemingly avowed opponent of strong federal and presidential power—as well as a strict reader of the Constitution—acquiesced.

Presidential exercise of inherent powers has become more frequent and a greater source of political controversy since Neustadt's time. One example of this is the growing use of *executive orders*. Technically, these are just administrative directives issued to further direct federal agencies and departments to carry out or define policies and programs in particular ways, but they have grown in importance and are sometimes more than mere administrative procedure. The same goes for *presidential proclamations,* which are generally broader in scope. They range from the mundane—the annual "Thanksgiving Day" proclamation—to those of high policy significance, such as Washington's Neutrality Proclamation of 1793 or Lincoln's Emancipation Proclamation of 1863. The use of presidential *signing statements*—statements of presidential interpretation that are appended to approved legislation—has also increased considerably. This practice raises questions about whether and how a president's intent should be factored into the proper legal interpretation of a law.

In the aftermath of the terrorist attacks of September 11, 2001, the issue of a president's inherent constitutional powers and other issues of presidential prerogative have taken on greater importance and meaning.[1] This was certainly the case for George W. Bush but remained true for Barack Obama, and likely will still be so for their successors in office. Presidential claims of war powers have increased and become a thornier issue. In the current undeclared war on terror, what constitutional powers does a president possess? What rights are applicable and in force for those on the opposing side?

This chapter focuses on exploring presidential claims to inherent powers and their use as a means for exercising power. We begin by going back to the Framers, at the different arguments of Hamilton and Madison as they battled it out on the constitutional merits of Washington's Neutrality Proclamation. In addition, we examine the views of three presidents—Theodore Roosevelt, William Howard Taft, and Abraham Lincoln—who each took different positions on what these powers might entail. On some occasions, the Supreme Court has reluctantly entered the fray, and we take a look at some of its key decisions. The court has provided some constitutional guidance, but not always wise guidance in some cases. We also discuss the very strong claims of executive power made by a more recent approach, the unitary theory of presidential power. Finally, we explore the recent upsurge in executive actions, grounded in claims about inherent powers, by the George W. Bush and Obama administrations. These actions have clearly increased in number and significance, but did they have constitutional merit and did they prove to be effective tools for these two presidents?

FRAMERS' AND PRESIDENTS' PERSPECTIVES ON PREROGATIVE POWERS

Executive prerogative has long been recognized through history. Most notably, even John Locke in his *Second Treatise on Government*—a seventeenth-century antimonarchical tract in favor of representative democracy—recognized that the executive must sometimes act without parliamentary authorization. In Locke's view there is inherent prerogative for an executive to act when the nation is under attack and no parliament is in session or can easily be brought to session.

The case for a broader interpretation of executive power—beyond the "nation under attack" justification—might also be grounded in the interpretation of broadly phrased words and clauses in Article II of the US Constitution. One source is the opening sentence of the article: "The executive Power shall be vested in a President." Another source is the charge that "he shall take Care that the Laws be faithfully executed." Broad powers have also been construed from the president's constitutional role as "Commander in Chief of the Army and Navy of the United States." That the president's oath of office is specified in the Constitution and that it states that the president "will *faithfully execute* the Office of President of the United States" provides another avenue for claims of power, as does the phrase that immediately follows: the president "will to the best of my Ability, preserve, protect and defend the Constitution of the United States."

At first glance, this might appear a shaky foundation for claims of more power; the words appear thin. But presidents have often made the most of it, and they have sometimes prevailed. In this section, we consider the reactions of Madison and Hamilton to Washington's first presidential proclamation to gauge their feelings on executive prerogative, and we look at the views of three presidents who are often cited as defining this terrain.

Hamilton and Madison Argue over Prerogative Powers

Although we do not have a clear statement from Washington framing his understanding of prerogative, he provided an important example of its practice when he issued the first presidential proclamation—the Neutrality Proclamation of 1793. At the time there were deep divisions as to whether the United States should support France or Britain, which were at war. Hamilton and his Federalists supported Britain. Jefferson and his followers favored France. Washington wished to remain neutral and wanted to act before events and political divisions got out of hand. He could call Congress back in session (a lengthy process at the time given difficult travel conditions)[2] and let them resolve it, or he could issue a proclamation. He chose the latter course. This proclamation was not just a vague statement of foreign policy intent; rather, it had real consequences of arrest and prosecution if violated.

The proclamation proved controversial. Both Hamilton and Madison sent letters to the press, just as they had done with the *Federalist Papers*. But on this issue they were on opposite sides. Hamilton, writing as "Pacificus," supported Washington's exercise of power. In the first of seven published essays, he argues that the president is "the organ of intercourse between the Nation and foreign nations."[3] Moreover, he argues that the Constitution vests executive power in the president, save for those exceptions it expressly carves out—a thought that Theodore Roosevelt would later support. Whereas Congress has the right to make war, it is "the duty of the executive to preserve peace till war is declared."[4] The Neutrality Proclamation made no new law in his view; it was just a statement of the status quo. Penalties for violating the proclamation, however, go unexamined in Hamilton's argument.

Madison responded, apparently urged on by Jefferson, who had initially supported neutrality but ended up resigning as secretary of state, in part, over the issue.[5] Writing as "Helvidius," Madison strongly attacked the constitutionality of the proclamation. In the first of his five essays, he opens with a heated statement, asserting that Pacificus's letters "have been read with singular pleasure and applause by the foreigners and degenerate citizens among us, who hate our republican government and the French Revolution."[6] According to Madison, Hamilton had it all reversed. Congress's constitutional power to declare war gives it primacy over foreign affairs, save those powers explicitly provided to the executive. For Madison, to argue otherwise was a violation of republican principles and smacked of British monarchism. To top it off, he quoted liberally from *Federalist No. 75*, which of course Hamilton himself had written, on the topic of Congress's treaty-making powers.[7]

As for Washington, although he initially acted unilaterally, he was able to gain Congress's support once it was back in session. In 1794, it passed the Neutrality Act, which gave the administration power to enforce Washington's proclamation. Historically, this set a precedent: subsequent agreement or prior authorization by Congress is a powerful chip for the president to have in justifying actions that might seem constitutionally unclear.

Abraham Lincoln: Life and Limb Theory

For Lincoln, the issue of presidential prerogative reared its head and took on special importance as he sought to preserve the Union. He took a number of immediate steps toward that end when he first took office. One week after the start of the Civil War, he issued a proclamation establishing a naval blockade of the Southern ports. His navy captured as war "prizes" ships that tried to run the blockade, which was common practice when a state of war existed between two nations. The problem was that there was no declared war between North and South, and the Lincoln administration went to great lengths to call it a "civil insurrection." Lincoln was also proactive in suspending writs of habeas corpus—the constitutional right of someone arrested to seek legal relief in a civilian court of law rather than being imprisoned for a prolonged and indefinite period or tried in military courts. It was not until two years later that Congress passed the Habeas Corpus Act of 1863, giving him statutory authorization to do so.

In Lincoln's view, particular constitutional guarantees sometimes need to be suspended to protect the larger project of the nation's survival—essentially, that sometimes a limb needs to be amputated in order to save a life. As he notes in an April 4, 1864, letter to Albert Hodges, the publisher of a Kentucky newspaper:

> I have never understood that the Presidency conferred upon me an unrestricted right to act officially upon this judgment and feeling. It was in the oath I took that I would, to the best of my ability, preserve, protect, and defend the Constitution of the United States. I could not take the office without taking the oath. Nor was it my view that I might take an oath to get power, and break the oath in using the power. . . . I did understand, however, that my oath to preserve the constitution to the best of my ability imposed upon me the duty of preserving, by every indispensable means, that government—that nation—of which that constitution was the organic law. Was it possible to lose the nation, and yet preserve the constitution? By general law life *and* limb must be protected; yet often a limb must be amputated to save a life; but a life is never wisely given to save a limb. I felt that measures, otherwise unconstitutional, might become lawful, by becoming indispensable to the preservation of the constitution, through the preservation of the nation. Right or wrong, I assumed this ground, and now avow it.[8]

Lincoln's view is somewhat akin to Locke's: national emergency and quick executive response justify extraconstitutional powers. The twist, however, was Lincoln's belief that depending on the nature of the emergency, the response could require suspension of some provisions of the Constitution. Louis Fisher, a constitutional scholar, picks up on this and posits that Lincoln's actions at the onset of the war were not grounded so much in claims of inherent powers but of *emergency* powers. Moreover, because Congress later assented to what Lincoln did, essentially combining Congress's powers as enumerated in Article I with the president's powers as implied by Article II, his actions might be regarded as having greater legitimacy.[9] But one must also ask: what are the limits here?

Theodore Roosevelt: Stewardship Theory

Theodore Roosevelt's view on presidential prerogative, like Hamilton's, is on the more expansive side, though unlike Lincoln, his actions were not in response to emergency situations. He was an activist president who expanded the role of the federal government as a political "progressive"—and from the Republican side of the Progressive Movement. This movement largely focused on breaking the power of political machines and party bosses by recommending greater democratic impact upon American politics—popular initiatives, recall of officeholders, direct election, and political primaries were among its chief efforts. However, Roosevelt coupled that with a generous reading of the president's constitutional powers, an effort that he shared with Woodrow Wilson, his progressive counterpart in the Democratic Party. Both saw themselves as representatives of the people against special interests, but that role was guided by a heavy dose of presidential direction. Neither saw themselves as mere instruments of the public will. As Roosevelt notes in his autobiography:

> The most important factor in getting the right spirit in my Administration . . . was my insistence upon the theory that the executive power was only limited by specific restrictions and prohibitions appearing in the Constitution or imposed by Congress under its Constitutional Powers. My view was that every executive officer, and above all every executive in high position, was a steward of the people bound actively and affirmatively to do all he could for the people. . . .
>
> I declined to adopt the view that what was imperatively necessary for the nation could not be done by the President unless he could find some specific

authorization for it. My belief was that it was not only his right but his duty to do anything that the needs of the nation demanded unless such action was forbidden by the Constitution or by the laws.[10]

Roosevelt's approach has been labeled *stewardship theory.* Power is grounded in service to the people, as well as the Constitution, on the president's terms—he is the public's somewhat independent "steward." Most importantly, unless the Constitution expressly prohibits something, the president is free to act.

William Howard Taft: Literalist Theory

Taft's alternative and more limited conception of presidential power was, in part, a response to Roosevelt's broader claims. Although Taft was Roosevelt's hand-picked successor in 1908, Roosevelt quickly soured on Taft's conduct as president. The two fought over the Republican nomination for president in 1912 and continued to clash after. The clearest statement of Taft's views comes from a series of lectures, delivered at Columbia University in the winter term of 1916, and later published as a book, *Our Chief Magistrate and His Powers.* (Note how he titles the presidential office in the work as chief *magistrate,* a term that normally connotes a judicial role.) According to Taft:

> The true view of the Executive functions is, as I conceive it, that the President can exercise no power which cannot be fairly and reasonably traced to some specific grant of power or justly implied and included within such express grant as proper and necessary to its exercise. Such specific grant must be either in the Federal Constitution or in an act of Congress passed in pursuance thereof. There is no undefined residuum of power. . . . The grants of Executive power are necessarily in general terms in order not to embarrass the Executive within the field of action plainly marked for him, but his jurisdiction must be justified and vindicated by affirmative constitutional or statutory provision, or it does not exist.[11]

Taft does not deny the need to interpret the Constitution, hence his proviso that presidential claims must be "justly implied." But he has a clearer and more confined view of the interpretive effort than Roosevelt; for Taft, there is no "undefined residuum of power." Taft also believed that the executive's interpretive power must be affirmed, and thus empowered, by reasonable constitutional interpretation, congressional assent, or both. Taft's conception of the office is not ungenerous to presidential power—it is no strict reading of the Constitution. That it is commonly termed a "literalist" interpretation of presidential power is a bit misleading though perhaps indicative of how we now take a more expansive view of presidential powers for granted.

In his autobiography, Roosevelt says that Taft took "a narrowly legalistic view that the President is the servant of Congress rather than the people," while noting that he himself embraced "substantially the course followed by both Andrew Jackson and Abraham Lincoln."[12] Taft examines this claim in his own book, countering that unlike Roosevelt, "Lincoln never claims that whatever authority in government was not expressly denied to him he could exercise. . . . Mr. Lincoln always pointed out the source of authority which in his opinion justified his acts."[13]

THE SUPREME COURT AND CONSTITUTIONAL DISPUTES OF PRESIDENTIAL POWER

So, is there some further, perhaps final resolution of this debate, especially by the Supreme Court? Alas, the court is generally not eager to resolve constitutional disputes over the powers of the other branches of government, because it regards many of these as "political questions," which it tends to avoid. Here, the court is concerned that resolving any disputes on the powers of the executive versus those of the legislative branch might overreach proper judicial bounds; that achieving a judicial solution might be beyond the expertise of the court; and that the court's own judicial powers could be weakened if the other branches were to ignore its judgment and findings. These concerns compound in disputes regarding the inherent powers of the presidency, an even grayer area where the applicable words of the Constitution are especially vague.

That said, there have been some cases in which the court has stepped into these constitutional disputes, as we will see in our examination of the court during Lincoln's presidency. We will also discuss two key twentieth-century cases that are generally regarded as landmark decisions in the area of presidential claims to inherent powers: *United States v. Curtiss-Wright Export Corp.* (1936)[14] and *Youngstown Sheet & Tube Co. v. Sawyer* (1952).[15] Although the line of judicial precedent is not as clearly established as in other areas of constitutional law, it is possible to discern some jurisprudence and reasoning in this area. That there is much that remains unclear is, of course, an invitation for presidents to use the command of their formal powers, whether clearly stated or not, as a tool for exercising influence and achieving political and policy ends. Although Neustadt would disagree, it can be an opportunity and means for the exercise of presidential power. But he is also right in noting that dangers can lurk should the president overreach (and should the court allow it), as we see in *Korematsu v. United States*.

Lincoln and the Court

During Lincoln's presidency, the Supreme Court at times responded to his claims of presidential power in the midst of the Civil War. In *The Prize Cases* (1863), which involved Lincoln's proclamation regarding the seizure of ships attempting to run Union blockades during the Civil War, the court upheld Lincoln's action by a narrow margin of 5–4, although four of the five Democrats on the court dissented.[16] The majority opinion stressed that the "President had a right, *jure belli* [right of war], to institute a blockade of ports . . . which neutrals are bound to regard." Moreover, the court noted that after Lincoln's proclamation, Congress passed a number of laws in 1861 enabling the prosecution of the war "with vigor and efficiency." Congress also passed an act making valid, post facto, all prior acts, orders, and proclamations of the president. Although the court did not declare the latter necessary, its attention to Congress's actions is notable.

On Lincoln's initial suspension of habeas corpus in April 1861, the result was more mixed. The first case, *Ex parte Merryman*, involved information that rebel supporters had planned attacks on railroad lines from Philadelphia through Maryland—vital links to Washington, DC. John Merryman was one of the men charged under Lincoln's order, accused and imprisoned without a judicial proceeding for cutting telegraph wires and burning bridges in Maryland. At the time, members of the Supreme Court "rode circuit," holding court and deciding cases in their assigned states before they reached the full Supreme Court. The member of the court assigned to Maryland was Chief Justice Roger Taney, a slave owner and the author of the court's opinion in the infamous *Dred Scott* case. He certainly was no ally of Lincoln. Taney, acting in his capacity as a circuit court judge, ruled in Merryman's favor, but Lincoln's attorney general ignored Taney's ruling and refused to bring him before a federal court.[17] In February 1862, Lincoln ordered the release of most prisoners involved in the episode, which rendered any further legal action moot. However, it took until March 1863 for the Congress to affirmatively respond and confirm Lincoln's habeas corpus suspension.[18]

By 1864, it seemed that suspension of the habeas corpus was settled, given that Congress had passed the necessary legislation so that Lincoln was no longer acting alone. However, that year Lambdin Milligan and four other Confederate supporters—all technically civilians—were accused of inciting insurrection and planning attacks on prisoner-of-war camps in Indiana. A civilian grand jury refused to indict Milligan. He was then tried before a military tribunal and sentenced to hang. Shortly before the sentence was to be carried out, Milligan applied for a habeas writ in federal court. In 1866, the Supreme Court heard the case and unanimously decided in Milligan's favor, reasoning that because civilian courts were operational in Indiana, he should have been tried there and not in a military court.[19] In fact, as a concurring opinion noted, the 1863 legislation explicitly contained language preserving habeas rights for civilians where federal courts remained open. But note that this was not just a test of Lincoln's war and emergency powers but directly involved the powers of the judicial branch. In *Ex parte Milligan,* when the federal judiciary's own powers were at stake, the court leaned in favor of its own branch of government—or at least that might be one interpretation.

United States v. Curtiss-Wright *and* Youngstown Sheet & Tube Co. v. Sawyer

In the twentieth century, there were two major Supreme Court cases on issues of the president's constitutional powers. One, *United States v. Curtiss-Wright* (1936), involved the sales of arms to Bolivia, which was engaged in a significant border dispute with Paraguay over control of the Gran Chaco region. In May 1934, Congress passed a joint resolution giving President Franklin D. Roosevelt the sole discretion to issue a proclamation prohibiting the sale of arms and other munitions to either nation; he immediately did so. The Curtiss-Wright firm was subsequently indicted for selling fifteen machine guns to Bolivia. In its defense, the firm argued that Congress had improperly delegated its legislative powers to the president and had provided unconstitutional discretion to the executive branch.

The firm's claim was likely to strike the court's interest: excessive delegation of power by Congress to the executive branch had been central to several cases in which the court struck down a number of laws that were part of FDR's New Deal. By a margin of 7–1, however, the court ruled in favor of the president; the issues raised were more complex than simple delegation and involved the president's own inherent powers. The majority opinion in the case, written by Justice George Sutherland, clearly differentiates a president's power in foreign affairs from that in domestic or internal affairs. As Sutherland—a conservative member of the court and an opponent of much of FDR's New Deal—notes, the "two classes of powers are different, both in respect of their origin and their nature. The broad statement that the federal government can exercise no powers except those specifically enumerated in the Constitution, and such implied powers as are necessary and proper to carry into effect the enumerated powers, is categorically true only in respect of our internal affairs."[20]

Moreover, Sutherland noted that "we are here dealing not alone with an authority vested in the President by an exertion of legislative power, but with such an authority plus the very delicate, *plenary and exclusive* power of the President as the *sole organ* of the federal government in the field of international relations—a power which does not require as a basis for its exercise an act of Congress" (emphasis added).[21] "Sole organ" and "plenary and exclusive power" are strong phrases. It is clear that the court was prepared to grant significant discretion, and thus acknowledgment of inherent constitutional power, to the president—at least in foreign matters.

We discussed the second case, *Youngstown Sheet & Tube Co. v. Sawyer* (1952), and Neustadt's analysis of its import for President Truman in Chapter 2, but the court's reasoning on the president's constitutional power is of interest here. In a 6–3 decision, the court ruled against Truman, and the jurisprudence of the majority opinion saw no justification of Truman's action. The court's analysis was much narrower than in *Curtiss-Wright,* especially in framing the seizure of the mills from a domestic rather than foreign affairs perspective. And unlike in the *Curtiss-Wright* case, there was no congressional authorization. Congress had discussed but rejected such seizure attempts and provided alternative means of resolution, which Truman did not follow. The court also rejected the administration's claims that Truman's order fell under the broad provisions of inherent power, which it had embraced in *Curtiss-Wright.* Even if previous presidents had successfully done what Truman attempted here without being challenged, his actions remained unconstitutional.

These two cases, essentially ruling and reasoning in opposite directions, set broad precedents on inherent powers. The central lessons we might take from these cases are that a president is likely to prevail in claims of inherent power if he or she has congressional authorization and if a convincing case can be made that the effort falls within the domain of foreign rather than domestic affairs. This analysis, however, is not particularly original on my part. In a concurring opinion to the majority view in *Youngstown,* Associate Justice Robert Jackson laid out a more elegant formulation. As he notes, "When the President acts pursuant to an express or implied authorization of Congress, his authority is at its maximum, for it includes all that he possesses in his own right plus all that Congress can delegate" but that "when the President takes measures incompatible with the expressed or implied will of Congress, his power is at its lowest ebb, for then he can rely only upon his own constitutional powers minus any constitutional powers of Congress over the matter."[22] He also addressed the middle ground, acknowledging that when a president acts without express assent or denial from Congress there is "a zone of twilight in which he and Congress may have concurrent authority, or in which its distribution is uncertain."[23] Jackson warned that presidential claims to "a power at once so conclusive and preclusive must be scrutinized with caution, for what is at stake is the equilibrium established by our constitutional system."[24]

Jackson's concurring opinion in *Youngstown* has been a special focus of attention at recent hearings on Supreme Court nominations in the aftermath of 9/11: Chief Justice John Roberts and Associate Justices Samuel Alito, Sonia Sotomayor, and Elena Kagan were each asked their views on it. People pay attention to Jackson's formulation, and rightfully so. He is reasoning through an area where the Constitution is not expressly clear, yet applying a sort of "constitutional logic" to resolve a difficult question. Where is the president on the strongest constitutional grounds? Where is the weakest point? What falls in the middle? How does Congress figure in?

We must ponder, however, the court's discernment in these two landmark cases with regard to the issue of foreign policy versus domestic policy. *Curtiss-Wright* involved the sale of fifteen machine guns; *Youngstown* involved a possibly prolonged strong strike in the steel industry in the midst of a major war. The court decided that *Youngstown* was a domestic issue, but it could be argued that the strike potentially had more of an impact on foreign affairs.

A Black Mark: Korematsu v. United States

I would be remiss if I did not direct attention to the darker side of Supreme Court involvement in presidential claims of inherent power—namely, *Korematsu v. United States* (1944). This case seems to fit the criteria that Jackson laid out in his opinion—there was congressional authorization and it was in the arena of foreign policy. However, its outcome is questionable if not repugnant. On March 19, 1942, several months after the attack on Pearl Harbor and the declaration of war against Japan, Congress passed legislation making it a crime to "enter, remain in, leave or commit any act in any military area"[25] specified by the president or the secretary of war. FDR had already created such a zone, encompassing California, Oregon, Washington, and parts of Arizona, through Executive Order 9066, issued on February 19, 1942. As a consequence, although no evidence of sabotage or acts of disloyalty were found among Japanese American *citizens*, they were all—some 120,000 in total—forced to leave their homes, farms, and businesses for government-run internment camps. Racial hysteria was rampant. According to Gen. John De Witt, who was in charge of the evacuation and internment process, absence of sabotage proved nothing: "A Jap's a Jap whether he's an American citizen or not. I don't want any of them."[26]

Fred Korematsu, a Japanese American citizen, was convicted of failing to report for internment. He challenged his conviction, and his case was eventually heard by the Supreme Court. By a 6–3 majority, the court ruled against him and upheld the constitutionality of the internments and FDR's executive order. Justice Hugo Black, often considered one of the court's great civil libertarians, wrote the majority opinion.[27] As Justice Stephen Breyer, a current member of the court, assessed: "To its long-lasting shame, the Court upheld the exclusion order based on racial and cultural stereotypes."[28] How did the court reach its decision in *Korematsu*? Breyer posits that although the court was not "unsympathetic to claims for protection of individual liberty," it reached the decision it did "because it could not find a way to protect individual liberties from invasion by the president without at the same time taking from the president discretionary powers that the war might require him to exercise."[29]

If we were to just take into account Justice Jackson's formula, then it would seem like an easy decision for the court to rule in favor of the president's actions. The president and Congress were acting in concert, and so power was at its highest. Unfortunately, it's not always so simple; in this case, real costs were borne by American citizens and no positive benefits were obtained. The *Korematsu* decision is a black mark upon the court.

THE UNITARY THEORY OF THE EXECUTIVE

A more recent theory—although there are historical antecedents—about executive power that has gained some traction is the ***unitary theory of the executive.***

It makes strong claims about a president's power, particularly about attempts by other branches of government to encroach upon it. As Louis Fisher explains, "This theory places all executive power directly under the control of the president, leaving no room for independent commissions, independent counsels, congressional involvement in administrative details, or statutory limitations on the president's power to remove executive officials."[30] It claims as its constitutional foundation Article II phrases such as "executive Power shall be vested in a President" and "he shall take Care that the Laws be faithfully executed" as well as the presidential oath of office to "preserve, protect and defend" the Constitution. These and others are then linked to create a strong theory of inherent, near-exclusive presidential control of the executive branch.

Those who argue in favor of it often trace its lineage back to specific claims of presidential power, such as Jefferson's refusal to recognize some of the commissions of appointment issued late in John Adams's presidency. But this might not be a particularly wise foundation on which to base a theory: it led to the case of *Marbury v. Madison* (1803) in which the court successfully asserted its own inherent power of judicial review. Additionally, Jefferson likely did not have a strong theory of presidential power in mind when he refused to honor Adams's commissions; he was mostly averse to a strong presidency and wanted the opportunity to appoint his own officials. Other claimed antecedents are Lincoln's suspension of habeas corpus, Theodore Roosevelt's stewardship theory, and Truman's seizure of the steel mills.[31] However, as we saw above, some of those claims were eventually constrained or rejected by the Supreme Court.

Perhaps the theory's greatest flaw is that it is difficult to square such a strong, unitary conception of executive control with Madison's theory of shared powers and checks and balances on each branch. Plus, should the other branches also interpret certain words in the Constitution with similar expansive generosity, it could result in significant impact and constraint upon the executive branch. The resurgence of Congress in the latter part of the Nixon presidency and in the post-Watergate period is an example of this. Of more important historical significance during this period was the Supreme Court's denial of Nixon's expansive claims to executive privilege concerning control of the "Watergate tapes"— Nixon's secret recordings of White House meetings. The latter was perhaps the most significant decision by the court concerning claims of inherent executive power: once the court ordered that the tapes must be released, their contents revealed a number of illegal actions on Nixon's part that quickly led to his resignation as president.[32]

Still, the theory has its proponents. One particular case from the Reagan presidency stands out: *Morrison v. Olson* (1988), which concerned the constitutionality of the Independent Counsel Act, which allowed for the appointment of special prosecutors during inquiries concerning alleged malfeasance by executive branch officials.[33] The legislation was a legacy of the Nixon presidency; the idea was that the Justice Department, as part of the executive branch, could not properly and impartially investigate misconduct within the administration. Although the Supreme Court upheld the constitutionality of appointing special prosecutors by a 7–1 margin, there was one dissenter—Justice Antonin Scalia. In his dissent, Scalia seems to embrace something close to a unitary theory. In his view, creation by law of special prosecutors usurped executive powers, especially shielding them from presidential dismissal. The constitutional problem here, in his reasoning, was that special prosecutors or independent counsels were technically executive branch officials. Congress could not take away or otherwise reduce those executive powers by law, presumably including the power of presidents to fire them.

The unitary theory of the executive achieved a stronger measure of influence in George W. Bush's presidency. One area that the Bush administration especially focused on was signing statements, which, by their nature, impose a president's thoughts and intents on a piece of legislation. In addition, many of Bush's statements included some reference to the "unitary executive." Bush was not the originator of this practice, nor the only one to do so: signing statements can be traced back, at least, to James Monroe's presidency. By Reagan's presidency we begin to find unitary thinking creeping into these statements. For example, Reagan's statement appended to the 1987 debt limit bill notes that: "If this provision were interpreted otherwise, so as to require the President to follow the orders of a subordinate, it would plainly constitute an unconstitutional infringement of the President's authority as head of a unitary executive branch."[34]

Signing statements accelerated in number under Bush. He issued more than all of his predecessors combined in just his first term. From Monroe through Carter, 75 statements were issued; from Reagan through Clinton, 322 were issued. Bush issued 436 in his first term alone. More importantly, the statements cited broad claims about presidential power. Bush used the term "unitary executive" 95 times in his signing statements and executive orders over this period.[35]

One example is Bush's statement accompanying the Intelligence Reform and Terrorism Prevention Act of 2004, a major piece of legislation that reconfigured the organization of the intelligence-gathering community and homeland security in the aftermath of 9/11. Arguably, it was the most significant reorganization of the executive branch since the creation of the Department of Defense in 1947, under President Truman. Most notably, it created the office of the Director of National Intelligence. As demonstrated in the language of the signing statement, the White House grants itself a significant measure of executive discretion. Note particularly the language in the second paragraph dealing with submission, and withholding, of information:

> The executive branch shall construe the Act, including amendments made by the Act, in a manner consistent with *the constitutional authority of the President* to conduct the Nation's foreign relations, as *Commander in Chief* of the Armed Forces, and to supervise the *unitary executive branch*, which encompass the *authority* to conduct intelligence operations.
>
> The executive branch shall construe provisions in the Act that *mandate submission of information* to the Congress, entities within or outside the executive branch, or the public, in a manner consistent with the *President's constitutional authority to supervise the unitary executive branch and to withhold information* that *could impair foreign relations, national security, the deliberative processes of the Executive, or the performance of the Executive's constitutional duties.* (emphasis added)[36]

Whether these signing statements matter much remains unclear; to date they do not seem to carry much weight. Although they have not regularly featured in court opinions when cases of controversy arise, they have not been wholly ignored either. In *INS v. Chadha* (1983), the court found the statutory power claimed by Congress to subsequently "veto" delegated administrative action to be unconstitutional. The court explored past presidential signing statements in a footnote in its majority opinion.[37]

It seems that presidential unilateralism is here to stay. As Barilleaux and Kelly conclude, "The long-term dynamics" of the presidency "favor the expansion of presidential power and therefore the consolidation of the unitary executive."[38] Although Obama has certainly not embraced the rhetoric of unilateralism his predecessor exhibited, his practices were often not all that different. Indeed, as a presidential candidate, he pledged to "not use signing statements to nullify or undermine congressional instructions as enacted into law." As president, however, Obama did use signing statements for the same purpose of protecting claims of presidential power—though not as many as Bush.[39]

CONTEMPORARY PRESIDENTS
AND EXECUTIVE ACTIONS

Although not unique to them, executive orders and presidential proclamations are particularly powerful tools that contemporary presidents have used to garner some result or outcome. In addition, presidents sometimes issue ***presidential memoranda,*** which, like executive orders, are directives for federal officials or governmental agencies. For example, in 1993, Bill Clinton issued a memorandum permitting abortions in military hospitals, although not at government expense.[40] In November 2014, Obama further expanded the number of undocumented persons exempt from deportation through a memorandum to his secretary of homeland security. In announcing the action, Obama made explicit reference to the failure of Congress to deliver on immigration reform. In the area of foreign policy, ***national security directives*** are yet another avenue of executive action. These are executive orders providing guidance for foreign, defense, and intelligence agencies and departments.[41]

Some of these executive actions derive from statutes that grant the president some power and some measure of discretion in how they might be carried out. Others stem from the president's general claim of broad constitutional authority. But, whatever the source, they can serve as tools of presidential power. In his study of executive orders from FDR's presidency through Clinton's, for example, Adam Warber found that "modern presidents have actively used executive orders to pursue major policy initiatives, to change existing policies made by their predecessors, and they have developed legal strategies to protect these directives from coming under political attack from Congress."[42] According to Phillip J. Cooper, executive orders might be used to

- Respond to emergencies
- Strike hard and fast in foreign policy matters
- Address private disputes with a public impact
- Generate favorable publicity
- Pay political debts, reward supporters, and send signals
- Make end runs around Congress
- Launch significant policy initiatives
- Control agency and departmental policy making
- Change policy direction from the previous administration[43]

In his work *Power Without Persuasion,* William G. Howell finds that executive actions can be a strong tool to attain presidential ends without relying on persuasion with Congress. The veto (an express rather than inherent power) can get Congress to make policy concessions, but, as Howell notes, it is still part of the normal legislative process. He believes presidents can use other executive office–specific tools and that they can accomplish quite a bit "by setting policy on their own, by acting unilaterally."[44] Howell also observes that the broader political context has an impact on the use and success of this category of presidential power. When Congress and the judiciary are weak, that's when the president can exert more unitary action, but when Congress is united and strong and the judiciary takes a restricted view of presidential power, then presidents aren't able to accomplish as much by themselves. In short, Howell believes that a president's ability to unilaterally set public policy depends upon the response from the other branches of government.[45]

In some ways, this harkens back to Neustadt's argument that professional reputation and public prestige can bolster a president's bargaining position. However, Howell's differs from Neustadt's thinking in an important way. For Howell, the stronger presidents resort to executive action to attain their ends, not the weaker ones who fail at bargaining and other strategies of influence.[46] Command is not the last resort for a weak president but rather the preferred course for a strong one. For both George W. Bush and Barack Obama, executive orders and related executive actions have proven useful instruments of presidential power. How has each administration used these tools, and what are the results and consequences of their executive actions?

Executive Actions in the George W. Bush Administration

Not surprisingly given the administration's strong adherence to the theory and practice of unitary executive power, Bush issued a number of orders and other executive actions to achieve his policy ends. For example, one of his initial legislative proposals was to permit greater leeway for religious organizations to administer a variety of social service programs. When Congress rejected it, the White House then issued executive orders directing agencies and departments to pursue the effort to the greatest degree legally possible. Stem cell research was another controversial area of action for the Bush administration. The use of stem cell lines obtained through the destruction of a human embryo raised ethical issues for the president, and so in 2001, Bush restricted funding for research on stem cells to those lines that had already been created. In 2006, the Republican-controlled Congress responded with legislation loosening the restrictions, but Bush successfully used his veto power to kill the bill; it was his first veto.

Perhaps the most important areas where the Bush administration used executive orders dealt with the war on terror in the aftermath of the 9/11 attacks.[47] Efforts here are interesting not only because of their far-reaching—and, at times, controversial—nature and consequences but also because many were coupled with claims stemming from a unitary theory of the executive. On November 13, 2001, Bush signed a military order that stripped combatants detained during the war on terror of their habeas corpus rights: they could potentially be held indefinitely or, at the government's choosing, have their case investigated and decided by a military tribunal in which they held few legal rights. Because the war on terror was against nonstate actors, entities that don't belong to any one nation, these were not traditional prisoners of war but were classified in the new, more nebulous category of "enemy combatants." Had they been combatants for a discernible state entity, treatment and responsibilities would have been more clear under various international conventions. Deliberations on the order were tightly held; neither Secretary of State Colin Powell nor National Security Adviser Condoleezza Rice were consulted before it was issued. Some of these prisoners were housed in foreign nations, others at the US detention facility at Guantanamo Bay, Cuba. The latter was explicitly selected because it was a secure facility but was thought by the administration to be beyond the jurisdiction of the federal courts.

Challenges to Bush's order and the thin procedural rights afforded detainees eventually made their way to the Supreme Court. In a series of decisions, the court ruled against the administration and Congress, which had passed legislation supporting the administration's position. The most important of these cases was *Hamdan v. Rumsfeld* (2006), in which the Supreme Court asserted that the military tribunals violated military law and the Geneva Conventions and were procedurally weak.[48] Congress then passed, with administration support, the Military Commissions Act of 2006, which sought to address the court's concerns in *Hamdan* but also explicitly stripped the federal court of habeas jurisdiction. In *Boumediene v. Bush* (2008), the Supreme Court struck down the act as unconstitutional and granted the Guantanamo detainees habeas rights.[49] This series of Supreme Court decisions rejected not only the administration's constitutional claims but also Congress's actions that supported them. Much like *Ex parte Milligan,* the constitutional questions in these cases were not just about presidential authority—and in this case the president acting in eventual concert with Congress—but also involved the powers of the judicial branch itself.

Another area of important executive action was in the use of enhanced interrogation techniques to seek, if not force, information from enemy combatants and other detainees. Although the Bush administration claimed that these did not constitute torture, were not prohibited by international law and the Geneva Conventions, and involved only a few individuals, they were arguably quite extreme. Among other acts, they included sensory deprivation, physical punishment, hypothermia, and waterboarding—the last was particularly controversial. One infamous memo from the Justice Department defined torture as only those actions that lead to pain equivalent to that of death or major organ failure. Anything less was apparently fair game. The development of such harsh interrogation policies led to strong disagreements within the administration. However, the president, Vice President Dick Cheney and some members of his staff, and some officials within the Justice Department prevailed in putting those policies in place. They justified these policies with logic and rhetoric that strongly epitomized the unitary executive theory. As James P. Pfiffner notes, the administration contended that in the war on terror, the Geneva Conventions do not apply, the laws of the United States do not apply, the president is not bound by international law, and the president's commander-in-chief authority can override any law.[50]

This particular case of presidential action raises an important question about the wisdom of such exercises of presidential power and the reasoning behind them. In the summer of 2003, photographs showing the extreme treatment of prisoners by US forces at the Abu Ghraib prison in Iraq became public, leading to an outpouring of outrage at home and abroad. In addition, some critics of the Bush administration have argued that the interrogation techniques, once publicized, strengthened the will and resolve of the enemy. Others have argued that little in the way of useful information was obtained through the use of these tactics, although some have countered that claim, most notably Cheney. Still, American prestige, both home and abroad, was damaged.

Another example is the covert surveillance of telephone and other electronic communications between suspected terrorists abroad and domestic sources the National Security Agency (NSA) conducted on the White House's order. Surveillance of foreign sources is permissible, but, as established by the Foreign Intelligence Surveillance Act of 1978 (FISA), domestic wiretapping for national security purposes requires the approval of a special court. The administration again claimed it had inherent constitutional authority to bypass FISA because it had privately consulted with Congress and because what the NSA was doing was not technically wiretapping specific conversations but looking at patterns of contact.

In addition, the administration justified this and other actions in the war on terror with the Authorization for Use of Military Force (AUMF), passed by Congress shortly after the 9/11 attacks. AUMF authorized the president to "use all necessary and appropriate force against those nations, organizations, or persons he determines planned, authorized, committed, or aided the terrorist attacks that occurred on September 11, 2001, or harbored such organizations or persons, in order to prevent any future acts of international terrorism against the United States by such nations, organizations or persons."[51] This was particularly salient for domestic wiretapping: because of the "unless authorized by statute" clause in FISA, AUMF could be interpreted as permitting the administration to bypass FISA.[52] Understandably, many citizens were unhappy to learn that their private communications were being monitored and collected by the NSA, and the White House came under heavy criticism for its actions. Many would argue that the Bush administration's executive actions during the war infringed on their constitutional rights, and as a result the administration's reputation and citizens' trust in government diminished. If results were achieved, they came at a very high cost. On June 2, 2015, President Obama signed into law the USA Freedom Act, which sharply curtailed the NSA's warrantless surveillance program.

Executive Actions in the Obama Administration

Bush is not alone—executive orders and other related actions also proved useful tools for the Obama administration. Interestingly, on his first day in office in 2001, Obama signed two executive orders. One banned the use of enhanced interrogation techniques on detainees, restricting methods to those in the Army Field Manual.[53] The other called for the closure of the Guantanamo detention facility within a year. However, two years later, the administration reversed course by executive order, continuing Guantanamo's use to house detainees. At this writing, seven years into the Obama presidency, "Gitmo" still remains open as a detention facility for accused terrorists.

The White House often employed executive orders and related actions to achieve policy ends when legislative action proved unproductive—especially during Obama's second term. Although the Democrats did reasonably well in the 2012 congressional elections, the Republicans still maintained a sizable majority in the House: 234 Republicans to 201 Democrats. And in the Senate, the split was 55–45 in favor of the Democrats, but not a sufficient margin to avoid Senate filibuster by the Republicans. As is the case for many second-term presidents, Obama had hoped to pursue an ambitious agenda. The year 2013, however, did not yield much in the way of legislative success. This was no surprise and followed the pattern of almost all, if not every, presidents' second term.

Obama's inaugural address in 2013 promised new efforts on gun control, climate change, and immigration reform. None gained traction. The major effort that year was battling with House Republicans over raising the debt ceiling, but attempts at a bipartisan "grand bargain" failed, which led to a sixteen-day shutdown of the federal government in October. Starting that same month and into early 2014, the White House also was preoccupied in dealing with the fallout from major technical glitches in the enrollment process for the Affordable Care Act (i.e., "Obamacare"), the signature achievement of Obama's first term. The rollout of Obama's second-term goals had largely failed.

It is perhaps not a surprise, then, that in his 2014 State of the Union address, Obama clearly signaled that he was willing to use his own presidential powers to further policy initiatives. The aim was to bypass a Congress that was increasingly polarized by party and unlikely to reach reasonable compromise. At the time, White House press secretary Jay Carney noted, "The President has been clear that he will work with Congress where Congress is willing to work with him, but where Congress refuses to move forward and cooperate on common sense ideas to help the economy, help the middle class, he's going to use every power that he has to advance that agenda."[54] In his weekly radio address on June 28, 2014, the president especially noted that Republican "obstruction keeps the system rigged for those at the top, and rigged against the middle class. And as long as they insist on doing it, I'll keep taking actions on my own—like the actions I've taken already to attract new jobs, lift workers' wages, and help students pay off their loans. I'll do my job."[55]

To date, Obama's various executive orders, memoranda, and presidential proclamations have included (or are planned to include) orders to

- Raise the minimum wage for employees of contractors doing business with the federal government

- Extend family leave policies to same-sex couples
- Require firms with federal contracts to have in place nondiscrimination policies for gay and lesbian employees
- Prohibit discrimination against federal employees based on gender identity
- Change the repayment options for college students with federal loans to more favorable terms
- Delay implementation of some of the provisions of the Affordable Care Act
- Allow the Environmental Protection Agency to enforce the reduction of carbon emissions from coal-fired power plants
- Expand background checks on those buying weapons at gun shows
- Prevent retaliation against employees who are prohibited from inquiring about, disclosing, or discussing their compensation with fellow workers
- Halt the deportation of children brought illegally to the United States by their parents and expand the number of undocumented immigrants exempt from deportation
- Create a vast marine sanctuary in the central Pacific Ocean, making it off-limits to fishing, oil exploration, and other activities

Each was a significant policy initiative. Taken together, they might be said to constitute a substantial political agenda.

On June 25, 2014, Speaker of the House John Boehner (R-OH) announced that he and a group of other House members planned to introduce legislation that would permit them to file suit against the president for his executive actions. Boehner saw Obama's actions as "an effort to erode the power of the legislative branch." Moreover, he believed that "the president is not faithfully executing the laws of our country, and on behalf of the institution and our Constitution, standing up and fighting for this is in the best long-term interest of the Congress."[56]

However, the effort was a hollow one, more for political consumption than likely judicial response. Federal courts have generally ruled that members of Congress lack "standing" to bring lawsuits against the president. Obama may even be out of office by the time the suit finally reaches federal court, likely rendering it moot. Still, it is important to bear in mind that executive orders and actions can be overturned. Congress can pass laws countermanding them, and successor presidents can write their own orders, altering or completely abolishing those of their predecessors. Presidents themselves can even do this for their own prior order as their term progresses (recall Obama on Guantanamo closure). As for Obama, his response to Boehner was: "So sue me," adding "as long as they're doing nothing, I'm not going to apologize for doing something."[57]

Yet Obama's executive actions, at least in terms of their sheer numbers, are not in any way more numerous than those of his recent predecessors. Indeed, Obama actually issued fewer executive orders, on average per year, than his two-term predecessors. Obama averaged 32.8 orders compared to Eisenhower's 60.5, Reagan's 47.6, Clinton's 45.5, and G. W. Bush's 36.4.[58] However, these numbers don't tell the full story. Although, much like his predecessors', Obama's executive actions range from the mundane and inconsequential (e.g., renaming the staff of the National Security Council) to the more significant (regulatory changes on climate policy), there is one major difference. The Obama administration claimed (publicly and loudly) to bypass Congress through executive action. Neither Clinton nor George W. Bush, and certainly not Truman, Eisenhower, Nixon, or Reagan, made such a public fuss about bypassing Congress through the executive branch's own initiatives.

Did it help? For Obama, despite these executive efforts, the political landscape as his term neared its end was not much better. Scandals in veterans' hospitals led to the resignation of the secretary of veterans' affairs. The president also faced several foreign policy challenges, including Russian incursions into the Ukraine, and the military advances of the Islamic State in Iraq and Syria (ISIS) that plunged these countries into chaos. The midterm congressional elections of 2014 did not bolster Obama's prospects for the remaining two years of his presidency. The Democrats lost 63 seats in the House and 9 seats in the Senate, putting both chambers under Republican control.

One question to consider is: If Obama had developed better relationships with members of Congress earlier in his presidency, would his use of executive actions have been less necessary later on? During his first term, many reports indicated that the White House was less inclined than previous administrations to schedule informal meetings and social functions with legislators—even those from his own party. One report noted that several Democrats believed that "if Obama had been more attentive to Congress, he would have more in his arsenal than executive actions."[59] Starting in 2014, Obama seems to have been more attentive to members' needs and requests and more amenable to the benefits of social interaction. It is indeed possible that Obama may not have had to resort to executive action as much had he been less insular throughout most of his presidency. He had contact with familiar aides and associates in his administration, but perhaps not with those he needed to win over to achieve success.

CONCLUSION: IMPLICATIONS AND QUESTIONS

Recent studies have emphasized that executive actions stemming from claims about the president's authority can be an important tool for exercising power. As Mayer concludes, "Presidential power must include a broader understanding of the president's formal power."[60] At the same time, executive orders and other actions, although offering opportunities for the successful exercise of presidential power, are not without their costs. Costs should be weighed against benefits, and both must be measured within the political context that prevails when executive actions are contemplated. What is the likely reaction of Congress? Will the courts eventually get involved? Clinton's hope, during his 1992 transition to the presidency, to use executive orders to overturn the ban on gays and lesbians serving in the military is the classic example of failure. Congressional and other opposition quickly arose, so Clinton backed down and was later forced to embrace the "Don't Ask, Don't Tell" directive. It was eventually overturned by legislation in December 2010, some seventeen years later.

According to Cooper, presidents and their advisers should follow three rules when contemplating the tools of executive action:

1. Understand the tools available as well as the risks involved in using each one.
2. Do not try to use too many of them at once.
3. Executive actions are especially tempting in emergencies and crises, real or imagined. A sober second look is necessary even when it seems most pertinent to move quickly.[61]

Richard Pious notes that presidents can benefit from "frontlash," or the early use of presidential action and prerogative to attempt to resolve controversy. Its exercise quiets critics, builds partisan support, and reassures the public. The president exercises power and successfully leads. The classic example is one of the earliest: Washington's Neutrality Proclamation. But Pious does warn that frontlash, if overplayed, can lead to presidential overconfidence and perhaps even an imperial presidency. Pious also discusses the danger of "backlash." Here, the effect is just the opposite: executive action is exercised, but it leads to a loss of support and a rise in opposition. Congress may even respond with constraining legislation or force a president into an unwelcome compromise. At the most extreme, perhaps even a crisis of constitutional authority occurs. Pious notes Nixon's Watergate and Reagan's Iran-Contra scandals as prime examples of this.[62] I agree.

There is no doubt that executive action, grounded in claims to inherent power, has become a more central resource in a president's toolkit in recent years. It has a long historical lineage all the way back to Washington, but its use is now more expected and routine. Indeed, I think it is fair to say that we will see not only the continued use of executive actions but perhaps even some acceleration of their use in the future because the political conditions that have led to their increase are unlikely to abate. Party and ideological polarization in Congress, which makes bargaining more difficult, is not likely to change and could get even worse. Instability in foreign affairs, especially the war on terror and dealing with rogue nations, is another factor that will continue to fuel the use of inherent powers. I suspect that future historians will look back at the George W. Bush and Obama presidencies not as abnormal blips but as trend points in presidential reliance on executive power.

At the same time, there are dangers to any branch of government single-handedly and successfully attaining goals without consideration of, and debate over, the merits or consequences of those ends. Harold Koh in *The National Security Constitution* frames this challenge best: the important question is not which branch has successfully achieved its goals, but what the broader policy implications of that effort are. As he notes, "Too many years of foreign policy dominance by any single branch of government will foster reactive interbranch conflict that will jeopardize the long-term interests of the nation as a whole."[63] Louis Fisher believes that presidents should hew more closely to a reasonable interpretation of the Constitution—a limited view of implied powers, not an expansive interpretation of inherent powers. He is especially critical of the George W. Bush administration's efforts in the aftermath of 9/11 to "advance a broad theory of presidential inherent power," one that is "not subject to constraint from other branches."[64] Going back to the Framers, Madison believed that competition among the branches of government would resolve these issues. Although this occurs on occasion, this competition for power lacks proper normative guidance.

When does the president go too far? Conversely, when has Congress exceeded its bounds? What are the reasonable limits of each branch's assertion of power?

Reliance on action grounded in inherent powers carries risk and even danger, as various scholars have noted. I would add that any risk might be avoided or at least lessened by understanding the proper place of executive actions in a wider array of means of exercising influence a president might turn to—one of which, bargaining, we have already explored in Chapter 2. We now turn to public appeals as yet another resource for the exercise of presidential power.

NOTES

1. For a good overview of presidential prerogative, see Richard Pious, "Prerogative Power and Presidential Politics," in *The Oxford Handbook of the American Presidency*, ed. George C. Edwards III and William G. Howell (New York: Oxford University Press, 2009), 455–476.

2. Travel from just Boston to Philadelphia, for example, was a journey of six or so days.

3. Alexander Hamilton, Document 14, Pacificus, No. 1, *The Founders' Constitution*, ed. Philip Kurland and Ralph Lerner (Chicago: University of Chicago Press, 2000), http://press-pubs.uchicago.edu/founders/documents/a2_2_2-3s14.html.

4. Ibid.

5. Madison's first Helvidius letter appeared on August 24, 1793. Thus, Jefferson was still secretary of state at the time and a member of Washington's cabinet (as was Secretary of the Treasury Hamilton). Jefferson did not resign his post until December 31, 1793.

6. James Madison, Helvidius, No. 1, *The Founders' Constitution*, ed. Philip Kurland and Ralph Lerner (Chicago: University of Chicago Press, 2000), http://press-pubs.uchicago.edu/founders/documents/a2_2_2-3s15.html.

7. Ibid.

8. Abraham Lincoln, "To Albert G. Hodges," in *Collected Works of Abraham Lincoln*, vol. 7 (Ann Arbor: University of Michigan Digital Library Production Services, 2001), 282, http://quod.lib.umich.edu/l/lincoln/lincoln7/1:617?hi=0;rgn=div1;view=fulltext.

9. Louis Fisher, "Invoking Inherent Powers: A Primer," *Presidential Studies Quarterly* 37, no. 1 (March 2007): 1–22.

10. Theodore Roosevelt, *The Autobiography of Theodore Roosevelt* (New York: Macmillan, 1913), 388–389.

11. William Howard Taft, *Our Chief Magistrate and His Powers* (New York: Columbia University Press, 1916), 139–140.

12. Roosevelt, *Autobiography*, 395.

13. Taft, *Our Chief Magistrate*, 147–148.

14. *US v. Curtiss-Wright Export Corp.*, 299 U.S. 304 (1936).

15. *Youngstown Sheet & Tube v. Sawyer*, 343 U.S. 579 (1952).

16. *The Prize Cases*, 67 U.S. 635 (1863).

17. *Ex parte Merryman*, 17 F. Case 144 (C.C.D. MD 1861).

18. According to Article I, section 9, "The Privilege of the Writ of Habeas Corpus shall not be suspended, unless when in Cases of Rebellion or Invasion the public Safety may require it." Since this clause is located in Article I, which deals with Congress, suspension is presumably a congressional power.

19. The case is *Ex parte Milligan*, 71 U.S. 4 (1866).

20. *US v. Curtiss-Wright Export Corp.*, 299 U.S. 315–316 (1936).

21. Ibid.

22. *Youngstown Sheet & Tube v. Sawyer*, 343 U.S. 635–638 (1952).

23. Ibid.

24. Ibid.

25. Public Law No. 503, 56 Stat. 173 (1942).

26. The Perilous Fight: America's World War II in Color, "Asian Americans," 2003, http://www.pbs.org/perilousfight/social/asian_americans/.

27. *Korematsu v. US*, 323 U.S. 214 (1944).

28. Stephen Breyer, *Making Our Democracy Work: A Judge's View* (New York: Alfred A. Knopf, 2010), 189–190.

29. Ibid.

30. Fisher, "Invoking Inherent Powers," 10.

31. For further discussion of unitary theory, with historical analysis of its use for all presidents from Washington through G. W. Bush, see Steven Calabresi and Christopher S. Yoo, *The Unitary Executive: Presidential Power from Washington to Bush* (New Haven, CT: Yale University Press, 2008). Another useful volume is the edited collection by Ryan Barilleaux and Christopher Kelly, eds., *The Unitary Executive and the Modern Presidency* (College Station: Texas A&M University Press, 2010). One of the strongest proponents of the view is John C. Yoo, a member of the Department of Justice's Office of Legal Counsel during the early G. W. Bush presidency. See John C. Yoo, *The Powers of War and Peace: The Constitution and Foreign Affairs after 9/11* (Chicago: University of Chicago Press, 2005) and *Crisis and Command: A History of Executive Power from George Washington to George W. Bush* (New York: Kaplan Publishing, 2010). Alternatively, for a view of presidential powers that is more constrained by Congress's participation and the Madisonian system of checks and balances, see Harold H. Koh, *The National Security Constitution: Sharing Power After the Iran-Contra Affair* (New Haven, CT: Yale University Press, 1990). Another set of important sources is the extensive writings of Louis Fisher, the most recent of which is *Law of the Executive Branch: Presidential Power* (New York: Oxford University Press, 2014).

32. *Unites States v. Nixon*, 418 U.S. 683 (1974).

33. *Morrison v. Olson*, 487 U.S. 654 (1988).

34. Ronald Reagan, "Statement on Signing the Federal Debt Limit and Deficit Reduction Bill," September 29, 1987, http://www.reagan.utexas.edu/archives/speeches/1987/092987d.htm.

35. Jennifer Van Bergen, "The Unitary Executive: Is the Doctrine Behind the Bush Presidency Consistent with a Democratic State?" FindLaw, January 9, 2006, http://writ.news.findlaw.com/commentary/20060109_bergen.html.

36. George W. Bush, "Statement on Signing the Intelligence Reform and Terrorism Prevention Act of 2004, December 17, 2004," in *Public Papers of the President, 2004* (Washington, DC: Government Printing Office, 2004), 2293.

37. *INS v. Chadha,* 462 U.S. 919 (1983). The footnote in the *Chadha* opinion is number 13. Another decision in this area is *Bowsher v. Synar,* 478 U.S. 714 (1986). Here the court ruled that a budget act, Gramm-Rudman-Hollings, was unconstitutional because it gave Congress the power to fire the comptroller general of the United States, an executive branch official.

38. Ryan Barilleaux and Christopher Kelly, "Conclusions: Going Forward," in *The Unitary Executive and the Modern Presidency,* ed. Ryan Barilleaux and Christopher Kelly (College Station: Texas A&M University Press, 2010), 224, 227.

39. According to one count, by July 1, 2014, Obama had issued 27 signing statements, 56 percent of which raised constitutional concerns compared to 79 percent of Bush's signing statements. Don Wolfensberger, "Defense Signing Statement Reveals President's Prescience/ Procedural Politics," Roll Call, July 1, 2014, http://blogs.rollcall.com/beltway-insiders/defense -signing-statement-reveals-presidents-prescience-procedural-politics/?dcz=.

40. Phillip J. Cooper, *By Order of the President: The Use and Abuse of Executive Direct Action* (Lawrence: University Press of Kansas, 2002), 81.

41. For more extensive discussion of executive orders, presidential proclamations, and national security directives, see Cooper, *By Order of the President.* On executive orders, also see Kenneth R. Mayer, *With the Stroke of a Pen: Executive Orders and Presidential Power* (Princeton, NJ: Princeton University Press, 2001).

42. Adam L. Warber, *Executive Orders and the Modern Presidency: Legislating from the Oval Office* (Boulder, CO: Lynne Rienner, 2006). Warber further notes, by carefully separating symbolic and routine orders from those that are more consequential policy-wise, that the number of the latter has not increased dramatically over time as might be expected.

43. Cooper, *By Order of the President,* 39–68.

44. William G. Howell, *Power Without Persuasion: The Politics of Direct Presidential Action* (Princeton, NJ: Princeton University Press, 2003), 175.

45. Howell, *Power Without Persuasion,* 176.

46. Ibid., 178.

47. For a fuller discussion of Bush's executive actions here and in the cases on torture and domestic surveillance policies, see James P. Pfiffner, *Power Play: The Bush Presidency and the Constitution* (Washington, DC: Brookings Institution, 2008).

48. *Hamdan v. Rumsfeld,* 548 U.S. 557 (2006). Other, earlier cases were *Hamdi v. Rumsfeld,* 542 U.S. 507 (2004), where the court did not resolve the habeas question but concluded that Hamdi, a US citizen, did have a right to at least challenge his detention by an impartial judge. *Rasul v. Bush,* 542 U.S. 466 (2004), the companion case to *Hamdi,* concerned a foreign national who was a detainee; the court also concluded that a court should decide Rasul's habeas claims.

49. *Boumediene v. Bush,* 553 U.S. 723 (2008).

50. Pfiffner, *Power Play,* 146.

51. Public Law 107-40, 115 Stat. 224 (2001).

52. For more extensive discussion, see Pfiffner, *Power Play,* 168–193. In the summer of 2007, the White House prevailed upon the Republican-controlled House and Senate to pass new legislation, the Protect America Act, which would essentially enable it to conduct surveillance and bypass FISA procedures if a foreign source was involved.

53. Per our discussion of Bush's signing statements and his use of language emphasizing the unitary executive, the one for this bill is also of interest: "The executive branch shall construe

Title X in Division A of the Act, relating to detainees, in a manner consistent with the constitutional authority of the President to *supervise the unitary executive branch* and as *Commander in Chief* and consistent with the *constitutional limitations on the judicial power*, which will assist in achieving the shared objective of the Congress and the President, evidenced in Title X, of protecting the American people from further terrorist attacks" (emphasis added).

54. "Press Briefing by Press Secretary Jay Carney, 1/24/14," The White House, January 24, 2014, http://www.whitehouse.gov/the-press-office/2014/01/27/press-briefing-press-secretary-jay-carney-12414.

55. Barack Obama, "Weekly Address: Focusing on the Economic Priorities for the Middle Class Nationwide," The White House, June 28, 2014, http://www.whitehouse.gov/the-press-office/2014/06/28/weekly-address-focusing-economic-priorities-middle-class-nationwide.

56. Dana Milbank, "John Boehner Wants to Sue President Obama," *Washington Post,* June 26, 2014, https://www.washingtonpost.com/opinions/dana-milbank-john-boehner-wants-to-sue-president-obama/2014/06/25/fc1e93e0-fc9d-11e3-932c-0a55b81f48ce_story.html.

57. Barack Obama, "Remarks by the President on the Economy," The White House, July 1, 2014, http://www.whitehouse.gov/the-press-office/2014/07/01/remarks-president-economy.

58. John Wooley and Gerhard Peters, "Executive Orders in the APP Collection: 2014," American Presidency Project, http://www.presidency.ucsb.edu/executive_orders.php. Data for Obama covers 6.5 years of his presidency. Also see Sebastian Payne, "How Obama Has Used Executive Powers Compared to His Predecessors," *Washington Post,* July 10, 2014, http://www.washingtonpost.com/blogs/the-fix/wp/2014/07/10/how-obama-has-used-executive-powers-compared-to-his-predecessors/.

59. Carrie Budoff Brown and Jennifer Epstein, "The Obama Paradox," Politico, June 4, 2014, http://www.politico.com/story/2014/06/the-obama-paradox-107304.html.

60. Mayer, *With the Stroke of a Pen,* 223.

61. Cooper, *By Order of the President,* 237–238.

62. Pious, "Prerogative Power and Presidential Politics," 462–465.

63. Koh, *National Security Constitution,* 156.

64. Fisher, "Invoking Inherent Powers," 10. Also see Louis Fisher, *The Constitution and 9/11: Recurring Threats to America's Freedoms* (Lawrence: University Press of Kansas, 2008).

4

Going Public and Presidential Power

A more robust interpretation of the president's constitutional powers is not the only tool recent presidents have used to strengthen their hand in dealing with Congress. Another potential way presidents can exercise power is by "*going public*," a term coined by Samuel Kernell to describe the act of appealing to the public and using that support as a means to influence Congress. This notion is not entirely new. We might even include George Washington's travels across the country as an early example, though it's not a wholly accurate one because the purpose of his tour was not to pressure, or bypass directly dealing with, Congress. Still, it was a first step in establishing the presidency as a national institution in the public mind.

We begin this chapter by considering two early-twentieth-century presidents—Theodore Roosevelt and Woodrow Wilson—who were ahead of their times in recognizing the mobilization of public support as a tool of presidential power. We then examine changes in the news media that made it easier for presidents to reach wide audiences, notably the emergence of radio and then television. Along with the changes in American politics in the 1970s that fractured the traditional ways of doing business, these gave rise to new conditions that made going public an even more successful and essential tool of presidential power. A number of scholars, however, have questioned the effectiveness of going public, and we explore their concerns. Finally, we look at how the Internet and social media have offered the public additional sources of political information, and how they have presented new challenges. In particular, we examine the Obama presidency as a case study of the opportunities for, and limitations of, public appeals in today's political and media landscape. Going public has undoubtedly become a primary resource in the exercise of presidential power today, but presidents must also remember that it poses its own risks and that it is not the only resource available to them.

EARLY EXAMPLES OF PUBLIC APPEALS: ROOSEVELT AND WILSON

Theodore Roosevelt and Woodrow Wilson both used public appeals to go around Congress to build support for their respective Progressive agendas. Roosevelt used his "bully pulpit," as he called it, to publicly take on those who opposed his "Square Deal" policy, including some Democrats in Congress and conservative opponents in his own Republican Party—the "old guard." His administration notched some major achievements, including successful legal efforts against business trusts as well as passing the Federal Meat Inspection Act, the Pure Food and Drug Act, and the Hepburn Act regulating railroad rates, all of which were enacted in 1906. In his last two years in office, he pushed more aggressively against business interests, but his efforts largely failed. It is not clear how much Roosevelt's bully pulpit strategy figured into his dealings with Congress, but it did at least build the perception of a popular president.

Wilson's use of public appeals and support grew out of both his scholarly interests and his political experience. As mentioned in Chapter 2, as a scholar Wilson advocated for a presidency-centered system. He envisioned the presidency as the heart of a new political energy that would move the nation in a more progressive direction by breaking through the gridlock of party elites, congressional committees, and special interests. In his view, the presidency could be further empowered by establishing strong public support for the president's program. Like Roosevelt, Wilson saw public appeals as a strong tool of executive leadership.

As president, Wilson recognized the importance that the press and favorable reports in the print media would play in this effort. Two days after his inauguration in 1913, he began to meet regularly with White House reporters, the first president to do so.[1] In addition, he resumed the practice of appearing before Congress to deliver what was then called "The President's Annual Message to Congress" (today's State of the Union address). In his second annual message to Congress, on December 8, 1914, Wilson summarized his approach:

I have tried to know what America is, what her people think, what they are, what they most cherish and hold dear. I hope that some of their finer passions are in my own heart—some of the great conceptions and desires which gave birth to this Government and which have made the voice of this people a voice of peace and hope and liberty among the peoples of the world, and that, in speaking my own thoughts, I shall, at least in part, speak theirs also.[2]

However, Wilson's most significant attempt at a public appeal would also prove his most disappointing, and it would ultimately cripple his presidency. In July 1919, he returned to Washington from France after pushing the Allies to craft a more moderate Treaty of Versailles at the end of World War I. Most importantly, he had successfully incorporated language into the treaty to create the League of Nations (a version of today's United Nations), a body that would help prevent future wars. It was central to Wilson's political agenda after the end of World War I. However, Article X of the treaty contained language that could force the United States to undertake war as a league member without Congress's approval. Wilson refused to compromise with some Senate Republicans—most notably Sen. Henry Cabot Lodge (R-MA)—who wanted to incorporate reservations that would protect Congress's war and constitutional powers. Instead, Wilson took his case to the American public. Starting in early September, he traveled by train, giving some forty speeches in various cities. While in Colorado, he collapsed from exhaustion, and he suffered a serious stroke on October 2, 1919, when he returned to Washington, DC. In November, it looked as if a treaty with reservations might pass the Senate, but Wilson, now in a debilitated state and his judgment perhaps impaired, refused to compromise. It was a major defeat for Wilson, and it is generally regarded as one of the most significant of presidential mistakes.

RADIO AND TELEVISION PROVIDE A MORE DIRECT PLATFORM

Theodore Roosevelt and Wilson largely dealt with newspapers, magazines, their press representatives, and however many members of the public that might hear them speak at an event. Public communication was relatively simple and limited. But this quickly changed with the advent of radio and again later with the development of television.

Radio

The first radio stations began broadcasting in 1920. By 1924, three million US households had radio and over fourteen hundred stations were operating. Ten years later, twenty-two million households had a radio. This changed the way people received and consumed the news and gave presidents a new, and more direct, platform to address the public. In 1920, a Pittsburgh radio station was first to announce that Warren Harding had been elected president. Later on, he was the first president to have a radio installed in the White House. In June 1922, Harding was the first president to speak over the radio at the dedication of a memorial to Francis Scott Key, the composer of "The Star Spangled Banner." In December 1923, President Calvin Coolidge delivered the first State of the Union address carried by radio; the *New York Times* reported that the address was a major success.[3] In addition, starting in the 1920s, the public could also see and sometimes hear the president in the short newsreels shown at movie theaters.

But perhaps the most effective use of radio was Franklin Roosevelt's "fireside chats" to the nation in the midst of the Great Depression. Speaking in a calm and friendly voice, FDR reassured the public and explained and built support for his programs. Although FDR gave only thirty of them during his presidency, they proved an effective presidential tool. But not one that was foolproof: despite public appeals, FDR's attempt in 1938 to block reelection of several conservative Democratic senators opposed to the New Deal effort largely failed.

Radio remains an important presidential tool of communication. Ronald Reagan revived the FDR tradition with his practice of delivering short radio addresses every Saturday. This has continued under his predecessors, but the American public is more likely to access them on YouTube or other websites, including that of the White House itself. However, talk radio can often be a strong source of political criticism of the president and the administration's policies. This is especially the case for a Democratic administration because national talk radio tilts conservative.[4] Rush Limbaugh's radio show, for example, attracts an estimated daily audience of over thirteen million listeners, the largest of any talk radio program.[5]

Television

Although public broadcasting on television began by the late 1930s, it was not until after World War II that television appeared on a large scale in the United

States. Television "sets," as they were then called, were initially expensive, but by the late 1940s and certainly into the early 1950s television ownership became more common. FDR was technically the first president to speak on television in 1939 at the opening of the New York World's Fair, but it was just an experimental broadcast to demonstrate the new technology. Truman gave the first presidential address from the White House on TV in October 1947, on the world food crisis. However, networks were still rudimentary, and the address was carried only on a local Washington, DC, station.

Broadcast of the national party conventions began in a very limited way when a local station broadcast the 1940 Republican convention held in Philadelphia, with links to stations in New York City and Schenectady (an odd locale, but it was the home office of General Electric, an early television pioneer). Estimates were that some five thousand TV sets were potentially able to pick up the broadcast.[6] By 1948, both parties' conventions were broadcast to a wider audience on the East Coast.

On August 15, 1948, CBS began broadcasting an evening news show. It lasted fifteen minutes, and it was not until 1963 that CBS expanded it to thirty minutes. The other networks quickly followed with evening news shows of their own. Between 1949 and 1951, the number of households with TV sets increased from three million to twelve million. By the mid-1950s, television had replaced radio as the chief broadcast media in US households, and by 1962, 90 percent of US households had a television set.

With television sets becoming common, politicians began using the new media to communicate their messages. In 1952, the first political advertising appeared on TV when Dwight Eisenhower's and Adlai Stevenson's presidential campaigns bought blocks of television time. In 1955, the Eisenhower White House permitted networks to film press conferences for later viewing; technology at the time was too cumbersome for live broadcasts. In 1960, the presidential debates between John F. Kennedy and Richard Nixon were the first to be broadcast. Nixon's poor appearance at the first one arguably cost him the election. In January 1961, President Kennedy held the first live, nationally broadcast presidential news conference. Over four hundred reporters were present, and the television audience was estimated at sixty-five million viewers—a milestone. Still, from the 1950s to the early 1970s, radio and television appeals were considered ancillary resources, and print media remained the dominant news source for the public. In addition, although public addresses and news conferences on radio and television did bolster presidents' approval ratings and did have a positive effect on presidential bargaining abilities, these efforts were largely not conducted for the purpose of gaining the public's support to bend congressional will.

The Pitfalls of Radio and Television

Despite all the benefits of radio and television, there were also some pitfalls. By early 1968, the rosy picture that the Johnson administration was projecting on progress in the Vietnam War was slowly being undermined by television reporters embedded in Saigon. Their less-than-optimistic reports were featured on the evening news broadcast—a first—and talk of a Johnson "credibility gap" developed. Walter Cronkite, well-watched and trusted CBS Evening News "anchorman," dealt an especially fatal blow when, after a trip to South Vietnam, he pessimistically concluded in the one-hour "Report from Vietnam" that the war was in stalemate and unwinnable. When he was told about the broadcast, LBJ apparently said, "If I've lost Cronkite, I've lost the country."[7]

Nixon faced a similar experience during the Watergate scandal that embroiled his administration at the start of his second term. Ironically, the Nixon administration was highly attentive to the news media and created the first White House Office of Communications. Prior to that point, relations with the press (largely the print media) were handled by the White House press secretary. Under Nixon, it was paramount that the White House, not the media, be in control of the message. David Gergen, who served on the Nixon, Ford, Reagan, and Clinton White House staffs, recalls that during his service under Nixon, before any event was put on the president's schedule, "you had to know what the headline out of the event was going to be, what the picture was going to be, and what the lead paragraph would be." In the White House pressroom, Nixon understood the importance of the tight sound bite, mandating that his statements be no more than one hundred words. He knew that if they were any longer, the media could pick and choose what was shown on the news and thus decide the point of his statement.[8] Yet, despite Nixon's efforts to encourage a positive picture of his presidency, as the Watergate scandal snowballed into a major crisis, there was little the White House could effectively do. Although it was the release of the secret White House tapes that eventually led to Nixon's resignation, his own press conferences built perceptions of a defensive, weakened president. When the president has to state "I am not a crook" in a press conference, as Nixon did, then something is decidedly wrong.

A CHANGING POLITICAL ENVIRONMENT NECESSITATES GOING PUBLIC

Starting with the Nixon presidency, and certainly accelerating in the post-Watergate years, American politics changed dramatically. The rules and procedures for party nominations of presidential candidates were significantly altered starting in 1972. More primaries and open caucuses weakened, if not largely eliminated, the control of party leaders over convention delegates. "Outsider" candidates have been able to prevail and gain nomination against better-known contenders, especially among Democrats; George McGovern in 1972, Jimmy Carter in 1976, Michael Dukakis in 1988, and Bill Clinton in 1992 are examples of this. We might also include Obama in 2008, then less than two years into his senate term, who successfully defeated the more established Sen. Hillary Clinton (D-NY).[9]

Congress changed in the post-Watergate years as well. Seniority rules were weakened, subcommittees and special interest caucuses became more prominent (although not necessarily more powerful), and new members felt freer to become more visible and vocal (both within Congress and in the broader media). In addition, members were more inclined to aggressively push legislation and challenge their elders. Standing firm mattered as much as trying to reach compromise or agreement, and so it's no surprise that internal polarization developed as well.

The two major parties also became more ideologically narrow, as noted earlier. For Democrats, the party's long hold on the South largely disappeared as many white southerners, who had been a more conservative counterweight in the party since the post–Reconstruction era, abandoned it. For Republicans, once staunch GOP areas in rural New England and the suburbs of northeastern cities became more solidly Democratic. Party bases have become more ideologically polarized, and this is reflected in the members they elect to Congress.

Samuel Kernell writes about this changing political environment in his book *Going Public: New Strategies of Presidential Leadership,* which was first published in 1986.[10] In his view, it changed the way the political game is played in Washington and paved the way for presidents to use public support as a primary strategy for exercising presidential power. Kernell posits that in this new political environment, going public is as important as traditional bargaining for presidents in attaining their goals.

From Institutionalized Pluralism to Individualized Pluralism

According to Kernell, the changes in the presidency, Congress, and the parties have altered not only the contours of our politics but also the presidential leadership required to operate within its parameters. In the 1940s and 1950s, when Neustadt was first studying and writing about presidential power, *institutionalized pluralism* prevailed, meaning that there was a small and relatively fixed group of political actors with stable rules of interaction and behavior. Neustadt's emphasis upon bargaining reflected this. Washington, DC, was a more insular political community, and it was a stable political context where all players understood the informal rules and behavioral expectations that encouraged bargaining and compromise. Political elders were expected to lead, and they were respected for their abilities to strike a deal, and so winning coalitions could be formed. New participants recognized that their future success depended upon working within the system. Showier Congress members who sought wider fame for themselves might capture media and public fancy, but their internal power was usually quite limited. This is perhaps one reason why Lyndon Johnson could not understand how Kennedy—a showboat in LBJ's view and with little legislative accomplishment to his credit—could best him for the Democratic nomination in 1960. Kennedy's triumph was an early warning sign of changes to come.

In addition, this "system" was also well understood by journalists (almost exclusively print at the time) who covered the Capitol and the White House. They, too, generally played by the rules, knowing that if they didn't their access would be cut off and they would be denied any inside scoop. As the old saying goes, "A reporter is only as good as his [or her] sources." One of the most interesting examples of this is the lack of news coverage of FDR's disability resulting from contracting polio in 1921. Although he was largely confined to a wheelchair, not a single photograph appeared in the print media indicating that.[11] Photos were usually shot of him in a car or behind his desk. The American public was in the dark about the extent of his condition because his appearances were carefully orchestrated by the White House staff and compliant journalists made sure that no news stories about the president's physical impairment appeared. The same practice persisted under JFK: his sexual dalliances were known among some reporters but only appeared in the news decades later. This was a different era, to say the least.

Kernell argues that in the post-Watergate years, and certainly by the time of the Reagan presidency, this system of institutionalized pluralism was replaced by one of *individualized pluralism,* in which there is a "propensity of members toward independence."[12] Many individuals seek to gain power rather than just a few established players, loyalty is lessened, and fewer incentives to engage in bargaining exist. Changes in the nomination process and the rise of "outsider" presidential candidates led to a different political reality. Their success was not the result of maneuvering and deal making among a select group of party leaders (with the occasional primary thrown in to demonstrate some public support). Rather, it was largely the result of their own ability to build a public base of support (and sufficient fund-raising, of course). This involved winning primaries and open caucuses week after week, month after month in the election year as well as carefully targeting fund-raising efforts for several years and campaigning early in states such as Iowa and New Hampshire.

Starting with creation of CNN in 1980, then Fox News and MSNBC in 1996, there has been a rapid proliferation of media outlets, which certainly contribute to this new environment of individualized pluralism. As Kernell notes, "Members must resort to their own devices to find their political fortunes,"[13] and a twenty-four-hour news cycle offers numerous opportunities for public visibility. Career opportunities in the media have also grown and broadened. Once upon a time, the aspiring journalist might have only a handful of places to move on to, perhaps to another paper or one of the national magazines such as *Life, Time,* or *Newsweek,* but this has changed since the rise of cable news and Internet news sites. Political reporting has also changed: getting the inside scoop and uncovering the truth are of paramount importance, and playing by the "rules" matters less. The media have long been seen as the "fourth estate" in American politics, but post-Watergate they have become an even stronger—albeit increasingly fragmented—force.

How does all this affect presidential leadership? Kernell argues that the path to success is less sure and more difficult now than it was when the system, rules, understandings, and mutual expectations of institutionalized pluralism were in place. In this new system of individualized pluralism, Neustadt's vision of a bargaining president is more difficult to imagine because "the leveled political topography offers fewer clues about where precisely his efforts at coalition-building should begin." Presidents have to deal not only with more players but also with weaker players—a near-impossible prospect, in Kernell's view. The alternative is to go public and use the public's support as a way to persuade Congress. A president who succeeds in going public, Kernell argues, "will find frequent opportunities for leadership in Washington."[14]

The Reagan Presidency: The Apogee of Going Public?

Kernell was inspired to research and write *Going Public* because of the early legislative success of Ronald Reagan's tax-cut and budget-reduction agenda of 1981, noting in the preface to the second edition of the work that it was Reagan's success that "so confirmed and clarified my own views on the direction of presidential leadership."[15] Reagan carefully crafted and targeted his speeches and comments to build public support for his proposals. Most notable was an address to Congress on April 28, 1981, shortly after his recovery from an assassination attempt in March; Kernell describes the reception by Congress as a "love feast."[16] Reagan also paid special attention to using public pressure to win over conservative Democrats in the districts that he had carried in the 1980 election. All of these efforts led to passage of the Reagan tax and budget plans by the end of the summer with little need for major compromises.

Yet Kernell notes that although Reagan's strategy initially worked, the effectiveness of his public appeals diminished as his approval ratings began to slide over time. Kernell observes that "Reagan exerted far less influence over the budget in 1982—both its substance and politics—than over the one in the preceding year."[17] And in 1983, as Reagan's popularity declined because of the weakened economy, his public appeals fell on deaf ears, so he was forced into a more traditional strategy of threatening to exercise his veto powers. Does this suggest that going public ultimately mattered less for Reagan than Kernell initially thought? I would argue that Reagan's success in 1981 was the result of multiple factors, not just his proactive use of public appeals as a tool to force Congress to accept his budget and tax proposals. These included an effective transition to office, a clear political agenda, and a public dissatisfied with the weak leadership of the Carter presidency. In other words, the Reagan White House strategically exploited favorable conditions. Once those conditions became less favorable, the potency of Reagan's going public efforts weakened. Still, at the end of his first term, as Kernell points out, Reagan "went on to amass one of the greatest landslides of this century."[18]

In particular, transition planning—determining which proposals to pursue, establishing connections to the Washington political community, and getting in place an effective White House team—had a major impact. In particular, Reagan's White House staff played a crucial role in Reagan's successes. During his first term, Reagan drew on the skills of Chief of Staff James Baker, Director of White House Communications David Gergen, and Michael Deaver, a longtime aide from his governorship who was very skilled at shaping the public face and visible imagery of the Reagan presidency. (We explore the importance of transition planning and the White House staff in more detail in Chapter 6.)

All three especially recognized the need to have a tightly focused policy agenda: just four or five key initiatives, not the laundry list of proposals that Jimmy Carter unwisely pursued. Baker pursued these initiatives strategically and successfully, chairing the daily meeting of the legislative strategy group that determined, among other things, how much they would compromise and when the president would make broader public appeals. Gergen, drawing on his experience in the Nixon and Ford White Houses, was a master at dealing with the press and controlling the message. As journalist Mark Hertsgaard noted, the Reagan administration paid special attention to how the media worked and how it could be manipulated to their advantage. The Reagan White House sought to control the public agenda and the terms of debate by planning ahead, staying on the offensive, controlling the flow of information, limiting reporters' access to Reagan, speaking in one voice, and repeating the same message many times.[19] As a result of putting these rules into practice, "bad stories rarely took root within the press."[20]

Deaver focused on carefully orchestrating and producing the Reagan seen by the public. "With his background in Hollywood image-making, President Reagan made certain that he had a publicity operation that would carry the message and actions of his presidency to the American people as well as to specific publics inside and outside of government that he wanted to reach," Martha Joynt Kumar notes in her study of the White House's communications efforts. "Reagan created a White House staff structure in which communications was important to those at the top level as well as throughout the organization."[21]

In my view, Reagan's first term was a moment, perhaps a fleeting one, when his efforts at going public were both easily controlled and effectively run. The media were manageable at the time; the Reagan administration only needed to contend with print journalism and the three major national networks. And more importantly, Reagan was a skilled public communicator, and his White House staff was especially adept at understanding how those skills might best be used. The deck was stacked in Reagan's favor in ways that might not be possible today. Unfortunately, Reagan's initial White House crew moved on to other positions during his second term. When the Iran-Contra scandal broke in 1986, less-adept hands were at the helm.

It is also important to note that bargaining during the Reagan years was not absent or ignored. Reagan successfully maneuvered his tax-cut bill in 1981 through Congress, but the White House also recognized the need to compromise and pulled back on tax legislation the next year. In 1986, Reagan oversaw another successful effort at tax reform where bargaining again played a major part; it was strategically timed and coupled with the *threat* of public appeal as well as actual appeals themselves.[22] According to Kernell: "No president has enlisted public strategies to better advantage than did Ronald Reagan. Throughout his tenure, he exhibited a full appreciation of *bargaining* and going public as the modern office's principal strategic alternatives" (emphasis added).[23] Note the combination of the two; bargaining remained an important tool in the Reagan administration, especially when strategically combined with public appeals.

THE CHALLENGES AND LIMITS OF GOING PUBLIC

Kernell does not claim that going public always works; his analysis of Reagan's first term and its uneven success is a clear indicator of that. My take is that the White House must adapt to meet the various challenges that surround going public; it is not just scheduling a public speech or event. As Reagan's first-term team well knew, the speech or event was just the last moment in a long and considerable planning and execution process. The contrast between Reagan and his immediate successor, George H. W. Bush, is interesting on this score. Bush correctly recognized that he was no Reagan; he was not the Great Communicator. But he had good interpersonal skills, especially with foreign leaders (if Reagan was the communicator, Bush was the master of "Rolodex diplomacy"). And although he was less adept at the set public speech, Bush was more open to the press than his predecessor, often appearing in the White House pressroom to take reporters' questions. Still, Bush Sr. did not enjoy these public efforts and the staff system that he developed reflected this disinterest in "presidential publicity."[24] And so, Bush was unable to control the airwaves in the same manner as Reagan did. One senior official from CBS News observed that "Reagan had something to say. It was consistent, and it redounded on what he was pushing on Capitol Hill. Bush doesn't have that."[25]

In addition, developments in the news media and the changing public complicated recent presidents' going public process. As Kernell notes, audience declined significantly, making presidential efforts to achieve public support more difficult. Over 50 percent of the public watched Nixon's public addresses, but by the time of Bill Clinton's presidency, that had declined to just over 30 percent.[26] Presidents now also face a media that is more assertive and independent. Going public does not operate in a vacuum, and presidential efforts at public outreach are increasingly likely to be met by media pushback and criticism. Going public now bears increasing costs as the media have become more prolific and diverse.

Another major limitation to going public, best analyzed in George C. Edwards III's work *On Deaf Ears*,[27] is that moving public opinion is incredibly difficult. Even Reagan and Clinton, who were both known to be good communicators in office and who both had staffs that were highly attentive to their public images as president, had dismal records when it comes to actually swaying public opinion their way.

Managing White House Communications Is Key to Going Public

As the Reagan versus Bush Sr. example shows, the ways that presidents and their staff approach going public can vary quite a bit. In Martha Joynt Kumar's view, these differences in their White House communication efforts can contribute to the difficulty of achieving a successful public relations effort. Bush's first chief of staff, former New Hampshire governor John Sununu, was very different from Baker, Reagan's chief of staff. Baker kept close watch on the media's coverage of the presidency, whereas Sununu claimed to rarely watch the news or pay attention to the press (though this was likely a political ploy). Baker and Gergen crafted both the "line of the day" and long-term strategy. Sununu was more interested in the substance of policy rather than the public message.

Furthermore, Bush reverted to the more traditional practice of using his White House press secretary as his most important communications adviser instead of the director of the White House Office of Communications.[28] Reliance on the press secretary worked in the days of FDR, Truman, and Kennedy, when the media landscape was much simpler. Today, the press secretary spends too much time on day-to-day operations to be effective in directing the "big picture." In addition, hundreds of aides are now involved in managing presidential communications. Some work on daily press briefings, and others are involved in long-range planning; some attend to local and regional reporters, while others monitor online news sites and social media. All of this complex communications machinery requires effective coordination and management by top-level White House officials.

As Kumar notes, "If there is no one to oversee the planning and implementation of communications, those jobs tend to end up haphazard or undone."[29]

Kumar also emphasizes that problems can arise from a president's individual communication style. For example, Reagan had difficulty in publicly admitting policy mistakes. A prime example was his initial poor response to the Iran-Contra scandal. He refused to publicly acknowledge that the United States had traded arms to Iran in hopes that they would exert influence in gaining the release of US hostages held in Lebanon. Public evidence about the deal was clear, yet it took weeks for Reagan to finally admit that it occurred. Bush Sr. faced difficulty in altering the perception that he was out of touch on domestic issues. As noted earlier, he was comfortable communicating in smaller venues but placed less value on wider publicity and public communication, and so it came as no surprise that he appeared detached from what was happening in the country at times. In my view, the organizational and the personal challenges are clearly related. It is no coincidence that Reagan's disastrous initial response to the Iran-Contra scandal happened in his second term, after a new team, who failed to understand and counteract Reagan's weaknesses, took over.

Communication skills clearly matter, and each president will have different strengths and weaknesses in this area. The trick for effective public leadership is to try to build on the strengths and figure out ways of countering the weaknesses. Occasionally, presidents take on this task themselves, but their White House communications staff plays a critical role in crafting an appealing presidential message, figuring out how this *specific* president can most effectively sell it, and developing strategies in dealing with the media to make sure that message is heard. In fact, building an effective presidential team is crucial to the overall success of a president's first term and second term, a subject we return to in Chapters 6 and 7.

Changing Media Landscape Alters Going Public Strategies

Changes in the media landscape and subsequent shifts in audiences' consumption habits must also be considered in gauging effective strategies for going public. In *The Presidency in the Era of 24-Hour News,* Jeffrey E. Cohen argues that the changing nature of the news media is a key factor in the diminishing effectiveness of presidential communication. "New media"—starting with twenty-four-hour cable news in the 1980s and continuing with the proliferation of online news sources—has generated obstacles for a president, including a decline in coverage of politics and the presidency, increased negativity in reporting, more competitive programming tailored to particular political views, and less public trust in the media. In his analysis of the media, Thomas E. Patterson also notes the decline in "hard" news stories and their replacement by "soft" news over the last several decades as another impediment to presidential efforts to mold or shift public opinion on particular policy issues.[30] Gaining public attention is difficult when soft news prevails, and it becomes even more problematic in a rapidly shifting news cycle where the latest story is what matters. Major presidential addresses simply do not have the effect that they once did.

These factors can limit the ability of presidents to lead the public, and so, as Cohen notes, presidents have had to increase "the amount of effort used to mobilize special interests, narrower publics, and/or their own partisan base."[31] Cohen refers to this targeting of specific audiences as "going narrow."[32] In a later book, *Going Local,* Cohen notes that we have now progressed beyond the two stages that Kernell lays out—institutionalized pluralism and individualized pluralism— to a third stage characterized by polarized parties and fragmented media. In this third phase, focus on the party base, supportive interest groups, and targeted local communities now matters, as he had anticipated in his earlier work. Although public appeals and their impact on public opinion remain important, "going national is no longer as effective a leadership strategy as it once was."[33] Instead, the White House needs to use a more narrow and finely tuned approach. Going narrow, however, has a price too: more targeted constituencies can have more extreme political and policy preferences than a broader national audience does. If this is the case, the presidential message may appear more extreme as well.[34]

The media landscape has shifted significantly, and audiences have fragmented and narrowed since the 1980s. As a result, it has become increasingly challenging for presidents to effectively and successfully go public. More recently, presidents and their staff have had to grapple with the rise of social media as a venue for the dissemination of political news and as a means of communicating with the public. And with today's rapidly changing world of information technology, yet another phase—and challenges of presidential communication—may loom.

Moving Public Opinion Is Difficult

In the preface of his book, George Edwards III presents the case of George W. Bush and his tax-cut legislation of his first year in office as an example of how little public opinion can change, despite a president's best efforts at appealing to the public. Bush is an especially interesting case because he was a controversial new president. He had just lost the popular vote to Vice President Al Gore by 543,816, and his victory in the Electoral College by the narrow margin of 271 to 266 came as the result of a lengthy legal challenge to the recount of Florida's popular vote. Despite the circumstances of his election, Bush pursued an ambitious policy agenda, with major tax-reduction legislation as its centerpiece—a bold move.

Edwards notes that in the early months of his presidency, Bush traveled extensively around the country pushing his legislative agenda. In his speeches and weekly radio addresses, Bush urged the public to support his plan and put pressure on their representatives in Congress to vote for it. With a bit of bargaining at the margin, Bush succeeded and the legislation passed. That a controversial and potentially weak president is able to skillfully use public support to move Congress seemingly makes a strong case for going public as a presidential strategy. However, there was actually little change in public support over time for Bush's tax proposal. A Gallup poll in early February 2001 indicated that 56 percent supported the tax cut, 34 percent were opposed, and 10 percent had no opinion. In late April, the numbers were virtually the same: 56 percent supported, 35 percent opposed, and 9 percent had no opinion. As Edwards points out, "It is one thing to go public. It is something quite different to succeed in moving public opinion."[35] Still, although Bush failed to move the public opinion needle, a solid majority supported his tax-cut plan.

To understand whether the public responds to presidential appeals, Edwards analyzes the records of two presidents thought to be great communicators: Reagan and Clinton. Their respective records, however, are surprisingly slim. Reagan was unable to build public support across a range of issues, and after his initial tax-cut and budget success with Congress, his later budget proposals were dead on arrival. In Edwards's view, Reagan's "image as The Great Communicator appears to owe more to his early success with Congress than to his ability to move the public in a reliable fashion."[36]

The Clinton White House was highly attentive to the president's public image; it extensively studied polls and conducted its own public surveys (including one on where the First Family should vacation). But the administration's efforts to move public opinion were not particularly productive. Early initiatives such as its economic plan and healthcare reform were particularly disappointing: despite Clinton's public appeals, support for both actually declined over time. In late February 1993, the end of his first month in office, support for his economic plan was at 59 percent, but it then dropped to 44 percent by late May. In September 1993, 59 percent supported the healthcare reform plan that Hillary Clinton had been charged with developing, but by June 1994, support had dropped to 42 percent. In addition, opposition to the plan increased from 33 percent to 50 percent.[37] The administration faced mounting criticisms from opponents of the plan, which even included a television ad campaign against it (opponents can go public, too).[38]

In my view, part of the problem can be attributed to presidents pushing too many policy proposals at once, making it difficult for them to properly frame and structure their message for the public. Clinton got off on the wrong track at the start of his presidency by proposing too much and by not prioritizing for the public what was *most* important to him. By contrast, George W. Bush was more focused: he made it absolutely clear that his tax-cut program was what mattered first and foremost.

Further compounding the problem is the fact that the White House has encountered increasing resistance to its requests for media time. The major networks once automatically granted presidential access to the airwaves but now balk at doing so. As Edwards notes, save for State of the Union addresses, speeches and addresses about major military actions, and responses to scandals, the president is not likely to be granted direct television access.[39] Coverage of the president now typically occurs at the media's choosing and is subject to its interpretation and commentary. Finally, the president is often speaking to the already converted. Supporters tend to remain convinced, but opponents also tend to remain opposed. According to Edwards, presidents need to overcome the public's predisposed notions if minds are to be changed—an incredibly tough thing to do.[40]

GOING PUBLIC IN THE AGE OF THE INTERNET AND SOCIAL MEDIA

The rise and rapid growth of the Internet and social media have changed the ways in which the public seeks and receives news and political information. With more and more people turning to the Internet and social media for news, new media have presented recent presidents with new opportunities for going public, but they have also created some new challenges.

The Internet was still in its infancy during Clinton's first term; in December 1995, only 16 million people used the Web worldwide.[41] By the end of Clinton's presidency, however, more than 250 million people, roughly 5 percent of the world's population, used the Internet. By 2015, that number had grown to over 3 billion users, 42 percent of the world's population. The first generation of Apple iPhones appeared in January 2007; the first android smartphones, in October 2008. By 2015, over 64 percent of all Americans used a smartphone. For those between the ages of eighteen and thirty-four, the number was over 85 percent.[42] Today, it's tough to imagine life without a smartphone—or, even more drastic, with no Internet connection.

More recently, the advent, and rapid growth, of social media has changed the way the public obtains and consumes news and political information. Facebook started in 2004, and in seven short years, it had reached one trillion hits per month. By 2015, Facebook had 1.5 billion subscribers, roughly half on mobile devices. A 2014 Pew Research Journalism project study[43] found that 64 percent of adults in the United States use Facebook and that 30 percent receive news from the site. However, for most people, getting news on Facebook is incidental: 78 percent of users see news items on Facebook when on the site for other reasons, but only 22 percent see the site as a useful source for news. Of the types of news accessed by Facebook users, the largest is entertainment (77 percent), followed by community information and events (65 percent) and sports (57 percent). Political and national news comes in next at 55 percent, while local government and politics (44 percent) and international news (39 percent) are farther down the list. Still, these data show that Facebook is a relatively strong source for political news, especially given its "social" nature.

Twitter, launched in 2007, is another source of news links. Although its membership is not as large as Facebook's, with only 16 percent of US adults using it, half (8 percent) report using it as a news source—roughly the same breakdown as for Facebook. Not all social media, however, are strong sources of news. Although YouTube followed Facebook as the second most important social networking site in the Pew study, with 51 percent of US adult users, only 10 percent said it was a source of news information. Member demographics also differ among social media. Twitter tends to skew younger, whereas Facebook skews older. Users aged eighteen to twenty-nine years comprised 45 percent of the news audience for Twitter but only 34 percent for Facebook. Users aged fifty and older comprised 16 percent of Twitter's membership but a larger 27 percent of Facebook's.[44] Still, despite the differences between the two, younger users tend to dominate social media sites.

Greater Audience Interactivity, Fragmentation, and Polarization

The spread of information through the Internet and social media seems to indicate that there is an increasing audience for political messages that is now much easier to reach. This is true in some regard: the Internet and social media do expose users to political news and communications from presidents and their staff. But whether this exposure "moves" or activates public opinion remains an open question. Still, some interesting trends in how the Internet and social media have changed the ways the public receives information could influence how presidents use these channels to go public.

One is the interactive nature of social media. Newspapers have long had their letters to the editor, and Internet news sources (including online versions of newspapers) have a comments section for their articles. Social media, however, is a more engaging and interactive process. As the Pew study notes: "Social and mobile developments are doing more than bringing consumers into the process—they are also changing the dynamics of the process itself."[45] Those dynamics reveal a potentially more attentive and participatory public: half of social network users share or repost news stories, images, or videos, whereas nearly 46 percent discuss news issues or events on social network sites. This is quite astounding. It potentially challenges the view of Robert Putnam and others who argue that the public is now less civically engaged and less inclined to join political and social groups.[46]

This interactivity also implies that news organizations now have less control over the dissemination of information, while individual users' efforts matter more. Because of the Internet and social media, citizens can submit their own videos, photos, and blog posts to news sites, as well as share Facebook updates or "live-tweet" events. The Pew study found that most people who get news on Facebook get it from links shared by friends in their network; only about a third of people follow a news organization or individual journalist.[47] The lessened control that news organizations have over information certainly applies to the White House, too. In this era, when nearly everyone has a smartphone with a video camera, it can be much more difficult for an administration to control the message going out to the public.

Another trend is fragmentation and polarization. A huge number of online sources of political information exist. (A recent Google search for "Obama presidency" turned up fifty-two million potential hits.[48]) It can be difficult for people to assess the legitimacy and trustworthiness of these sources when there are so many. And for presidents seeking to go public, this can mean that their message may get muddied, simply because the public is receiving information from many more, and different, sources. More importantly, this growth in online news sources has also resulted in more *targeted* news sources that are directed at specific audiences—they have become increasingly polarized. For example, *Media Matters for America* has a liberal bent, while *The Drudge Report* has a conservative voice. As a result, the public can seek out information from media sources that most closely match their own political views. This is a phenomenon that came to the forefront with cable news—the familiar case of Republicans watching Fox News and Democrats turning to MSNBC—but the Internet and social media have intensified this polarization.[49]

Although the Internet does connect people and create social and political connections, it is not a guaranteed forum for democratic discourse and the open exchange of ideas. It could in fact induce a dangerous cycle: self-reinforcing news sources can lead people to have isolating experiences with like-minded others, which can further encourage the consumption of news sources that simply reaffirm a particular worldview.[50] The Pew study found some interesting evidence of polarization in social media. In the aftermath of the Newtown, Connecticut, school shooting in 2012, 64 percent of tweets called for stricter gun control, while only 21 percent opposed stricter control. By contrast, Pew's own public opinion survey at the time found that the general public was evenly split: 49 percent supported stricter gun control, while 42 percent were opposed. This indicates that although social media can be a place for administrations to get a sense of public opinion, it might not offer the most balanced or reliable picture. The increasing polarization and fragmentation in audiences can also be incredibly challenging for presidents looking to communicate a unified message to the broad public. It is just that much easier for liberals to tune out a Republican president and for conservatives to do the same with a Democrat. As Dan Pfeiffer, who served as director of White House communications and then as senior adviser in the Obama administration, observes: "In every year, this project gets harder, the media gets more disaggregated, people get more options to choose from, and they self-select outlets that speak to their preconceived notions."[51]

Presidents Directly Connect with the Public Online

On a more positive note, the Internet and social media now enable presidents to establish direct connections with supporters in ways far more sophisticated than in the past. The first candidate to use the Internet, albeit tentatively and on a small scale, was Bill Clinton in 1992. Today, an online and social media presence is central to a presidential campaign. For the Obama campaign, for example, its site (barackobama.com) not only enabled supporters to reach them, get information about the candidate, and make donations but also was a place for supporters to form blogs, find videos they could share on their own social media accounts, and create their own volunteer groups. It also then permitted the campaign to engage in proactive efforts to contact supporters, both in large-scale emails and in more finely tuned messages to thirty thousand special listservs.

Once the president is in office, this Internet audience can be used to maintain a base of support and can be expanded—something the Obama White House excelled at. At the start of his second term, Obama's site was renamed and became the online presence for "Organizing for Action," a 501(c)(4) organization with a mission to be "a grassroots movement built by millions of Americans to pass the agenda we voted for in 2012."[52] Obama and his former campaign aides remained heavily involved in this technically nonpartisan organization's launch and management. Its chief founder was Jim Messina, a longtime Obama senior adviser, and its executive director was Jon Carson, a former White House director of public engagement. Obama himself emailed his supporters about the new group, noting that it would be actively "mobilizing around and speaking out in support of important legislation" during his second term.[53]

In 1994, during Clinton's presidency, the White House capitalized on the ability to reach the public without needing to go through the White House press corps and launched the official White House website (www.whitehouse.gov). Under George W. Bush, the site became more interactive: live streaming of events debuted in 2001; live web chats with administration officials started in 2003; and presidential speeches, news conferences, and press briefings were made downloadable in 2005.[54] Under Obama, it has become even more sophisticated, with news about the presidency and presidential efforts and initiatives appearing throughout the site. It also offers a collation of the White House's social media feeds, a mobile app that supplies the latest White House news, as well as a section for people to submit public petitions. The Obama administration became particularly active on Twitter, with several accounts. As of January 2016, @BarackObama (run by Organizing for Action) had 68.9 million followers, @WhiteHouse (the official White House account) had 8.8 million, and @POTUS (Obama's own account, which he started in 2013) had 6.0 million. The Office of the First Lady also has its own Twitter account (@FLOTUS). With the exception of the @POTUS account, staffers do almost all of the tweeting. All of these accounts are used to disseminate information and build support for the administration's policy issues. In addition, there have been Twitter town hall events, a virtual "big block of cheese day" using the hashtag #AsktheWH, and, most notably for Obama's efforts at going public, requests to have followers tweet members of Congress to support the president's initiatives. In his second term, Obama expanded his online and social media reach even more with interviews on the podcast *WTF with Marc Maron* and the online comedy talk show *Between Two Ferns with Zack Galifinakis* as well as hosting an "Ask Me Anything" Q&A session on Reddit.

The Obama administration continued to engage in traditional outreach, albeit in a much narrower and targeted way. When a major climate initiative was about to be launched in 2014, for example, local television meteorologists from around the nation—not the White House press corps—were briefed by cabinet members in the Roosevelt Room of the White House and offered Rose Garden interviews with the president.[55] I suspect not a single local television station failed to run the story of their weatherperson at this White House event. Obama's public events have been structured so that he can feel his most comfortable. This is not a new development, but there has been a decided shift away from standard speeches at the White House.

One effect of the shift to the Internet and social media is that recent presidents have been able to hem in the traditional media, like Nixon and Reagan attempted to do, without seeming completely unavailable. The Obama White House initially pledged to be the most transparent presidency ever, and in some ways the administration's online presence has given the public direct access to the president and seemingly created an aura of openness. But opportunities for questions from the press have been curtailed, and press access to some events has also been restricted, especially for political fund-raisers. According to one account, "Press access to the president has shrunk steadily in each of the last three administrations—two Democrats and one Republican—and seems virtually certain to continue to do so in coming administrations."[56] Press photographers have also had their access restricted; their images have largely been replaced by those shot by White House photographers. Although all presidents have had official photographers, social media sites such as Flickr, Instagram, and Twitter have enabled Obama and his staff to have even more control over shaping his persona. Images that the White House wants seen far and wide can be instantaneously shared through this "massive distribution channel simply not available to past presidents."[57] One picture of the president with a kid in a Spiderman costume—showing Obama's lighthearted side—had three million hits on Flickr.

But Has Going Public Worked for Obama?

Despite initial promise as a public speaker during his 2008 campaign, and despite all the new channels for going public open to him, Obama has not been particularly successful in selling his policy proposals to the American public. As noted earlier, efforts at going public have become more difficult for recent presidents, including Obama, as a variety of media, and especially online, sources have become politically polarized and fragmented. Reaching Obama supporters may have become easier technologically speaking, but gaining (and holding) the attention of the broader public is now more difficult.

Support for his signature first-term policy achievement—the 2010 Affordable Care Act—has remained tepid. Even in his second term, disapproval of the act remained higher than approval. In May 2014, after the glitches in initial enrollment during fall 2013 had largely been fixed and healthcare exchanges (where people could sign up for a plan) were closed, Gallup polling found that 51 percent still disapproved of the act and only 43 percent approved.[58] Of those surveyed 59 percent believed that the act had no effect on their own health care, whereas 24 percent believed they had been hurt by it. Only 14 percent believed their healthcare situation was improved.[59] Although some controversial provisions were included, the act's lackluster reception was in part because Obama had mostly failed to sell it to the American public. According to Robert Reich, former secretary of labor under Clinton, Obama's general inability to have much impact on the public through his speeches and travel is surprising, noting that despite some "stirring speeches," Obama "seems not to be able to make the sale, not only to the American people, but to members of Congress."[60]

Yet even when public support seemed to be present, Obama was not able to turn it to his benefit in dealing with Congress. Perhaps the most significant example was the failure to pass tougher gun control legislation in the aftermath of the mass shooting at the Sandy Hook Elementary School in Newtown, Connecticut, on December 14, 2012. It was one of the deadliest mass shootings at a school in US history, with twenty children and six adults killed. Before the shooting, Gallup polling revealed that the public was evenly divided: 44 percent wanted stricter gun control laws, while 43 percent wanted them to be less strict. After the shooting, those supporting stricter laws increased to 58 percent, while those wanting fewer restrictions dropped to 34 percent.[61]

The White House recognized this as an opportunity to push for stricter legislation, and the president made a number of public appeals in support of it. The chief proposal that seemed to have the best chance of passage was a bipartisan compromise proposed by Senators Joe Manchin (D-WV) and Patrick Toomey (R-PA), which involved expanded background checks on the sale of guns at shows and over the Internet. However, despite extensive effort by the White House both with the public and in lobbying members of Congress, the legislation did not have sufficient support in the Senate to overcome filibuster: 54 senators voted "aye," a majority, but fewer than the 60 votes needed; 46 senators voted against it, with only 4 Republicans voting in favor of the amendment. The National Rifle Association and other gun lobbies were particularly active in opposing the bill; traditional interest group politics prevailed. According to Ross K. Baker, a Rutgers political scientist, "If you ever wanted a textbook example of intensity trumping preference, this is it. . . . You can't translate poll results into public policy."[62] A Gallup poll taken a week after the defeat of the legislation in April 2013 indicated that 65 percent of those polled wanted the background check legislation to pass, while 29 percent were opposed to it. The proposal even divided Republicans: 45 percent believed it should have passed, while 50 percent remained against it.[63]

Obama's difficulties with going public can certainly be attributed to the increasing fragmentation and polarization of the public today. He might have been reaching and even mobilizing his supporters, but he was not necessarily convincing anybody else. His inability to have some effect on public opinion was further compounded by his low approval ratings. Since the start of his second term, he did not score above the 50 percent approval mark, and since June 2013 his disapproval ratings were higher than his approval ratings through 2015. Underlying support for both the president and the specific proposal is needed for successful appeals to the public and to Congress. It is not just all about the selling—the public needs to be receptive to *who* is doing the selling and *what* the president is selling.

GOING PUBLIC IS NOT IMPOSSIBLE—AND IT IS NECESSARY

All of this analysis suggests that going public is difficult, but not impossible. And perhaps we are asking for too much when it comes to assessing the effectiveness of public appeals as a strategic effort. As Brandon Rottinghaus observes, public lead-ership is provisional: "Presidents may lead at the margins but they still lead."[64] In short, maybe effectively going public does not require that the president *actually* move public opinion. Perhaps going public can be successful simply with the *perception* of public support and a president willing to make public efforts.

The Bush 2001 tax-cuts proposal is a prime example of this: he did not move public opinion, but he did succeed in getting the legislation passed. In this case, a majority of the public did already support Bush's tax-cut plan. Even if public efforts serve only to mobilize the president's support base rather than create new supporters, they swing presidential supporters into action, which may then have some impact upon congressional representatives. Also, Bush had several internal political advantages working in his favor. Because his legislation was part of a budget plan, under the rules of the Senate it could pass by a simple majority and no filibuster was permitted—thus, there was no need to garner sixty Senate votes. The Republicans narrowly controlled the Senate 50–50, with Vice Presi-dent Cheney casting the tie vote to give the GOP control. The Republicans also continued to control the House of Representatives (222–213) at the start of the 107th Congress.[65] These broader political circumstances suggest the importance of *context* for presidential power, a subject we consider in subsequent chapters.

Of course, going public has its risks. Taken too far it can negatively affect presidents' ability to bargain, which remains an important tool of presidential power. Some members of Congress could resent the president for using the pub-lic to pressure them, making them less willing to strike a deal with the president. In addition, presidents may be forced into public statements from which it might later be difficult to back down. Finally, it weakens the legitimacy of other political actors: going public presumes that the president is the articulator and master of the public will, while Congress is just a servant.[66]

Even so, presidents persist in believing that going public is worthwhile, and perhaps they are correct to do so. Although presidents may not be able to move public opinion in a favorable direction as much as they might hope, if they do not attempt to go public, it may come back to negatively affect them—they run the risk of being perceived as weak, isolated, imperiled, and lacking political will. For example, in July 2014 when the missile attack on a Malaysian airliner occurred as it flew over Ukrainian airspace, Obama made brief, appropriate comments but then returned to his planned schedule, including flying to California and Seat-tle for fund-raising events several days later. Although it was unclear what more Obama might have done, some Republicans accused "the president of failing to show Americans he was in charge of the situation."[67] Bush faced even more dev-astating media criticism for his response in the aftermath of Hurricane Katrina in 2005. Rather than returning immediately to the White House, Bush continued with plans to give three scheduled speeches in California and then returned to his Texas ranch for two days. On his way back to Washington, DC, three days after Katrina, Bush simply conducted a flyover of the affected states. Although he later made a number of subsequent appearances in New Orleans and other areas hit by the storm, the media's live coverage of the devastating conditions only emphasized the Bush administration's weak initial response and belated efforts—an image that stuck. A better-crafted public presence at the onset of the disaster might have helped Bush.

CONCLUSION: IMPLICATIONS AND QUESTIONS

Going public is not a panacea for the deadlock in Washington politics. Some presidential efforts have succeeded, while others have failed. Still, it has become more than the ancillary resource that Neustadt initially posited. It does not just bolster perceptions of a president's bargaining and persuasion powers. On occasion, it has been a useful and direct presidential tool for exercising influence over Congress. At the same time, more traditional forms of presidential power remain important. Presidents must still exercise influence, and they must still bargain. Even examples of successful going public efforts include some element of strategic bargaining: Reagan in 1981 on tax and budget cuts and again in 1985–1986 on further tax reforms, and Bush in 2001 with his tax-cut plan.

However, it seems that successful going public efforts have become rarer as media technology has advanced. The public audience is now more fragmented and focused on sources of information that confirm rather than question or deepen their own predetermined views. Recent presidents—George W. Bush and especially Obama—have sought to use their own organizational resources as well as the Internet and social media to mobilize their supporters, their public allies, in exercising influence. However, the extent to which these efforts are successful remains unknown. Does Congress simply consider this partisan "noise," or do these efforts have some effect? Still, presidents today cannot avoid having a public presence, nor can they appear to have a weak one: note George W. Bush with Hurricane Katrina and Obama with a number of foreign policy issues. If presidents make few, or weak, efforts at a "public presidency," they suffer because the public expects them to be front and center. The paradox, as Edwards cautions, is that much of the substance falls on deaf ears.

A final point: important *normative* stakes are involved when going public goes too far. As Jeffrey Tulis has noted, Woodrow Wilson's theory and practice of a presidency-centered system based on public appeals were a marked departure from the "separate but shared powers" expectation of the Constitution. The Framers worried about political demagogues and were concerned about an over-reliance on popular will. Recall that the main theme of Madison's *Federalist No. 51* is about controlling the power of those who govern, about pitting "ambition against ambition."[68] Madison wanted energy in the executive but abhorred executive dominance. Tulis argues that too much of a shift toward going public endangers that constitutional balance by moving the nation in the direction of a presidency that is not constitutionally guided or specified.[69]

Tulis is partially correct to be concerned: the problem is that a presidency grounded in popular will and shaped by presidential appeals to the public may move the nation into the constitutionally uncharted waters of presidential prerogative.[70] Much becomes defined by the president's own view of the office. And as we saw in the previous chapter, prerogative and the proper determination of presidents' inherent claims to power are areas of less-than-clear constitutional guidance, and ones that are often subject to reluctant judicial interpretation. Moreover, that judicial resolution is sometimes questionable—recall the *Korematsu* decision.

At the same time, the framework and dynamics of US politics have changed. The public now matters more—and should matter more—than it did in 1787 amid the fears of the Framers of mob rule and political demagogues. Just as the question of the end result of power raises issues for the "Neustadtian" president, a presidency based largely on public appeal poses its own significant political and constitutional concerns. What is the proper democratic balance between popular will and knowledgeable and wise political leadership? That is a very difficult question to answer. However, one thing that is sure is that presidents should take care in using going public as their *primary* strategy for exercising power, and those who do will not likely succeed. Pursuing it as the *sole* means to power is risky. Not only is Madison's idea of checks and balances lost, but, perhaps more importantly, a presidency so reliant on public appeals can impede citizen participation and threaten democratic accountability.[71] The public expects and wants presidents to lead but does not need them to dominate and manipulate.

NOTES

1. Wilson's meetings with the press began to dwindle off in June 1915 as he began to turn increasingly to foreign affairs and the war in Europe.

2. Woodrow Wilson, "Second Annual Message to Congress, December 8, 1914," in *President Wilson's State Papers and Addresses* (New York: George H. Doran, 1918), 76, http://babel .hathitrust.org/cgi/pt?id=hvd.hx4il8;view=1up;seq=102.

3. Learning Network, "Dec. 6, 1923: Calvin Coolidge Delivers First Presidential Address on Radio," December 6, 2011, http://learning.blogs.nytimes.com/2011/12/06/dec-6-1923-calvin -coolidge-delivers-first-presidential-address-on-radio/?_r=1.

4. See Kathleen Hall Jamieson and Joseph N. Cappella, *Echo Chamber: Rush Limbaugh and the Conservative Media Establishment* (New York: Oxford University Press, 2008).

5. Talkers, "The Top Talk Radio Audiences," 2015, http://www.talkers.com/top-talk-radio -audiences/.

6. Broadcast Pioneers of Philadelphia, description of the televised National Convention of the Republican Party, 2005, http://www.broadcastpioneers.com/40gop.html. According to this source, "NBC estimated that 40,000 to 50,000 people saw some part of its coverage on TV. The network based this estimate on their belief that 8 to 10 people would make up their audience in front of each receiver."

7. Douglas Brinkley, *Cronkite* (New York: HarperCollins, 2012), 379, 383. Some versions have it as, "I've lost Middle America."

8. Hedrick Smith, *The Power Game: How Washington Works* (New York: Random House, 1988), 405–406.

9. An interesting question: Does Ronald Reagan also fit as an outsider? In 1976, he came very close to denying President Ford the GOP nomination. In 1980, he successfully ran against a number of impressive "insiders"—Senate minority leader Howard Baker (R-TN); Senator Bob Dole (R-KS), who had been the vice presidential nominee in 1976; John Connolly, who had been governor of Texas and Nixon's secretary of the treasury; and George H. W. Bush, who had held a variety of high-level elected and appointed positions.

10. Samuel Kernell, *Going Public: New Strategies of Presidential Leadership,* 1st ed. (Washington, DC: CQ Press, 1986). The second edition of the work appeared in 1993, the third in 1997, and the fourth in 2006.

11. Three photographs of FDR in a wheelchair exist, apparently taken by family members at private gatherings. That he suffered from polio was known. FDR was one of the founders of the March of Dimes, which initially was created as a charitable foundation devoted to curing polio. That he had braces on his legs was apparent; his use of crutches for mobility was less publicized. According to the Franklin D. Roosevelt Presidential Library and Museum, "There was a gentlemen's understanding with the press that photographs displaying FDR's disability were not published. Consequently, only candid photos of FDR in his wheelchairs have survived. The Roosevelt Library owns three of them." Franklin D. Roosevelt Presidential Library and Museum, "Roosevelt Facts and Figures," http://www.fdrlibrary.marist.edu/facts.html.

12. Kernell, *Going Public,* 3rd ed., 27.

13. Ibid., 27.

14. Ibid., 28.

15. Kernell, *Going Public*, 2nd ed., xvi.

16. Ibid., 130.

17. Kernell, *Going Public*, 3rd ed., 159.

18. Ibid., 170.

19. Mark Hertsgaard, *On Bended Knee: The Press and the Reagan Presidency* (New York: Schocken Books, 1989).

20. Ibid., 261.

21. Martha Joynt Kumar, *Managing the President's Message: The White House Communications Operation* (Baltimore: Johns Hopkins University Press, 2007), 301.

22. Kernell, *Going Public,* 3rd ed., 6–7. Kernell especially notes the contrast with John Kennedy here. When his legislative agenda became stalled in Congress, there were no reports of any effort to threaten to go public or actually make some public appeal as a device to pressure Congress.

23. Ibid., 5.

24. Kumar, *Managing the President's Message,* 301.

25. Hertsgaard, *On Bended Knee,* xiii–xiv.

26. Kernell, *Going Public,* 3rd ed., 132.

27. George C. Edwards III, *On Deaf Ears: The Limits of the Bully Pulpit* (New Haven, CT: Yale University Press, 2003).

28. Kumar, *Managing the President's Message,* 301.

29. Ibid., 288.

30. Thomas E. Patterson, *Out of Control* (New York: Vintage, 1994).

31. Jeffrey E. Cohen, *The Presidency in the Era of 24-Hour News* (Princeton, NJ: Princeton University Press, 2008), 15.

32. Ibid., 189–191.

33. Jeffrey E. Cohen, *Going Local: Presidential Leadership in the Post-Broadcast Age* (New York: Cambridge University Press, 2010), 210.

34. Cohen, *Presidency in the Era of 24-Hour News,* 190.

35. Edwards, *On Deaf Ears,* ix.

36. Ibid., 74.

37. Ibid., 36–37.

38. One that was widely distributed (I remember seeing it a number of times) focused on a mythical married couple, "Harry" and "Louise"; it was sponsored by a group of health insurances companies. See http://www.youtube.com/watch?v=Dt31nhleeCg.

39. Edwards, *On Deaf Ears,* 217.

40. Ibid., 238.

41. See Internet World Stats, "Internet Growth Statistics," 2015, http://www.internetworld stats.com/emarketing.htm.

42. Aaron Smith, "U.S. Smartphone Use in 2015: Chapter One: A Portrait of Smartphone Ownership," Pew Research Center, April 1, 2015, http://www.pewinternet.org/2015/04/01 /chapter-one-a-portrait-of-smartphone-ownership/.

43. Katerina Matsa and Amy Mitchell, "Eight Key Takeaways About Social Media and News," March 26, 2014, http://www.journalism.org/2014/03/26/8-key-takeaways-about-social-media -and-news/.

44. Amy Mitchell, "State of the News Media 2014," Recent Changes in the Media: Pew Research Journalism Project, March 26, 2014, http://www.journalism.org/2014/03/26/state-of-the-news-media-2014-overview/.

45. Amy Mitchell, "State of the News Media."

46. Robert D. Putnam, *Bowling Alone: The Collapse and Revival of American Community* (New York: Simon & Schuster, 2000).

47. Matsa and Mitchell, "Eight Key Takeaways."

48. The search was done on December 15, 2015.

49. See Shanto Iyengar and Kyu S. Hahn, "Red Media, Blue Media: Evidence of Ideological Selectivity in Media Usage," *Journal of Communication* 59, no. 1 (March 2009): 19–39; Cohen, *Presidency in the Era of the 24-Hour News,* 14–15.

50. On the general issue of "selective exposure" in a variety of news sources, including the media, see Nathalie J. Stroud, *Niche News: The Politics of News Choice* (New York: Oxford University Press, 2011). Although they tend to be more positive about the Internet's effects on politics, also see the discussion of selective patterns of Internet usage in Jason Gainous and Kevin M. Wagner, *Rebooting American Politics: The Internet Revolution* (Lanham, MD: Rowman and Littlefield, 2011), 32–34.

51. Zachary A. Goldfarb and Juliet Eilperin, "White House Looking for New Ways to Penetrate Polarized Media," *Washington Post,* May 6, 2014, https://www.washingtonpost.com/politics/white-house-looking-for-new-ways-to-penetrate-polarized-media/2014/05/06/ebd39b6c-d532-11e3-aae8-c2d44bd79778_story.html.

52. Its mission statement can be found at http://www.barackobama.com/#get-the-latest/.

53. Glenn Thrush, Reid Epstein, and Byron Tau, "Obama Unveils 'Organizing for Action,'" *Politico,* January 17, 2013, http://www.politico.com/story/2013/01/obama-campaign-to-relaunch-as-tax-exempt-group-86375.html#ixzz394EEuN6M.

54. On Bush efforts, see Kevin F. Sullivan, "Bush Pioneered Use of Internet, Obama Mastering It," Real Clear Politics, June 27, 2009, http://www.realclearpolitics.com/articles/2009/06/27/bush_pioneered_use_of_internet_obama_mastering_it.html. Sullivan served as one of Bush's directors of the Office of White House Communications.

55. Goldfarb and Eilperin, "White House Looking for New Ways."

56. Chris Cillizza, "No This Isn't the Most Transparent Administration Ever. And the Next One Will Be Even Worse," *Washington Post,* July 24, 2014, http://www.washingtonpost.com/blogs/the-fix/wp/2014/07/24/no-this-isnt-the-most-transparent-administration-ever-and-the-next-one-will-be-worse/.

57. Chris Cillizza, "How Pete Souza Became President Obama's Secret Weapon," *Washington Post,* December 19, 2012, http://www.washingtonpost.com/blogs/the-fix/wp/2012/12/19/pete-souza-president-obamas-secret-weapon/.

58. Andrew Dugan, "Despite Enrollment Success, Healthcare Law Still Unpopular," Gallup, May 29, 2014, http://www.gallup.com/poll/170750/despite-enrollment-success-healthcare-law-remains-unpopular.aspx.

59. Frank Newport, "Few Americans Say Healthcare Law Has Helped Them," Gallup, May 29, 2014, http://www.gallup.com/poll/170756/few-americans-say-healthcare-law-helped.aspx.

60. Edward-Isaac Dovere, "The 'Meh' of a Salesman," Politico, September 20, 2013, http://www.politico.com/story/2013/09/obama-messaging-97098.html.

61. Lydia Saad, "Americans Want Stricter Gun Laws, Still Oppose Bans," Gallup, December 27, 2012, http://www.gallup.com/poll/159569/americans-stricter-gun-laws-oppose-bans.aspx.

62. Dan Balz, "Gun Vote Shows Gulf Between Washington, Country," *Washington Post,* April 17, 2013, https://www.washingtonpost.com/politics/gun-vote-shows-gulf-between-washington-country/2013/04/17/e50ede04-a793-11e2-8302-3c7e0ea97057_story.html.

63. Frank Newport, "Americans Wanted Gun Background Checks to Pass Senate," Gallup, April 29, 2013, http://www.gallup.com/poll/162083/americans-wanted-gun-background-checks-pass-senate.aspx.

64. Brandon Rottinghaus, *The Provisional Pulpit: Modern Presidential Leadership of Public Opinion* (College Station: Texas A&M University Press, 2010), 196–197.

65. G. W. Bush is also an interesting case study because, at the start of his second term, not only did a signature policy proposal, Social Security reform, fail to receive public support but also public opinion moved in the opposite direction (much like Clinton's early healthcare initiative). From March to May 2005, Bush and other administration officials went on a sixty-day campaign to sixty cities to sell the proposal. At the start of the effort, 44 percent approved of the administration's plan, while 50 percent opposed it. By late July, approval had sunk to 29 percent, and disapproval had increased to 62 percent (see Kumar, *Managing the President's Message,* 285). As Bush later concedes in his memoirs, "If I had it to do over again, I would have pushed for immigration reform rather than Social Security . . . immigration reform had bipartisan support." George W. Bush, *Decision Points* (New York: Crown, 2010), 306.

66. Kernell, *Going Public,* 3rd ed., 3–4.

67. Michael D. Shear, "Sticking to His Travel Plans, at Risk of Looking Bad," *New York Times,* July 19, 2014, http://www.nytimes.com/2014/07/20/us/politics/obama-sticks-to-schedule-despite-world-crises.html?_r=0.

68. James Madison, "Federalist No. 51," *Federalist Papers,* Library of Congress edition, http://thomas.loc.gov/home/histdox/fedpapers.html.

69. Jeffrey K. Tulis, *The Rhetorical Presidency* (Princeton, NJ: Princeton University Press, 1987).

70. Ibid., 202–204.

71. Craig A. Rimmerman, *Presidency by Plebiscite: The Reagan-Bush Era in Institutional Perspective* (Boulder, CO: Westview Press, 1993), 134–135.

5

Presidential Power and Historical Time, Variously Interpreted

Time and history matter in the study of presidential power. Presidencies do not occur in a vacuum; they are located at a particular point in history. As a result, presidents may face different challenges and opportunities, depending on the forces at play during their time in office. These forces can work for them or against them, making their leadership tasks easier or more difficult. Still, presidents are active agents within a particular historical context and should not be regarded as passive participants nor historically determined instruments. As Stephen Skowronek notes, "Political time does not turn presidents into automatons or negate the substantive significance of the choices they make."[1] Some leaders are highly attuned to their place in history, whereas others may be more oblivious. However, even if presidents are cognizant of historical context, their individual impact and their skills and abilities to exercise influence can vary. Some presidents seize the moment and achieve great things, while others struggle and sometimes even fail.

Moreover, some methods of exercising power may work well at one point in time but poorly at others. That leads to the question of adaptability: If one way of exercising influence is failing to achieve policy ends, are presidents able to shift to other means and strategies? Sometimes, a president's adaptability may not even matter. Policies that are embraced and achievable at one point may be rejected and unsuccessful at another, and vice versa. For example, Harry Truman first proposed comprehensive national health care, but it was not enacted into law until Barack Obama took office over sixty years later. In short, whether individual presidents, their strategies and tactics for exercising power, and the ends they pursue fail or succeed can be, in large part, the result of the historical moment.

George Washington is a good example of a president who understood the situation he faced and crafted a presidency to successfully meet it. But what if someone had been elected in his place who was more deferential to Congress or, on the other hand, more arrogant in the exercise of power? Moving forward in history, suppose that Abraham Lincoln had been elected in 1856 rather than 1860. Did it take a civil war to make Lincoln a great president? Like Lincoln, Franklin Roosevelt faced the most difficult of challenges—the height of the Great Depression—yet his leadership largely prevailed. But did it take a massive economic crisis to make Congress and the nation receptive to FDR's message? Would some of his policies—Social Security, federal housing projects, collective bargaining rights for unions, a federal minimum wage, to list but a few—have been achieved had he served during a different political period and under better economic times?

Likewise, presidents who have been regarded as failures in office might have proven more successful had they served at a different time. Herbert Hoover, for example, became president in March 1929 but by October faced a massive crash in the stock market and the start of the Great Depression. We often think of Hoover as a curmudgeonly old man, ill-equipped to deal with the Great Depression. He certainly lacked the communicative skills of his successor, FDR. Yet, there were some signs that Hoover would have been a more successful president at another time. He came from the progressive wing of his party and was regarded as a technocrat and a reformer. Few remember it today, but Hoover was in charge of massive and successful relief efforts in post–World War I Europe and after the devastating flood of the Mississippi River in 1927.

One interesting twist: sometimes presidents make choices that were considered ill-advised at the time they were made but that history eventually vindicates. The classic example is when Gerald Ford pardoned Richard Nixon shortly after Ford took office. Ford's approval ratings declined after he issued the pardon. Had Ford not pardoned Nixon, he might have preserved his popularity and won the 1976 election. However, in my view at least, Ford did the right thing. Nixon may not have deserved a pardon, but the country deserved to avoid the distraction of a likely criminal trial and to get on with national business.

These are individual cases. The challenge is to more generally understand how *historical time* might affect a presidency. That is, what broad historical cycles or patterns help determine or explain a president's success or failure, and which have the greatest impact upon the exercise of presidential power? We examine these issues in this chapter, beginning with a look at two historical political trends: congressional versus presidential dominance, and divided versus unified government. We explore in depth Stephen Skowronek's theory of political time, which argues that there are dominant political regimes in US political history, that these regimes are cyclical in nature, and that presidents located at different points within a regime cycle face very different opportunities and constraints for exercising leadership. We then consider other plausible historical cycles such as those grounded in stages of policy development as well as swings in political ideology. We also discuss James David Barber's theory of presidential character and its resonance with his assertion that there are historical cycles of changing public moods. As we shall see, these various attempts to bring history to bear concerning the exercise of presidential power can be revealing in hindsight, though they are far from perfect as predictors of presidential success. Moreover, it is difficult for sitting presidents to determine where they are located in the ebb and flow of history and what practical lessons in exercising presidential power might be gleaned from this determination. Still, there is no denying that historical context is a contributing factor to the success or failure of a presidency, so although understanding their place in history might be difficult for future presidents, they must at least attempt to do so.

HISTORICAL TRENDS IN THE RELATIONSHIP BETWEEN CONGRESS AND THE EXECUTIVE

To understand the impact of historical forces on presidential power, we begin with two broad trends: congressional versus presidential dominance, and divided versus united government. Both trends emanate from the relationship between the legislative branch and the executive branch.

Congressional Versus Presidential Dominance

Bert Rockman posits that there are four phases in the changing power balance between the legislative branch and the executive branch, or congressional versus presidential dominance.[2] In the first phase, from 1789 to 1860, presidential relations with Congress were adversarial but with some measure of congressional dominance. In the second phase, from 1876 to roughly 1910, Congress took the lead and was the dominant force in guiding and setting the legislative agenda. However, in the third phase, from 1920 to 1965, the president had the upper hand, though seniority prevailed in the Congress and "committee barons"—the chairs of congressional committees—still held great power. The fourth phase, from the mid-1960s into the early 1980s, was a time of adversarial and mutually assertive relations coupled with a decline in the seniority system and an increase in the influence of congressional subcommittees.

Since the 1980s, in my view, the balance of power has worsened for presidents seeking to exercise influence. The seniority system has weakened in terms of committee assignments, especially for chairs. In addition, individual members of Congress are now more independent, and they often have become policy and political entrepreneurs in their own right. They are also more adept at building their own base of financial support for their election campaigns. The balance of power today makes the exercise of presidential leadership more difficult. Depending on the balance of power, the strategies and tactics used by presidents to exercise influence have had to vary. At a time when the executive branch is more dominant, bargaining and going public might be most successful. But at a time when Congress is more dominant, a president may have to rely more on executive actions, as we have seen with Barack Obama.

Divided Versus United Government

Another historical political approach is to look at party control of the executive branch versus that of Congress: a divided government versus a unified one. The Democrats controlled both the House and the Senate from 1955 until 1981, a period covering six of Eisenhower's eight years in office and all of the Nixon and Ford presidencies. Republicans regained control of the Senate in 1981 only to lose it after the 1986 midterms under Reagan. The House remained under Democratic control from 1955 until after the 1994 midterms, a period of forty years. Thus, all Republican presidents, including Reagan and George H. W. Bush, faced at least some measure of divided government through 1992.

Does a divided government hamper presidential power? Some believe that it does. The lack of responsible, unified, and energetic government both within Congress and between the president and Congress was a theme of Woodrow Wilson's first book as a young academic, *Congressional Government*.[3] More recently, Ginsberg and Shefter note that divided government doesn't just make the passage of presidential proposals more difficult, it can lead to "institutional combat" between the executive and congressional branches. During the Nixon presidency, for example, a divided government led to the White House strengthening its administrative powers. And on Congress's part, it has resulted in a greater degree of investigation of the executive branch, both by congressional committees and, for a period, with legislation that empowered the appointment of special prosecutors. The Democrats did this to Nixon, while the Republicans did it to Clinton. According to Ginsberg and Shefter, the struggle between institutions "is most likely to occur when the major branches of government are controlled by hostile political forces."[4]

Other scholars are less sure about the effects of divided government. David Mayhew's extensive empirical research indicates that, in the end, divided government does not matter much. He found that a roughly equal number of major pieces of legislation are passed whether there is unified or divided government; in particular, Mayhew notes that it "has probably not made a notable difference during the post-war era."[5] Nor, he argues, does it explain the likelihood of Congress to conduct high-publicity investigations of the executive branch.[6] Morris Fiorina agrees, noting that "some divided governments are legislatively active, some are legislatively passive." While Fiorina admits that divided government can exacerbate the level of conflict, he does not necessarily see this as a bad thing.[7]

Although divided government can create political difficulties in achieving presidential goals and presidents are better positioned to succeed if their party also controls Congress, it should not be taken as an excuse for presidential inaction or passivity. In fact, divided government can be an invitation for greater and more creative efforts at exercising power. Recall, for example, Eisenhower's indirect, hidden-hand strategy in dealing with congressional Democrats that we discussed in Chapter 2. Divided government may not matter much not because it is unimportant but rather because presidents need to be adept enough to exercise power in ways that overcome the limitations and constraints of divided government.

STEPHEN SKOWRONEK'S
THEORY OF POLITICAL TIME

Perhaps one of the most prominent theories of historical time is Stephen Skowronek's theory of *political time.* Skowronek originated this theory in his 1993 book *The Politics Presidents Make* and later expanded upon it in subsequent articles and in collections of his writings.[8] In a nutshell, he argues that at various points in history some presidents come to power by creating political coalitions and policy agendas that coalesce into a new political regime. These political regimes endure through subsequent presidencies but eventually come to an end. Depending on where a president falls within the cycle of a particular regime, he faces different challenges and opportunities in terms of presidential power and, hence, a need for different types and exercises of leadership.

Interestingly, in Skowronek's view, Neustadt's analysis of presidential power illustrates the merits of his own approach. In the first edition of his work, Neustadt examined a specific historical period: FDR's New Deal policies and the successors to his particular brand of politics—Truman and Eisenhower. However, Neustadt judged Truman and Eisenhower against the model of presidential power embodied and established by FDR and restricted his analysis to the individual president's ability to wield power through bargaining and persuasion. They largely paled in comparison. Skowronek argues that this is unsurprising because Neustadt disregards the broader dynamics and political context. FDR did not simply influence; he dominated and ushered American politics into a new era. Truman and Eisenhower came into the presidency at a different political time from FDR; they were constrained by the regime FDR created and its subsequent historical arc.

For Skowronek, the weaknesses in Neustadt's theory prove that a broader view is needed. The standard perspective among many scholars—and Neustadt is one of them—is that FDR's administration marks the end of the "traditional" presidency and the beginning of the "modern" presidency, which continues to this day. For Skowronek, the story is more complex. He lays out four eras of American presidential history: (1) a patrician period when presidents' personal reputations among a small group of political elites mattered most (1789–1832); (2) a highly partisan period when political patronage and brokering deals with party bosses dominated (1832–1900); (3) a pluralist period in which the presidency became the focal point of policy initiative, and bargaining with a wider variety of elites and organized interests developed (1900–1972); and (4) a plebiscitary period with a more public presidency (1972 to the present).[9] Each era changed the political landscape, which then informed the specific opportunities and challenges of the regime cycles within that period.

The Regime Cycle: Reconstruction, Articulation, and Disjunction

Now for the central question: What exactly is the regime cycle? Skowronek posits that there are three stages in each cycle, beginning with reconstruction, then

FIGURE 5.1. Skowronek's Political Regime Cycle

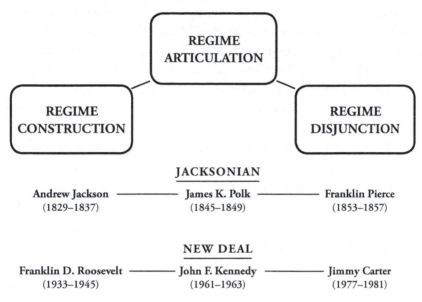

moving to articulation, and ending with disjunction (see Figure 5.1). Skowronek argues that presidents cannot be compared as equals; we have to factor in where a president fits within a regime's cycle—regardless of which era of presidential history the president occupies or whether he is considered "traditional" or "modern." Depending on the stage of the regime cycle, presidents face different challenges in exercising power and possess different resources for doing so. To be effective, presidents must recognize where they fit, and then figure out how to exercise leadership accordingly.

Reconstructive presidents establish new regimes within the historical periods mentioned earlier. They understand the weaknesses of the past and seize the moment to form new political coalitions, apply new strategies to attain their goals, and take the political agenda on a different course. In this category, Skowronek places Thomas Jefferson, Andrew Jackson, Abraham Lincoln, Franklin Roosevelt, and, with some qualification, Ronald Reagan. Jefferson was a notable patrician, but he adapted to emerging partisan politics and offered a new political program that differed substantially from Washington's and John Adams's. Jackson's regime was a repudiation of the patrician elite. It was grounded in broader democratic politics and wary of national financial institutions but embraced stronger executive powers. Lincoln guided the country through the Civil War and was at the forefront of the emergence of the Republican Party as a political force. The Republican Party formed in the mid-1850s, and its focus on ending slavery built a political coalition that peeled off voters from the Jacksonian Democrats and the Whigs (which disappeared as a political party in the United States).

The political winds changed yet again with the election of FDR. He created a new political coalition that displaced the Republican majority. FDR's policies during his first and second terms provided the eventual groundwork that would keep the Democrats dominant for several more decades. Except for a brief two-year period under Truman and at the start of the Eisenhower presidency, the Democrats largely remained in control of Congress. Although the Republicans had a majority in the Senate during the first six years of the Reagan presidency, the House remained under Democratic control from the 1954 midterm elections until after the 1994 midterms, a span of forty years. As for Reagan, Skowronek does classify him as a reconstructive president, but one whose regime was somewhat stillborn. As evidence of Reagan as a reconstructive president, Skowronek notes his great success in bringing his program of tax reductions and budget cuts during his first year in office to successful fruition. But Skowronek then concludes that after Reagan's first year, "the administration was a spent force so far as reconstruction was concerned."[10] We discuss the Reagan regime in more depth in the following section.

Reconstructive presidencies may ignite the beginning of a new regime, but who carries on their work? The next phase of a regime's cycle is occupied by *articulators;* they are partisans of the same regime, but their role is to fine-tune and continue the policies set in motion by reconstructors. Reconstructors transform the political landscape, but the continuing hard work is left to others. In the Jeffersonian cycle, James Madison and James Monroe are the articulators. Monroe's leadership, according to Skowronek, was a "purely constructive elaboration of received premises."[11] Other articulators include James K. Polk in Jacksonian democracy; Theodore Roosevelt for the Lincoln regime; and Harry Truman, John F. Kennedy, and Lyndon B. Johnson in FDR's regime. Skowronek also classifies George H. W. Bush as an articulator within the Reagan regime. Note, however, that his achievements were largely in international affairs, and his domestic record was slim save for a brokered agreement to raise taxes slightly, which infuriated the Reaganite Republicans.

Articulators face the common task of keeping the regime's political coalition together while adapting to new policy challenges that threaten to fracture it. Although articulators share the politics and policies of the reconstructive president in their regime cycle, they arguably have more in common with their fellow articulators in terms of the challenges they face and the exercise of presidential power and leadership. For example, Kennedy and LBJ have more in common with Polk than they do with FDR. For Polk, the challenge was to keep the geographical wings of his party together as the debate over slavery proved increasingly divisive. For JFK and LBJ, the challenge was to keep white southerners within the Democratic fold while responding to increased concern about the civil rights of African Americans.

The articulators are followed by those poor presidential souls who eke out a win as a regime peters out. *Disjunctive presidents* come at the end of a regime cycle and attempt to stave off disaster as best they can. John Quincy Adams for the Jeffersonians, Franklin Pierce for the Jackson regime, Herbert Hoover for the Lincoln Republicans, and Jimmy Carter for FDR's New Deal are all disjunctive presidents, according to Skowronek. Adams and Pierce tried to bargain their way out of difficulty, but they fell victim to accusations of engaging in corrupt deals.[12] Carter's ineptitude was the result of political inexperience, especially in legislative politics. Rather than invigorating—or even sustaining—the legacy of the New Deal as a populist southern governor with broad appeal, he generated doubts about his leadership.[13] In addition, despite being a born-again Christian, he did not have much influence over white southerners, who continued to desert the Democratic Party. The regime's coalition fragmented and was no longer electorally viable at the regional level. The South was moving toward the Republicans, and Ronald Reagan was waiting in the wings to usher in a new alternative regime.

The Reagan Presidency: A Failed Reconstruction?

The Reagan presidency warrants extra attention. For Skowronek, it was essentially a failed reconstruction, one marked by the initial success of his economic program but with a less settled legacy. It was a story with two sides: "the economic success and the political failure," according to Skowronek.[14] Yet, to play devil's advocate, I might also reverse that formula: economic difficulty but political success. The improvement of the economy under Reagan may have had more to do with the Federal Reserve's staunch attempt to control inflation. Furthermore, Reagan's record on the national debt is startling: tax cuts and increased defense expenditures yielded significant increases in the national debt. In the last fiscal year of the Carter presidency, the debt stood at $930 billion (33.3 percent of GDP); by the end of the Reagan presidency it rose to $2.68 trillion (52.6 percent of GDP). Still, some credit Reagan's tax cuts for leading to the economic boom years of the 1980s.

As for political success, his appeal to blue-collar Democrats led to his defeat of Carter in 1980 and a resounding reelection victory in 1984. Only DC and Minnesota, the home state of his opponent, former vice president Walter Mondale, cast electoral votes against him. Although the Republicans did not assert prolonged control over Congress the way that Democrats did during FDR's regime cycle, Republicans still controlled the Senate for six of the eight years of Reagan's presidency. They then resumed control of it after the 1994 midterms through the early months of George W. Bush's presidency, and again after the 2002 midterms. The GOP lost their majority in the Senate in 2006 and did not regain it until the 2014 midterms. As for the House of Representatives, the GOP finally achieved a majority after the 1994 midterms and remained in control until the 2006 midterms; it later returned to GOP control after the 2010 midterms. In addition, Reagan's international policies arguably played a role in ending the Cold War, a significant achievement. The resumption of tensions with Russia didn't occur until more recent administrations, most notably Obama's, as that nation was confronted with its own version of a likely reconstructor: Vladimir Putin.

We might quibble with Reagan's economic record or point out that after his first year he encountered increasing policy opposition with a divided Congress. However, in my view, there is no denying that Reagan defined a new political landscape and regime. For many Republicans, Reagan has achieved the iconic status that FDR held for decades among Democrats. His tax-cut policies remain GOP orthodoxy; his suspiciousness of federal policy still holds sway for many. As Skowronek notes in a later collection of essays, "each of Reagan's successors has been subject to political expectations that he set."[15] That sounds like more than just a stillborn regime to me.

ISSUES WITH SKOWRONEK'S THEORY

Although Skowronek makes one of the most compelling arguments for the impact of historical time on presidential power, his theory is not without gaps and issues. In fact, the example of Reagan's presidency and the debate over its classification as a failed reconstruction by Skowronek is a good example of how the presidential categories or phases in Skowronek's regime cycle are not always clear-cut.

Addressing Periods of Regime Uncertainty

One of the most obvious gaps in Skowronek's work is that he largely glosses over some of the historical periods in which the results of political battle are unclear. For example, after Ulysses S. Grant's presidency ended in early 1877, the nation was politically divided. Grant's successor, Rutherford Hayes, became president under questionable electoral circumstances. Democrat Grover Cleveland served two nonconsecutive terms: he became president in 1884 but lost the electoral vote to Benjamin Harrison in 1888 before becoming president again after the 1892 election. Most elections during this period were closely contested—a clear sign of regime uncertainty, in my view. It is not until William McKinley's election in 1896, often regarded as a "realigning" one, that a more dominant Republican coalition emerged, solidified, and persisted until 1932.

Skowronek does not really discuss or categorize any of the pre-McKinley presidents in the Lincoln regime. Instead, he jumps from Lincoln as the regime constructor to Theodore Roosevelt as its subsequent articulator. In my view, the divided politics in the immediate post–Civil War era suggests there is no clear political regime cycle during this period. Lincoln brings the Republicans into major party status, but there is a subsequent era of regime uncertainty. It could also be the case that Lincoln is really just a precursor and that perhaps McKinley—or even Theodore Roosevelt, an articulator in the Lincoln cycle according to Skowronek— is really the constructor of a more dominant Republican regime.

Accounting for the Differences in Presidents Occupying the Same Phase

Even with the presidents that Skowronek neatly situates within a regime cycle, there are issues and unanswered questions. Presidents occupying the same phase in the cycle may experience similar moments in political history and face common tasks, but that does not necessarily mean they have equal amounts of success (or failure), as we saw with the Reagan example, nor does it mean that they go about achieving their goals in the same way. Skowronek notes in a later work that reconstructive presidents are all advantaged by the failing and faltering regimes of their predecessors and that they share a "moment in a political sequence in which presidential authority is at its most compelling, a moment when opponents stand indicted in the court of public opinion and allies are not yet secure."[16] But Skowronek is a little vague on exactly why and how reconstructive presidents are able to mark out a new political era. (Although Skowronek does observe that reconstructors come to power because they are "perceived as the only alternatives to national ruin" and because they are "not only great communicators but also great repudiators" of their predecessors' policies.[17])

Reconstructors assemble pieces into new political alliances that endure over time, but there is little consistency from one reconstructive president to another on how they get this done. FDR and his New Deal coalition is perhaps the best example of this. The traditional Democratic Party base of the southern states and large cities was broadened as organized labor became stronger and the party's blue-collar membership increased, as progressives became more strongly allied to the party, and as African Americans moved away from the party of Lincoln. Yet the substance of the New Deal itself was a changing array of policies and programs. Although the administration recognized that the federal government needed to act more vigorously with respect to the economic sector and to respond to social needs, it had no consistent policy agenda. FDR was a pragmatist, willing to test whatever new plausible ideas surfaced, not an ideologue with a clear program that guided his efforts from the start. Indeed, one of his early initiatives in 1933 was to try to balance the federal budget. It was an ill-conceived effort and was quickly abandoned in favor of large-scale federal spending on a variety of public projects as well as efforts at regulating industrial and agricultural production. FDR was successful at reconstruction—arguably, the most successful—largely because he was Franklin D. Roosevelt: a skilled communicator who inspired confidence, and a shrewd and often manipulative politician. The lessons I draw from FDR and the New Deal are essentially about his leadership and personal skills, not broader generalities that might be applied to successive reconstructive presidents.

With articulators as well, some clearly fared better than others. Why? Skowronek observes in later commentary that presidents who fall quickly on the heels of a reconstructor face more difficulty than do articulators who come later in the cycle. The latter have more distance, whereas early articulators tend to be in the shadow of the reconstructive president and suffer more by comparison.[18] For example, Truman, coming right on the heels of FDR, faced a more difficult task than did Kennedy and LBJ, his Democratic successors. But even with Kennedy, it is difficult to draw concrete evaluations of the articulator role or lessons about exercising power as an articulator. History has denied us a sufficient range of time to judge whether John F. Kennedy might have provided useful and positive lessons for keeping a regime intact while building toward a different future. We do not know how a second-term Kennedy presidency might have handled Vietnam or made further progress on the issue of African American civil rights. As such, Skowronek focuses on Lyndon Johnson. LBJ was certainly skilled in legislative politics, and his domestic achievements were great. He extrapolated the social safety nets that FDR had laid the foundation for, such as establishing Medicare and Medicaid, championing urban redevelopment, and introducing a variety of programs as part of his War on Poverty. Yet his decision to expand the war in Vietnam clouded his overall record.

This bifurcation of LBJ's achievements is important: it shows how international and national security issues, not just domestic regime politics and political coalitions, now greatly affect a presidency. Skowronek would likely argue that Polk, a fellow articulator, faced similar choices to LBJ with the Mexican-American War in 1846–1847. But the truth is that much has changed since then, particularly for LBJ and other post–World War II presidents. The foreign policy piece of the equation has become increasingly important, given the growth of US leadership in world affairs. After the dissolution of the Soviet Union, many thought that there would be, at least, a somewhat peaceful interlude because the major ideological tensions between East and West had seemingly been resolved. However, we might argue that things got worse—they certainly got more complex. Since the terrorist attacks during the Clinton presidency and 9/11, the United States is in conflict not only with other countries but also with nonstate entities such as Al-Qaeda, the Taliban, and the Islamic State of Iraq and Syria (ISIS). The United States also faces danger from their rogue followers within US borders, as was the case with the killings in San Bernardino, California, in December 2015. And our nation is still dealing with other nation-states: our relationship with Russia has become strained once again, and China has become a superpower with international interests that differ from our own. Iran and North Korea remain longtime adversaries. The impact of presidential regimes and their respective cycles is even harder to figure out today given the dynamic forces beyond our borders.

Addressing Oppositional Presidents

In *The Politics Presidents Make,* Skowronek does not extensively address the presidents who do not fit into the political time of a regime cycle: oppositional presidents, also known as preemptive presidents.[19] ***Oppositional presidents*** come from the political party outside of the regime and attempt, in varying degrees, to alter the policy course of the existing regime. Some even aggressively seek to construct regimes of their own but end up failing. Oppositional presidents are numerous, every regime is punctuated with them from time to time, and their historical impact is sometimes quite significant. The administrations of some even rank high on lists of historic presidencies, including those of Grover Cleveland, Woodrow Wilson, and Eisenhower. Others, such as the terms of Nixon and Clinton, are subject to varied interpretations. Still, the contributions of these oppositional presidents and the impact they have on public policy should not be underestimated.

In his later work, *Presidential Leadership in Political Time*, Skowronek does offer some insight: "opposition leaders will be more authoritative in political action to the extent that received commitments are vulnerable," while leaders affiliated with a regime "will be more authoritative in political action to the extent received commitments are resilient."[20] Yet the importance of these oppositional leaders remains a bit undeveloped in his theory. Fortunately, a number of oppositional presidents are analyzed—with specific reference to Skowronek's theory—by David A. Crockett in *The Opposition Presidency*.[21] Crockett's analysis is important because he delves more deeply into how oppositional presidents exercised power and what lessons we might draw from them.

In Crockett's view, oppositional presidents must adapt to the context of the existing regime, even if they want to establish their own ideal political agenda. They can propose policy alternatives, but those policies must be tempered and molded around the political realities of the regime. They should govern with moderation and understand that a steady administration can be their best asset. Choosing their political battles carefully also helps oppositional presidents be successful, because they tend not to hold the upper hand in the zero-sum politics game. As such, they should exercise their veto powers judiciously. Although it is enticing for oppositional presidents to try to enact change through rhetorical appeals and going public, the historical record of success here is not encouraging. Still, there are some scenarios in which oppositional presidents can gain more power. For example, shifting the ideological base of their own party even slightly or establishing cross-party alliances can be hugely beneficial. And if their party happens to attain control of the House or the Senate or both, oppositional presidents will have greater degrees of freedom.

In short, according to Crockett, "A strategy of moderation and tempered goals, one that avoids frontal assaults on the reigning governing philosophy, provides for greater success for the opposition president and the political system as a whole."[22] However, Crockett also notes that personal character matters. Some oppositional leaders who lack what he calls a "prudent temperament" can take matters too far. The temptations of power can cause them to push constitutional boundaries too much, which then fosters "pathological outcomes."[23] Andrew Johnson, Nixon, and Clinton clearly come to mind: all faced the impeachment process and a divided public.[24]

The Difficulty in Assessing Recent Presidencies: Where Do Bush and Obama Fit?

Where do George W. Bush and Barack Obama fit in the regime cycle? For Bush, the obvious question is whether he is a disjunctive president in the Reagan cycle, a regime ender, a Republican Jimmy Carter. Or is he a midregime articulator, like his father? Skowronek locates him within the Reagan legacy, labeling him an "orthodox innovator," presidents who are not just affiliates of their regime but stalwart defenders of it, aiming to advance its agenda even further.[25] In my view, frankly, it is still difficult to tell—even years after the end of Bush's presidency—whether this label is appropriate. He seemed to be a regime innovator at the beginning of his presidency, touting "compassionate conservatism" as his slogan, but by the end of his presidency, his weakened reputation and growing disfavor among the public seem to indicate that his was a disjunctive presidency, marking the end of the Reagan regime. Even Skowronek notes that although Bush "came to power in 2000 determined to complete and secure the 'Reagan Revolution'; he enters his final year in office amid charges that he betrayed it and shattered the political foundations of conservative governance."[26]

As for Barack Obama, his campaign rhetoric was that of a reconstructor: he promised a new kind of politics with his slogan "change we can believe in." His path to the presidency was certainly reminiscent of a reconstructor. He defeated the perceived frontrunner Sen. Hillary Clinton (D-NY) for the nomination and then went on to beat Sen. John McCain (R-AZ) in the general election. Both were more experienced Washington insiders, whereas Obama was barely into his first two years as a member of the Senate when he made his presidential bid. Writing in 2011, Skowronek posited that Obama could be a transformational president and a game changer.[27]

However, this has largely not been the case—something that Skowronek also acknowledged.[28] Although Obama was able to pass comprehensive national healthcare reform, an accomplishment that eluded his Democratic predecessors since the Truman years, it generated controversy and lacked majority public support. In addition, his party suffered significant losses in the aftermath of the 2010 midterms, which returned control of the House to the Republicans, effectively ending major White House initiatives. Although Obama was reelected in 2012, his second term did not result in major domestic advances either. Instead, the turmoil of international politics assumed center stage, and his record is somewhat spotty here as well. Although he ended American military presence in Iraq in 2011 and significantly reduced the number of troops in Afghanistan in 2011–2014, political and military instability in both countries remained. And in the fall of 2014, Obama redeployed American military forces to the Middle East in the fight against ISIS. Troubles also brewed with Russia and Ukraine, with Libya, and with Iran's continuing quest for nuclear armament. In the 2014 midterm elections, the Republicans regained control of the Senate and increased their numbers in the House to historic levels. As Skowronek observes, in the end Obama's presidency may seem "more consistent with the preemptive pattern."[29] I would note, though, the Obama administration might be more easily explained in terms of the internal rhythms of a presidency, especially his waning power and performance during the second term, rather than by the external rhythms of the regime cycle. We explore this dynamic in Chapters 6 and 7.

Both the Bush and Obama examples illustrate the difficulty in categorizing more recent presidencies within Skowronek's political regime cycle. Also, in my view, the difficulty of classifying Obama points to the fact that it is unclear whether the Reagan cycle has yet to be played out. Perhaps it has already ended? Or is there future life to it? The presidential election of 2016 will tell, perhaps; but, then again, we might need to wait until 2020, or even after that. That we must defer to future analysis is very revealing of a significant conceptual problem in Skowronek's theory. If we have trouble in categorizing particular presidents even years after they have left office, how do sitting presidents know where they stand in political time? And if they can't know, then how are they to factor in the historical opportunities and constraints in their exercise of presidential power and influence? In all honesty, for sitting presidents there does not seem to be a clear answer to the question: "Where am I in political history?" Perhaps the great presidents of the past have simply sensed their role and proceeded accordingly.

Regime Politics: A Thing of the Past?

Recognizing their own place in the political regime cycle may not even be relevant for future presidents. Skowronek has observed that regime politics may be a thing of the past. He believes that we are now possibly entering a period of "perpetual preemption," where pragmatism rather than regime construction becomes more typical.[30] It is certainly true that parties, especially their respective members in Congress, have become more ideologically polarized, while the middle, the legislative audience most amenable to compromise, has shrunk. The absence of regimes binding supporters together both politically and programmatically could have significant consequences for presidential power. The president's task could prove difficult if Congress is controlled by the opposite party. But by the same token, should a president's party achieve both presidential and congressional control, it will likely become easier for the president to exercise power.

Furthermore, the weakening of party ties and the increasing polarization make both the president and Congress independent policy entrepreneurs, less likely to engage in behind-the-scenes negotiations. In addition, the proliferation of news media gives these "entrepreneurs" a place to hawk and build their individual political brand. Temptations drawing Congress members away from yielding to the presidential position and policy preference increasingly abound. All of this means it is increasingly difficult to build a regime coalition in the first place, never mind sustaining it through several presidencies. Note how this description of weakening party ties and the rise of members of Congress as independent entrepreneurs echoes the reasoning that Kernell and others provide for going public. In the days of political regime building, bargaining would undoubtedly have been the primary resource of presidential power. But in this age of perpetual preemption, going public could be the more useful tool.

THE IMPACT OF THE POLICY CYCLE

The cycle of a *political* regime is not the only form of historical time that can affect a presidency. Erwin Hargrove and Michael Nelson have explored the impact of the *policy* cycle on a president's exercise of power and an administration's degree of activity.[31] After all, it is rare for a president to simply introduce a new policy out of the blue, gain public support and congressional acceptance, and implement the policy before the end of his or her term. FDR is perhaps the only example, but he was president at a time of extraordinary acquiescence to presidential leadership given the economic crisis of the Great Depression. By contrast, most presidents will find that policy development takes time, and they will be helped if that process has begun even before they take office.

The Policy Cycle: Preparation, Achievement, Consolidation

Much like Skowronek's regime cycle, Hargrove and Nelson's policy cycle has three phases: preparation, achievement, and consolidation (see Figure 5.2). *Preparation presidents* are dissatisfied with existing policies and distrustful of existing bureaucracies and the cabinet as a source of policy development. As such, they often turn to their own White House staff and other advisers to bring in fresh ideas. JFK fits in this category, as does Jimmy Carter. Although Hargrove and Nelson do not elaborate in detail on JFK's proposals, we might include his commitment to landing a man on the moon by the end of the 1960s, his efforts to cut federal taxes, as well as his initial development of a comprehensive civil rights bill that would have more enforcement power than the one passed in 1957 during the Eisenhower administration. However, JFK was unable to see any of these efforts come to fruition (arguably perhaps in part because his presidency was tragically cut short).

FIGURE 5.2. Hargrove and Nelson's Policy Cycle

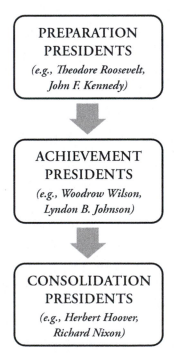

As for Carter, Hargrove and Nelson note that because he "trusted less in persons than in mechanisms" he embraced more technocratic reforms such as departmental reorganization and changes in the federal civil service bureaucracy.[32] Carter also sought a comprehensive national energy policy, especially to reduce dependence on the import of foreign oil. Congress, the energy sector, and the public were not willing to accept the large-scale reforms that the Carter White House proposed. It was a seemingly major defeat of his administration. Yet I would argue that although Carter failed at grander reform, he did have some achievements in this area. He established the Department of Energy, and his extensive efforts to deregulate industries such as trucking, airlines, and oil and natural gas made it through Congress—no small matters. In the airline industry, for example, there was little competition on fares prior to Carter's efforts. After regulations were removed, airlines became more competitive and ticket prices dropped. Perhaps contrary to their classification in the "preparation" phase, presidents at this stage of the cycle often do achieve some of their policy goals.

Presidents in the subsequent stage are known as *achievement presidents.* These presidents capitalize on the groundwork of their preparation predecessors to successfully push policies through Congress. Hargrove and Nelson include FDR, LBJ, and Reagan in this category. In addition to getting Kennedy's proposed tax cuts passed in Congress, LBJ was also able to bring Kennedy's civil rights efforts to fruition with the Civil Rights Bill of 1964. However, Hargrove and Nelson note that *how* achievement presidents implement their policies can often be problematic. They often turn to reorganizing governmental units to secure their aims, but these frequently deliver less than they promise and in some cases considerably less and with negative consequences. FDR is an example of this: during his efforts to deal with the Great Depression, one New Deal agency would be created only to be replaced by another, and perhaps each by a third or fourth.[33] Critics charged his administration with waste and incompetence. LBJ created political forces that could not be managed or controlled in his quest for a "Great Society." As part of his war on poverty, a number of community action groups were created, designed to increase citizen participation and involvement. However, they were often located in cities under Democratic Party control, and they often challenged the power of elected leaders, which resulted in numerous political battles and turmoil that weakened the party at the local level. Reagan's policies reduced federal programs and allowed federal responsibilities to fall to the states. Both LBJ and Reagan gave over responsibility for policy implementation from their administrations to others, yielding power to those who were not necessarily allied with the White House or its policy goals.

Finally, there are *consolidation presidents.* They tend to be from the opposite party, and they aim to "direct policy development primarily to the *modification and consolidation of existing programs*" (emphasis added).[34] Note the emphasis on modification: consolidation presidents do not just solidify the policies of their predecessors, nor do they chart a wholly new policy course. Rather, they tend to continue or implement programs in a similar vein as existing policies but perhaps with slight adjustments to better align with their own governing philosophies. Hargrove and Nelson single out Eisenhower and Nixon here. Eisenhower approved federal aid for school construction, an issue that had been lingering since Truman's presidency, and created an interstate highway system, which built upon prior federal highway initiatives. Nixon launched comprehensive welfare reform and a number of other initiatives designed to make existing policy efforts more effective but in a more Republican direction.

Comparing the Regime Cycle and the Policy Cycle

In Hargrove and Nelson's policy cycle, Eisenhower and Nixon are categorized as presidents of consolidation, while in Skowronek's regime cycle, they are designated as oppositional presidents. Which theory best captures the aims and records of these two presidents? In my view, Hargrove and Nelson may be more right about Eisenhower as a consolidator, whereas the assessment of Nixon as an oppositional president in Skowronek's cycle is more on the money. Eisenhower accepted the broad framework of FDR's New Deal while attempting to curb its budgetary excesses, a process of consolidation. Nixon, however, sought a sharper break with the Democratic past and began the process of moving the southern states into the Republican Party, more along the lines of a potential reconstructor. He was unsuccessful at reconstruction, which makes him an oppositional president.

In fact, in comparing Skowronek's theory with that of Hargrove and Nelson, the categorizations differ for almost every president, highlighting a fundamental point: both theories seek to bring history to bear on the presidency, but they use very different constructs. For Skowronek, within the rise and fall of political regimes, Kennedy is an articulator who built on the foundation laid by FDR, while Carter is a disjunctive president at the end of the FDR regime. But for Hargrove and Nelson, in the cycle of policy development and implementation, they are both preparation presidents, sowing the seeds for the future. For Skowronek, FDR and Reagan are both regime reconstructors. For Hargrove and Nelson, they are midpoint policy achievers. Carter's differing fate in each theory is especially stark: he is at the tail end of a regime cycle for Skowronek but at the beginning of a policy cycle for Hargrove and Nelson. Only Lyndon Johnson, as an articulator in Skowronek's cycle and an achiever in Hargrove and Nelson's, sits at the midway point in both schemas.

These differences further highlight how difficult it can be for presidents not only to situate themselves within historical context but also to decide which type of historical context should be taken into account when determining an achievable agenda and the best course of action for exercising presidential power. For example, following Skowronek's theory, FDR and Reagan as regime constructors should be looking forward and striving to build a new political regime. But following Hargrove and Nelson's theory, they, as policy achievers, should be looking back and working to realize the policy vision of a preparatory predecessor. There is no simple answer to the question of which form of historical time will be most relevant to future presidents—it remains a dilemma of presidential power.

THE IDEOLOGICAL PENDULUM

Another notable attempt to think about how historical cycles can have some bearing on the presidency and what presidents might reasonably achieve is Arthur M. Schlesinger's attempt to discern ideological cycles in American political history. This is not just an effort at historical periodization (e.g., Jacksonian Democracy, post–Civil War Reconstruction, FDR's New Deal) but a more ambitious argument that the nation goes through regular, measurable swings from liberalism to conservatism and back again to liberalism: an ideological pendulum.

Schlesinger, a prominent Harvard historian from the mid-1920s through the mid-1950s, argued that there are "deep forces" at work in American politics, which he unfortunately does not explain in much detail save that they are "oscillations of sentiment" and "shifts of mood" that do not involve party control of the presidency.[35] Unlike Skowronek's later claim of the importance of regime cycles, Schlesinger noted that "the two major parties have seldom advocated well-defined alternative programs and never for long."[36] For Schlesinger, there is a roughly fifteen- to sixteen-year swing in favor of one ideology and then the other so that overall the total cycle is some thirty to thirty-two years. He even traces the cycle back to 1765, the start of a "liberal" shift with the Stamp Act rebellion against Britain that then culminates in 1787 with the more conservative, antidemocratic reaction of the Framers of the Constitution.

Schlesinger's theory does broadly capture the major points of political change in American history—although not all of these moments are "liberal" or "conservative" in today's ideological terms. Schlesinger notes a more liberal ascendency around 1801, which coincides with the start of the Jeffersonian period. Although Jacksonian democracy beginning in 1829 was hardly liberal, it did mark a major political change and was right around the time another cycle would be starting according to Schlesinger's theory. Lincoln's landmark presidency in 1861 shows that after thirty-two years, the pendulum had again swung a full cycle. The year 1901 (the timing is a little off here) marks the start of the progressive presidencies of Theodore Roosevelt and Woodrow Wilson. Wilson's waning influence at the end of his second term is roughly on target with the pendulum's swing to the right. At the time Schlesinger was writing, the nation had moved from a liberal high point in 1930 to a conservative one by 1947. This portended a Republican victory in 1948, because the pendulum supposedly was in its conservative phase. Alas, Harry Truman proved Schlesinger wrong—liberalism was to have another four years. Yet, to be fair to Schlesinger, it proved to be a difficult four years for Truman, as we have seen.

Although Schlesinger's timing seems roughly (perhaps, very roughly) on point, what is lacking from his analysis is an account of *why* these shifts occur. Theories in history or politics should be not only predictive but also explanatory, and in the latter Schlesinger falls short. As he concedes, "The reason for the ebb and flow seems singularly elusive."[37] Yet, he wrote in 1949 that "the next conservative epoch will then be due around 1978," which was a mere two years or so from the start of the Reagan presidency.[38] Not a bad prediction—even if it's lacking explanation.

His son, Arthur M. Schlesinger Jr., took up his father's work in his 1986 book *The Cycles of American History*.[39] Schlesinger Jr. is troubled by the lack of a hypothesis and underlying theory in his father's original work.[40] In his view, the key is to recharacterize the pendulum swing as a shift between "public purpose" and "private interest." He believes that this shift between public purpose and private interest is a primarily internal and self-generating one, where movement toward a new phase flows "from the conditions—and contradictions—of the phase before."[41] This still does not take us very far; he, like his father, is somewhat vague about what exactly these conditions and contradictions are. By contrast, Skowronek is more incisive in terms of the internal dynamics of political time.

Schlesinger Jr. believed this theory held up well in the years between his father's work and the publication of his book in 1986. The 1960s saw a swing toward liberalism/public purpose, but its troubles—the Vietnam War, assassinations, riots, cultural discontent, and economic difficulty in the 1970s—led to the antigovernment reaction of the Reagan years. We seem to be roughly on target here. But how has the theory fared in subsequent years? The answer is somewhat mixed and subject to interpretation and complications. The early 1990s should have marked the pendulum's place at the high mark of liberalism/public purpose. Although this lands us in the early Clinton presidency, the Republicans regained control of the House of Representatives for the first time in forty years and recaptured control of the Senate at this point in time. And if we were indeed at the high point in the swing to liberalism, Clinton should have had an easy time in getting comprehensive healthcare reform and other liberal measures passed by Congress, which did not occur. Something is amiss in the ideological timing of the early Clinton presidency. But the remaining years of the Clinton presidency may offer some hope for the theory: as the pendulum began to swing toward the right again, Clinton moved toward the political center. In addition, the late 1990s were times of economic prosperity, which fits with the reformulation of the theory not as liberal versus conservative but as public purpose versus private interest. Private interest increasingly prevailed then.

The George W. Bush presidency presents an interesting case. On the one hand, he pursued conservative tax, social, and regulatory policies, which fits with what should have been the pendulum's shift to private interest and the conservative Right. However, some of the social policies his administration and the Republicans favored involved significant exercise of governmental power restricting individual liberty: abortion and other privacy rights most notably. Moreover, in the aftermath of 9/11, governmental powers—hence, public purpose—expanded, and to an extent not seen since World War II. As noted in previous chapters, these included claims to broader presidential powers—the unitary theory of the executive—as well as expansive efforts in dealing with homeland and national security, including a variety of domestic surveillance activities. In fact, we might argue that this expansion in "public purpose" accounted for the rise of the Tea Party movement; for those folks, governmental power had grown too great.

As for the Obama presidency, according to Schlesinger, 1978 marked a conservative high point, so thirty years later in 2008, we should have come full circle.

This hardly matches Obama's election. Yet it may shed some light upon his presidential difficulties. Other than passing comprehensive healthcare reform early on, the remainder of his domestic record—as far as formal legislation—is slim. But, according to the Schlesingers, Obama should have had an easier time in the latter years of his presidency, as the pendulum began to swing leftward. This was not the case: by the end of the Obama presidency, Congress was solidly under Republican control, a process that began in 2010 when the Democrats lost the House and that culminated in 2014 with the loss of the Senate. This suggests that the impact of divided government may offer a better explanation for the Obama presidency than any purported ideological swings.

One problem with the theory is its own timing. Both Schlesingers allow a bit of wiggle room. Schlesinger Sr. permits "a possible margin of a year or two in one direction or the other."[42] Over time these additional years add up, making it difficult to determine precisely where a more recent administration is located in the pendulum's swing. And as we can see from the Bush example, another difficulty is that the "public purpose" and "private interest" phases are now too muddled to be of practical use in distinguishing among presidential programs. Or more likely, with the changes in domestic and international politics since the Schlesingers developed their theories, we are simply in different historical times and with different ideological forces at work. Unfortunately, because much remains vague about the underlying forces driving the rhythms and shifts in the Schlesingers' interpretation of political history, it is increasingly difficult to extrapolate and expand this theory to cover recent, and future, presidencies.

PRESIDENTIAL CHARACTER AND CYCLES OF PUBLIC MOOD

Still another approach is that of James David Barber, professor of political science at Yale and then at Duke University. He marries his early work on categorizing presidential character with his later work on the cycles of public mood as a predictor of the likelihood of presidential success.

Barber's Categories of Presidential Character

Barber achieved great fame for his initial work on presidential character. In *The Presidential Character*, Barber attempts to explain and predict how well presidents of different personality types will fare in office. The first edition was published in

1972 and it predicted that trouble was brewing in the Nixon presidency. That, of course, came to pass, in no small measure based on Nixon's own personality and his inner demons.

Barber does not delve into an in-depth psychological or psychoanalytic analysis of individual presidents. Instead, as a good social scientist should do, he generalizes and boils down presidents into a simple theory (too simple, as some of his critics would argue) with two key dimensions. The first dimension is psychological satisfaction: essentially, if the person enjoys the job, then he or she is a "positive" president. If the job is more of a burden or struggle, then that is a sign of a "negative" president. The second dimension is the level of activity that is invested: is it "active" or more "passive"? For Barber, these two dimensions yield four combinations of presidential character:

- **Active-positive presidents** enjoy the office and actively pursue their political goals. This type of president is flexible in response to challenge and adaptable to change. Examples include Jefferson, Theodore Roosevelt, FDR, Truman, Kennedy, Clinton, and, oddly, Carter. Active-positives are likely to achieve success in office.
- **Active-negative presidents,** by contrast, are problematic. They work hard but are compulsive and driven; they lack the psychological balance and "rational mastery" of the active-positives. Their aggressive tendencies and self-image problems often lead them on a disastrous course. Examples include John Adams, Lincoln, Wilson, Hoover, and Nixon.
- **Passive-positive presidents** are happy presidential campers. However, underneath the pleasant veneer and superficial optimism is a sense of low self-esteem. They seek acceptance and turn to others for initiative. Examples include Madison, Harding, Taft, and Reagan.
- **Passive-negative presidents** are the slackers. They serve out of a sense of duty, but they hate being in office. They too suffer from low self-esteem, although this comes from a sense of feeling useless rather than unloved. They tend to be aloof, dislike the nitty-gritty of politics, and retreat into vague principles as guardians of the right and proper way. Examples include Washington, Coolidge, and Eisenhower.

I could devote a whole chapter to analyzing the strengths and weaknesses of Barber's account of presidential character, but I will just note here that these categories are not perfect indicators of a president's success. Some presidents are not the favored active-positives, yet they did well in office, Washington (a passive-negative) most notably. Lincoln (an active-negative) is especially problematic for Barber's theory. He was often vexed with depression, yet he surmounted that difficulty and is ranked by almost all as one of the greatest of presidents. As for Eisenhower (a passive-negative), his "hidden-hand" presidency and seeming reluctance to enter politics might have been a deliberate strategy of passivity concealing a more active agenda.

Pairing Presidential Character with Public Mood

In his later book, *The Pulse of Politics,* Barber sought to square this understanding of presidential personality with its efficacy and fit in historical time, especially for those presidents who were not active-positives yet seemed to attain a measure of success. In his view, there is a regular cycle of presidencies of conflict, conscience, and then conciliation, based on shifting public moods.[43] Each period lasts four years, for a twelve-year cycle in all. During periods of *conflict,* the country is divided in its politics, it "itches for adventure," and both sides are primed to do battle. A classic example of a conflict election is the 1960 contest between Kennedy and Nixon.

Four years after conflict elections and the resulting presidencies, the public retreats to a mood of *conscience,* turning away from sharp partisan divisions toward a president who embodies broader principles and "American values." The classic example here is Jimmy Carter in 1976. He was the quintessential Washington outsider who aimed to restore ethics and decency to the presidency. But when policy problems persist, presidential morality comes to be negatively perceived as self-righteousness, and the public once again becomes dissatisfied.

The public then yearns for quieter times, a presidency of *conciliation.* The nation wants a president it likes and wants to be friends with, someone who brings "tolerance, comfort, goodwill, patient forgiveness, even laughter, and especially confidence." Barber cites Warren Harding as an example: a president who followed the moralistic, conscience-driven Woodrow Wilson. However, public dissatisfaction again looms, and the cycle begins anew as a conflictual mood emerges.[44]

Barber notes that although all three moods are present in every presidency, more often than not one seems to predominate. However, second-term presidencies seem particularly problematic for the theory because these presidents span two moods. In fact, in FDR's case, we have the only presidency that runs across all three periods and started the cycle once again when he was elected to his fourth term. FDR starts and ends as a conciliator according to Barber's schema.

Connecting back to his work on presidential character, Barber notes that although candidates who do not match the public mood can get elected, a mismatch can spell trouble for the presidency. An active-positive president is generally a recipe for success across all moods. However, presidents from the other three categories—active-negative, passive-negative, passive-positive—are successful when they fit well with the political mood at the time. According to Barber, the active-negative president pairs well with a mood of conflict, whereas the passive-negative president pairs well with a mood of conscience. The passive-positive triumphs in a mood of conciliation (see Figure 5.3). In Barber's view, this explains Reagan's arguably successful first term: a passive-positive president

FIGURE 5.3. Barber's Theory of Presidential Character and Public Mood

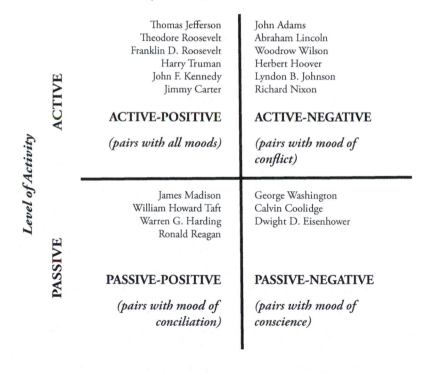

elected at a time of conciliation. Eisenhower's election in 1952 also works: it pairs a passive-negative president with a period of conscience. We should note that this theory is not a foolproof predictor of presidential success. In Barber's earlier theory of presidential character, Nixon's categorization as an active-negative indicated signs of a problematic presidency. But Barber's argument in *Pulse of Politics* complicates things. At the time Nixon was seeking a second term, the country was in a period of conflict. This should have been a positive fit for success: his character matched the public mood. As we know, Nixon did not achieve success: he was forced to resign by August 1974. Perhaps Nixon was so off the chart as an active-negative that even a mood match did not help.

Where are we now? According to Barber's theory, Clinton's reelection in 1996 was one of conflict, George W. Bush's election in 2000 was one of conscience, and his reelection in 2004 was one of conciliation. Obama's election in 2008 was during a mood of conflict, while his reelection in 2012 was one of conscience. The election of 2016, if Barber is correct, should mark a public mood of conciliation. As for presidential character, Barber stopped categorizing after Clinton, so we lack an assessment of his successors. But that is something we might ponder. How would we characterize G. W. Bush and Barack Obama? Moreover, do their respective characterizations match the public moods in the years they were elected, as posited by Barber? How helpful are Barber's works—*Pulse of Politics* and *Presidential Character*—in understanding these presidencies?

Weaknesses in Barber's Theory

Although Barber's theory of the four presidential character categories admittedly oversimplifies the diversity of the presidencies, it does capture clusters of presidential personalities in an orderly way. And it is a well-known and widely used theory: if I were to ask a colleague in my field whether candidate X is an "active-positive" or an "active-negative," that person would understand my question precisely. Finally, its goal of attempting to predict presidential performance in office is an important one. As noted earlier, Barber's effort to both explain and predict outcomes is a valuable contribution to the social science of presidential scholarship.

More problematic are his claims in the *Pulse of Politics*. Like the Schlesingers' ideological swing theory, Barber's theory of a public mood cycle leaves us puzzling over why the shifts occur. Barber attempts an answer. But his explanation is vague if not conceptually very odd. He describes the impetus for these mood shifts as a "mythic pulse." For Barber, the three moods resonate in "human memories." The mood of conflict can be linked back to preliterate hunter stories, he argues, while the conscience theme is like a mother's warning to a child moving too close to the hearth. As for conciliation, Barber claims that it may "draw upon the appeal of ancient acts of union," whatever that might mean.[45] Although Barber is attempting to take into account the broader historical environment a president faces, the mood swings of conflict, conciliation, and conscience, though provocative, lack any firm grounding in historical time. Where do these moods come from, and why does each emerge regularly at the end of four years? Barber's explanation is ambiguous at best. Yes, dissatisfaction with presidential performance arises, but Barber does not make it clear why this occurs like clockwork and in this particular sequence.

Finally, Barber's analysis of moods and the cycle it forms is largely linked to presidential elections, but he does not touch much upon its effects once a president is in office. We could assume, of course, that a president whose character is a poor fit with the mood at the time of his or her election might be headed for trouble. We might also posit that, even when there is a good fit, a president might slowly be headed for trouble as time passes and the signs of a new public mood begin to develop.

CONCLUSION: IMPLICATIONS AND QUESTIONS

Historical time obviously has implications for presidential power. The central and most important lesson here is that a president's opportunities for exercising influence likely differ depending upon the historical context he or she as president faces. The same goes for the strategies and tactics most appropriate and most likely to be successful in attaining presidential goals. Another important lesson to bear in mind is that historical context should affect our expectations of what a president can reasonably achieve. A reconstructive president faces a higher bar than a disjunctive one. A president of policy preparation has a different set of tasks than a president of consolidation. So too for presidents who find themselves at various points along ideological cycles and shifts in public moods. The proper perspective is to focus not upon an ideal presidency but on one that takes account of the actual challenges of politics and the actual capacities presidents possess in responding to them at particular points in historical time.[46]

Each of the theories discussed in this chapter—from Rockman's congressional versus presidential dominance to Barber's analysis of public moods—offers some insight into the historical factors that can affect a presidency. The dilemma is that each approach emphasizes very different historical factors, meaning that a president's place or categorization in each theory can vary greatly. The problem is in deciding which one matters most, which one a president should focus upon. In my view, Skowronek's political time theory and Hargrove and Nelson's policy cycle theory are the most promising. They are clearer on the forces that undergird their cycles: the growth and fall of regime coalitions and the stages of policy development and implementation, respectively. By contrast, the Schlesingers' ideological swing and Barber's public moods are vague in accounting for what causes the change and movement in their cycles. At best, they are predictive, but not explanatory, and historical theories should be both.

In *The Cycles of American History,* Schlesinger Jr. provides a lengthy quote from R. G. Collingwood, a prominent British philosopher of history, which I find of great interest. Collingwood observes that although the historical cycle is a "permanent feature of all historical thought," it comes from a particular perspective at a specific point in time: "the historian's field of vision at a given moment." It is much like a person's shadow. We all cast one, but it shifts, and its shape even alters, as we move about. So, too, for the observer of history: the "cyclical view of history will shift and dissolve, decompose and recompose itself anew, with every advance in the historical knowledge of the individual."[47] Collingwood's main point is that history is an interpretive process and that our view of historical events shifts and changes with time and new understanding and knowledge. For our purposes, this notion influences how presidents identify their "historical moment," how they perceive and seize the opportunities and tactics of exercising power available to them, as well as how we evaluate them for that effort. And given the somewhat fluid nature of history, how can presidents properly ascertain where they stand within a historical cycle in the midst of their presidency? The short answer is: it's a difficult task, and presidents may get it wrong, but in my view it is one they must at least grapple with because what is absolutely clear is that history does matter.

It is possible too that our existing theories of historical time and presidential power are inadequate both as means for evaluating contemporary presidents and as blueprints for future presidents. Skowronek posits that contemporary politics may bode the end of political time, as least as he has defined it. He notes that "we are witness to the waning of political time, to the practical disintegration of the medium through which presidents have claimed authority for the exercise of their powers since the beginning of our constitutional history."[48] Skowronek may be a bit dire in his language, but he has a point. In recent years, it is less necessary for a president to have a strong connection to a predecessor's regime to success-fully exercise power. Essentially, presidents have greater freedom to strike out on their own and thus greater chances for success (or failure). But in some ways, this reinforces the difficulties of presidential power, because without the "glue" of a political regime, a president's attendant resources become weaker and they are much more on their own. It is also important to note that we are increasingly moving beyond a nationally defined context of historical relevance to one where international and global factors increasingly matter. Terrorism, cyber security, climate change, and even epidemics such as the Ebola virus have generated a new dimension in our politics that is not accounted for in any of the theories we discuss in this chapter.

NOTES

1. Stephen Skowronek, *Presidential Leadership in Political Time: Reprise and Reappraisal,* 2nd ed. revised (Lawrence: University Press of Kansas, 2011), 78.

2. Bert A. Rockman, *The Leadership Question: The Presidency and the American System* (New York: Praeger, 1984), 96–98.

3. Woodrow Wilson, *Congressional Government* (Boston: Houghton Mifflin, 1885).

4. Benjamin Ginsberg and Martin Shefter, *Politics by Other Means: Politicians, Prosecutors, and the Press from Watergate to Whitewater,* 3rd ed. (New York: W. W. Norton, 2002), 21–23.

5. David R. Mayhew, *Divided We Govern: Party Control, Lawmaking, and Investigations, 1946–2002,* 2nd ed. (New Haven, CT: Yale University Press, 2005), 177–178.

6. Ibid., 31–33, 175.

7. Morris Fiorina, *Divided Government,* 2nd ed. (Boston: Allyn and Bacon, 1996). Further analysis of divided government can be found in an edited collection on the topic: Gary W. Cox and Samuel Kernell, eds., *The Politics of Divided Government* (Boulder, CO: Westview Press, 1991).

8. Stephen Skowronek, *The Politics Presidents Make: Leadership from John Adams to George Bush* (Cambridge, MA: Harvard University Press, 1993). In subsequent years, Skowronek pub-lished a number of articles expanding on his thesis of political time, particularly with attention to the Clinton, G. W. Bush, and Obama presidencies. These were then collected and revised in *Presidential Leadership in Political Time: Reprise and Reappraisal,* 2nd ed. (Lawrence: Kansas University Press, 2011).

9. Skowronek, *Politics Presidents Make,* 53.

10. Ibid., 421.

11. Ibid., 88.

12. Ibid., 191.

13. Ibid., 386, 393.

14. Ibid., 429.

15. Skowronek, *Presidential Leadership in Political Time,* 4, 97.

16. Ibid., 94.

17. Ibid., 94.

18. Ibid., 100.

19. For the discussion he does offer, see Skowronek, *Politics Presidents Make,* 43–47.

20. Skowronek, *Presidential Leadership in Political Time,* 83.

21. David A. Crockett, *The Opposition Presidency: Leadership and the Constraints of History* (College Station: Texas A&M University Press, 2002).

22. Ibid., 219.

23. Ibid., 235.

24. Skowronek finds that John Tyler, Andrew Johnson, Woodrow Wilson, and Nixon fall into this problematic group (Skowronek, *Politics Presidents Make,* 44).

25. Skowronek, *Presidential Leadership in Political Time,* 100.

26. Ibid., 4.

27. Ibid., 172.

28. Ibid., 176.

29. Ibid., 293.

30. Skowronek, *Politics Presidents Make,* 444.

31. Erwin C. Hargrove and Michael Nelson, *Presidents, Politics, and Policy* (New York: Alfred A. Knopf, 1984).

32. Ibid., 264.

33. For example, in efforts to get people back to work, a number of successive public employment projects were initiated. Early in 1933, a Civil Works Administration (CWA) was established, but it was soon disbanded. Later that year, the Public Works Administration (PWA) was created. By 1935, it had morphed into the Works Progress Administration (WPA).

34. Hargrove and Nelson, *Presidents, Politics, and Policy,* 265.

35. Arthur M. Schlesinger, *Paths to the Present* (New York: Macmillan, 1949), 77, 81. Schlesinger's theory on the ideological swing first appeared in "Tides of American Politics," *Yale Review,* XXIX (December 1939): 217–230. It was later updated in a chapter by that same title in *Paths to the Present.* Schlesinger was also an early popularizer of presidential "greatness" rankings, an activity that still remains with us today. His survey on presidential greatness also appears in *Paths to the Present* in a chapter titled "A Yardstick for Presidents," 93–111.

36. Ibid., 77, 79.

37. Ibid., 89.

38. Ibid., 85.

39. Arthur M. Schlesinger Jr., *The Cycles of American History* (Boston: Houghton Mifflin, 1986).

40. Ibid., 25.

41. Ibid., 27. Schlesinger Jr. adds that the public grows tired during each period: high levels of public commitment become exhausting and people yearn for a private life, but this in turn gives way to discontentment as public needs go unaddressed and inequality widens (28–29).

42. Schlesinger, *Paths to the Present,* 85.

43. James David Barber, *The Pulse of Politics: Electing Presidents in the Media Age* (New York: W. W. Norton, 1980).

44. Ibid., 3–4.

45. Ibid., 20.

46. Skowronek, *Presidential Leadership in Political Time,* xi.

47. Schlesinger, *Cycles of American History,* 31. He quotes from R. G. Collingwood, *Essays on the Philosophy of History,* ed. William Debbins (Austin: University of Texas Press, 1965), 75, 89. Collingwood was the Waynflete Professor of Metaphysical Philosophy at Magdalen College, Oxford. He died in 1943, at the age of fifty-three, with many of his essays published posthumously.

48. Skowronek, *Politics Presidents Make,* 442.

6

The First Term: Internal Time and Presidential Power

The preceding chapter demonstrates how *external* historical forces can have an impact upon the exercise of presidential power and its success. However, equally important forces are at work *within* a president's term of office, and the first term and second term each have their own dynamics. I call this the **internal time** of a presidency. In this chapter, we explore the key moments in a president's first term—from election and transition to office to the midterm elections and planning for a second term—and consider how the dynamics at each stage might affect presidential power.

We begin by examining how election results generally do not enable newly elected presidents to claim broad public support for their policy agendas. Without this claim, presidents-elect must build a base of power, which begins during the transition to office. We consider the crucial role that this transition plays in early presidencies; it sets the stage for whether a president hits the ground running or stumbles out of the gate. One of the most important goals of the transition and early presidency is creating a lean and strategic policy agenda, and we explore how different presidents have responded to this challenge. Next, we examine the midterm election—a crucial turning point during the first term. The party of the president almost always suffers a loss of seats in Congress, and we discuss how a number of recent presidents have sought to deal with this setback. Finally, we look at the problems presidents encounter as the next election looms and the need to start developing policies for a possible second term arises.

Recognizing how presidents navigate the internal time of the first term is an important dimension in understanding the successful exercise of presidential power.

THE MYTH OF A PRESIDENTIAL MANDATE

On election night, or shortly thereafter, newly elected (or reelected) presidents often claim that the election results have delivered them a *mandate.* That is, the nation has spoken with its vote for the winning candidate and, by extension, his or her policy stances, and Congress must follow the public voice and its implied presidential support. However, a mandate rarely occurs and this is largely rhetorical bluster.[1] It is a clever claim on a president's part, but not one often grounded in the realities of electoral politics.

What circumstances would need to occur for a mandate to exist? First, presidents clearly need to do well electorally. Conventional wisdom suggests a landslide in a two-candidate race; this is usually pegged at around 60 percent of the popular vote. Where there are strong third-party candidates, a 10 percent margin for the winner often counts as a significant victory. Second, mandates should imply issue and policy agreement between the winning candidate and the electorate. If the presidential election is mainly about personalities rather than the substance of policy, then there can be no *policy* mandate. Related to this is a third factor: there ought to be broader political change and consequences. This means that the election not only involves a presidential triumph but also sweeps into office the president's fellow partisans. This is often termed the *coattail effect:* members of the president's party, down the ballot, are literally elected by clinging to the presidential candidate's coattails. If not for a significant presidential victory, those down-ballot candidates—especially members of Congress—would not have been elected to office.

Considering all of these factors, the number of actual mandates is slim (see Table 6.1). In the post–World War II era, Eisenhower was one president who could possibly claim a mandate. Although he did not achieve a landslide victory of 60 percent plus, Eisenhower came close with 55 percent of the popular vote, a 10 percent margin over his opponent, former Illinois governor Adlai Stevenson. The electoral vote result was even more significant: 442 for Eisenhower versus 89 for Stevenson. Party control of Congress shifted from the Democrats to the Republicans, with gains of 22 seats for the Republicans in the House and 1 in the Senate. The latter was just enough to yield a very narrow 50–50 margin in the

TABLE 6.1. First-Term Presidential Election Performance

Year	President	Party	Vote (%)	Margin (%)	House	Senate
1952	Eisenhower	R	55.2	9.9	22	1
1960	Kennedy	D	49.7	0.2	−22	2
1964	Johnson	D	61.1	22.6	37	1
1968	Nixon	R	43.4	0.7	5	6
1976	Carter	D	50.1	2.1	1	0
1980	Reagan	R	50.7	9.7	34	12
1988	G. H. W. Bush	R	53.4	7.8	−2	0
1992	Clinton	D	43.0	5.6	−10	0
2000	G. W. Bush	R	47.9	−0.5	−3	−4
2008	Obama	D	52.9	7.2	23	8
	Averages		**50.7**	**7.3**	**9**	**2.6**

SOURCES: Gerhard Peters, "Seats in Congress Gained or Lost by the President's Party in Presidential Election Years," in *The American Presidency Project,* ed. John T. Woolley and Gerhard Peters (Santa Barbara: University of California, Santa Barbara, 1999–2013), http://www.presidency.ucsb.edu/data/presidential_elections_seats.php; History, Art and Archives, US House of Representatives, "Election Statistics, 1920 to Present," 2015, http://history.house.gov/Institution/Election-Statistics/Election-Statistics/; and History, Art and Archives, US House of Representatives, "Party Divisions of the House of Representatives," 2015, http://history.house.gov/Institution/Party-Divisions/Party-Divisions/.

Senate, with Vice President Nixon casting the deciding vote to give control to the GOP. Although not a sweeping margin, the Republicans regained control of both chambers of Congress, which they briefly held for two years after the 1946 midterms. However, Eisenhower was a World War II military hero, widely revered as the Supreme Allied Commander in Europe. As a result, we might argue that 1952 was an election in which personal popularity loomed large, even though there were some issue differences among the presidential candidates.

The second president of this era who could possibly claim a mandate was President Lyndon Johnson. In 1964, he was elected with a popular vote over the 60 percent mark. He also had clear issue differences over his conservative opponent, Sen. Barry Goldwater (R-AZ). In addition, Democrats gained substantial seats in the House and one in the Senate, which Johnson took advantage of to push a broad domestic agenda. All of this would suggest that LBJ had a mandate, but his was also an unusual situation: LBJ was a sitting president, because he had taken the office just less than a year before, following Kennedy's assassination. Interestingly, he ran on a peace platform, opposing the introduction of American ground troops in South Vietnam, but by July 1965 LBJ had made significant force commitments. If LBJ had a mandate, it was for peace, not war—and he chose to ignore it.

The third election during this period that also might suggest something of a mandate was Reagan's defeat of Carter in 1980. Here, a third-party candidate—Rep. John Anderson (R-IL)—captured 6.6 percent of the popular vote, and Reagan received only 51 percent. However, he still won by a margin of almost 10 percent over Carter, and Reagan claimed a decisive electoral vote majority with 489 votes compared to Carter's 49. Moreover, the Republicans made double-digit gains in both the House (+34) and Senate (+12), the largest of all of the presidents listed in Table 6.1. The Senate results are particularly important: they gave the GOP control of the Senate for the first time since after the 1954 midterms.

For the remaining presidents, the case for a mandate appears very weak. Either the popular vote margin was narrower or seat gains in Congress were slim. In 1960, Kennedy's very narrow win—slightly over one hundred thousand in the popular vote—was coupled with a twenty-two-seat decline for the Democrats in the House. To be fair, Democrats had done very well in the preceding midterms in 1958. Still, just a shift of *one* vote in every precinct or ward across the United States would have given Nixon a majority of the popular vote. In 1968, Nixon was the first president-elect not to have his party gain control of Congress since Zachary Taylor's election in 1848. In 1976, Carter won a bare majority of the popular vote while the Democrats gained just one seat in the House and none in the Senate. George H. W. Bush's and Clinton's parties both lost seats in the House and gained nothing in the Senate in their respective first-term elections.

Even when gains are made by the president-elect's party, the coattail effect has less of an impact than we might think. Note that for all the elections listed in Table 6.1, most House and Senate gains are in the single digits, with an average of 9 House seats and 2.6 Senate seats. Moreover, even when the increase in seats is more substantial, it is not clear that the members who are newly elected feel beholden to the new president. Imagine a candidate who has worked hard for over a year to win a seat in the US House of Representatives in a swing district. Much time and effort were spent campaigning and soliciting campaign contributions.

According to a 2012 Brookings Institution study, the average expenditure for a challenger beating an incumbent member of the House was $2.48 million.[2] That is a lot of money to raise. The candidate wins a seat, but by a couple of points fewer than the president. Does the new member feel like the election is owed to the president's pull at the top of the ballot? I suspect that the president and the coattail effect are the least of the new representative's concerns on election night. This is the *candidate's* victory alone, and the new member does not feel beholden to, or the need to support, the president.

Perhaps the key to successfully using the presidential mandate as justification for exercising influence is not in the actual numbers but in the *perception* of the election results. For example, George W. Bush's election in 2000 was the most contested election since 1876, requiring intervention from the US Supreme Court. Not only did Bush eke out a narrow Electoral College victory but also his opponent, Vice President Al Gore, won the popular vote. In addition, Bush's party lost seats in both the House and the Senate. Bush was arguably in the worst position of any of the post–World War II presidents. However, he ignored these factors, this negative landscape, and strategically positioned himself to govern *as if* he had been elected with substantial popular support. This posture did yield some success, even before national politics changed in the aftermath of September 11, 2001. This could be encouraging news for presidents who don't have much of a mandate based solely on the numbers.

It is also important to bear in mind that positive election results might be tempered by what happened in preceding elections. For example, Reagan's Republicans gained a notable 12 seats in 1980. This Senate class, however, had been elected or reelected in the 1974 midterms, right after the Watergate scandal and Nixon's resignation—not a good year for Republicans. Viewed in this context, a gain of 12 seats for Republicans in 1980 after doing poorly in 1974 might not be as remarkable. In 2008, Obama's Democrats gained 8 Senate seats. However, this class of senators was previously elected or reelected in 2002, a year when G. W. Bush's popularity was still very high—he was the only elected president since FDR in 1934 to gain seats in both the House and Senate in his first midterm election. As such, the Democrats' Senate gains could be seen as more of a return to the earlier numerical status quo rather than as a massive increase for their party.

Given what constitutes a mandate and how few of these presidents measure up, largely resting on the laurels of election results is not likely to be a workable strategy for exercising presidential influence. Most presidents will likely be on their own, receiving little help from down-ballot elected candidates. Even the rare few who might plausibly claim a mandate still have much work to do in building relationships with Congress and establishing support for their agendas. A strong electoral victory does not usually translate into, or guarantee, subsequent policy and political success.

THE TRANSITION TO OFFICE

What has more of an impact on a president's success is the transition to office, that is, how presidents-elect plan for their new presidency. It is the opening act in the exercise of presidential power. Odd as it may seem, for much of presidential history, this was not terribly important. Prior to passage of the Twentieth Amendment to the Constitution in 1933, presidents were inaugurated in March, and Congress often held just a short special session to confirm nominees, convening for a real session later in the year. We might think that this broader time frame enabled greater planning efforts. Yet, expectations for a new president were different at the time—presidents were not under pressure to start office with an ambitious policy agenda and a plan of attack already in place. The White House staff was small and had virtually no advisory functions. There were cabinet appointments to handle, but that was about it.

Franklin D. Roosevelt's presidency marked the beginning of a change. His historic first one hundred days in office is testimony to this.[3] He spent the time from his election in November until he took office in March planning his cabinet appointments and crafting policy proposals. Once he took office, he called Congress back into a special session to deal with the crisis of the Great Depression and to pass needed legislation, which it readily did. Eisenhower's election in 1952 was the first time that a newly elected president needed to deal with a transition to office by January 20 rather than in March. Kennedy was the first to start planning for the presidency prior to Election Day. In the fall of 1960, Kennedy enlisted Richard Neustadt (see Chapter 2) and Clark Clifford, a former Truman aide and Washington power broker, to start planning for a possible presidency. They produced several important memos—a far cry from what occurs today. In 1968, Nixon's team undertook some efforts to assemble dossiers on potential appointees, but little came of it: many ended up piled in a bathtub in one of the rooms of the Hotel Pierre in New York City, the headquarters of Nixon's campaign and, later, transition team.

In 1976, with Jimmy Carter's candidacy, a major shift in presidential transition planning occurred. After he clinched his party's nomination in April with a victory in the Pennsylvania primary, Carter realized that he needed to begin planning for his presidency, particularly because he was a Washington outsider. He devoted some of his scarce resources to staff a group to plan for a potential presidency. Although this effort created tension in his campaign staff, who worried about this new group hijacking future appointments in a Carter administration, it marked a new era in planning for a successful presidency.[4] Carter and his successors provide a number of important lessons on how to best utilize the transition period to secure the launch of a successful presidency.

First, it is now custom—and vitally important—for presidential candidates to begin transition planning before the November general election. At a minimum, they must understand the legal and organizational tasks ahead. What executive orders do they need to, or want to, examine? What vacancies do they need to fill? What organizational issues do they need to address, especially with respect to the White House staff? If possible, they might discreetly consider the appointment of key staff members.

Second, after Election Day, a president-elect must move quickly to assemble a transition team and key White House staff. George H. W. Bush, George W. Bush, and Obama are good examples of this. All three had a list of key transition officials and had essentially settled on the appointment of a White House chief of staff before Election Day. Although much public attention focuses on cabinet appointments, the early selection of a chief of staff is in some ways more critical. The position is not subject to Senate confirmation, so the appointed person can take office immediately after the president is sworn into office. More importantly, the designated chief of staff is responsible for building the organization and personnel of the White House staff during the transition period. The same is true for the president's primary, in-house source of foreign policy counsel—the national security adviser—who also heads up a large staff.[5]

Failure to speedily appoint a chief of staff or national security adviser can impair efforts to have at least the top levels of the staff in place by Inauguration Day, making it much harder for a seamless transition into office. Three other key positions need to be filled early. First is the director of the White House personnel office. In recent transitions, this person has played a central role in appointments during the transition. Another important appointment is the head of the White House's office of legal counsel, which advises the president on a range of legal and constitutional matters, including reviewing the executive actions of prior admin-istrations and vetting legal issues concerning new appointees. The person who occupies this role is also the one who is usually responsible for these tasks during the transition. The third position is the head of the White House congressional affairs staff. The congressional affairs unit plays a critical role as the president's lobbyist with Congress, and establishing good relations with Congress is a task that starts during the transition. In short, a president does not work alone, so having a well-functioning staff, on the job at the very start of an administration, is crucial to presidential success.[6]

Some newly elected presidents fail to understand this. For example, internal discord and disorganization in the Carter and Clinton transition efforts led to delays in establishing a team and selecting key White House personnel. Carter refused to designate someone as chief of staff and did not understand the im-portance of the White House staff. The staff he did appoint comprised former aides and other associates from his time as governor of Georgia. They were loyal to Carter, but few had a handle on how Washington politics worked. As such, his early presidency was fraught with ineffectiveness and strategic mistakes. Only later in his presidency was this error partially corrected with the appointment of a chief of staff. Even then, he still clung to an outdated model of cabinet govern-ment and a flawed decision-making style.

Clinton's White House staff was poorly organized. He had waited until mid-December to appoint a chief of staff, which was too long after he had been elected. In addition, the person he picked was ill-equipped to do the job and lacked prior Washington experience. Clinton's own poor managerial habits con-tributed to the disorder. People showed up at White House meetings uninvited, and Clinton let the meetings turn into long, rambling, and unfocused discussions. The staff was divided into a variety of camps. Clinton had the "resources"—and on balance they were better choices than Carter had made—but Clinton used them poorly. It took until the appointment of Leon Panetta as chief of staff in 1994 for some semblance of order to be imposed. As a result, Clinton lost valu-able time early in his presidency, and as we shall see later in the chapter, this cost him in terms of his legislative agenda.

Third, the transition is an important period for moving from a campaign mode to a presidential one. The public needs to be "reintroduced" to the winning can-didate as the president rather than as just a contender for the office. At the same time, presidents-elect are still somewhat in "campaign mode." Ties to political constituencies must be maintained and even strengthened, and a strong political message must be delivered to the public, because future support remains necessary for a successful presidency. Successfully managing this transition is even more critical with today's twenty-four-hour cable news and online news attentively reporting and monitoring every appointment and every action presidents-elect and their staffs make. Perceptions of presidential power by the public and by Congress can diminish if transition activities are not skillfully navigated.

To the extent that presidents-elect make good use of the transition period to settle on these staff appointments early and effectively project a successful transition process and political message, the better off they will be in positioning their early policy initiatives. Power is fleeting, fading fairly quickly over the course of the first term, and so newly elected presidents must take full advantage of the transition process to be ahead of the curve. Carter and Clinton failed to recognize this: their early presidencies were handicapped because they did not take the early appointment of key staffers seriously. George W. Bush and Obama, by contrast, settled on a staff early. Although their presidencies encountered trouble later on, their early efforts proceeded more smoothly.

DEVELOPING A STRATEGIC AGENDA EARLY

Once key White House officials have been identified and selected, the new administration needs to turn its attention to examining and homing in on the substance of the initial legislative agenda. During the campaign, many issues are addressed and policies proposed. But during the transition period, presidents-elect need to carve away and settle upon the three or four most important proposals that they wish to pursue. Here is where the early selection of staff is particularly important. Potential cabinet members and their chief lieutenants (the subcabinet) are all subject to Senate confirmation. Whereas most cabinet members are confirmed shortly after Inauguration Day, subcabinet confirmations take more time, often many months. So, until that is settled, the brunt of developing the early agenda falls on the White House staff.

Strategies for Crafting an Agenda and Working with Congress

Given that a president's legislative agenda cannot pass without Congress, what lessons can we learn from past presidents on the pitfalls to avoid and the strategies to employ? The first is not to overload Congress with requests. Here, Carter is the cautionary tale. He developed a laundry list of items he wanted Congress to enact, including a comprehensive energy plan, welfare reform, an economic stimulus proposal, new policies for urban areas, changes in Social Security, and increases in the minimum wage, to list just a few of the major proposals. All of these were perfectly legitimate in the abstract, but Carter failed to recognize that Congress needed set and limited priorities, even though the Democrats controlled both the House and the Senate by large margins. What was most important to the new president? Where should members of Congress focus their attention? In this, Carter failed to provide guidance, which resulted in too much being pushed through the legislative pipeline, ineffective lobbying efforts from an inexperienced White House, and increasing concern among Democratic congressional leaders that they were dealing with arrogant amateurs.[7]

The second is to take into consideration the needs and desires of Congress and to recognize that some political maneuvering and bargaining is required to have a successful, symbiotic relationship with Congress. This was another area where Carter foundered—political calculation was anathema to him. In his view, reason and logic should dictate the legislative course, not politics. Carter wanted a minor tax cut for the middle class and succeeded in getting the House to pass a $50 tax rebate. However, economic conditions changed for the better, so he dumped the proposal before it reached the Senate, leaving some House members out on a limb and wondering why they supported him in the first place. Carter also opposed federal funds for a variety of pork-barrel projects, which are vital to House and Senate members' electoral success back home. These projects were often the result of years of congressional effort: horse trading and deal making at their political finest. Carter did back off on most of his objections, once opposition mounted, but damage was done.[8] It was an error typical of a political novice; wiser hands in the White House, surely, would have counseled a president differently.[9]

George W. Bush was much more successful in this regard. According to Steven Schier, the Bush administration's "coalitional and bargaining skills during this time produced frequent success with Congress."[10] To pass legislation that sought to improve the quality of elementary and secondary education, the Bush administration bargained and built alliances with prominent Democrats, Senator Ted Kennedy (D-MA) most notably. Bush's efforts here included dropping his insistence on a voucher program to permit parents to place students in alternative public or private schools. But Bush also charmed the elder Kennedy, inviting him to White House functions, notably for a special screening of the film *Thirteen Days,* about JFK's deliberations during the Cuban Missile Crisis in 1962. The No Child Left Behind Act passed in December 2001 and was signed into law in early

January 2002.[11] To be fair, Bush also benefited from external circumstances: he was helped by the discipline among the Republican members of the House and by the period of bipartisan goodwill in the aftermath of September 11.

Another important lesson is to be realistic about what Congress (and the public) is willing to accept, and to not be *too* ambitious. For Clinton, relations with Congress got off to a rocky start when he floated the possibility of issuing an executive order to allow gays to serve in the military. It was a major miscalculation. It smacked of unilateral action in what was then a controversial proposal, one for which he neglected to pave the way in a favorable direction. He encountered immediate opposition from both the Joint Chiefs of Staff, especially Chairman General Colin Powell, and key members of Congress. Clinton anticipated that Congress would not be open to enacting legislation allowing gays to serve in the military, hence his plan to take the lead and use an executive order to bring about change. But he did not recognize just how controversial the issue was at the time, nor did he realize that Congress could pass a law overturning his order. Clinton quickly backed off and ended up compromising with the "Don't Ask, Don't Tell" policy. Clinton later admitted enacting this policy was a mistake, and it was finally revoked during the Obama presidency.

Finally, presidents *do* need to develop a substantive policy agenda. Failing to do so could cost them reelection, as it did for George H. W. Bush. His 1988 campaign focused primarily on the weaknesses of Michael Dukakis, the Democratic nominee, rather than on Bush's own policy plans, although there was some talk about the importance of private charitable efforts to cure social ills. Bush's major domestic achievements were new civil rights legislation to address concerns in recent Supreme Court decisions and a new law dealing with accommodations for persons with a variety of disabilities. Although each was no doubt important, this was thin gruel for a reelection effort despite the Bush administration's attempts to control domestic spending. Whereas Bush had his strengths in foreign affairs—fighting the Persian Gulf War and dealing with the collapse of the Soviet empire—the lack of a strong domestic and economic record cost him reelection.

Time Is of the Essence

Not only do presidents need to establish a strong and strategic agenda but also they need to do so early on because time begins to work against them. Paul Light notes that although there is a cycle of "increasing effectiveness," as the president grows comfortable with the office and learns over time, and as the administration's staff becomes more familiar with their responsibilities, there is also undeniably a cycle of "decreasing influence." Presidential power is at its peak in the first year of a presidency, after which there is usually a "decline in presidential capital, time, and energy."[12] The waning effectiveness of George W. Bush's strategy of bargaining with Congress, and his increasing reliance on other tools, particularly the use of executive action, to attain his policy goals, is an example of this. In fact, using executive action to secure policy began early in his administration. Bush favored a change in federal regulations concerning religious groups that sought to introduce religious meetings and practices in dealing with substance abuse and other health-related issues. Congress balked, so the Bush administration resorted to executive orders in directing a variety of governmental departments and agencies to attain these ends.

Presidents need to hit the ground running and develop legislation to present to Congress during the transition and in the early months of a new presidency because delay by the White House results in delay of the legislative process on Capitol Hill. That lost time, in turn, may push crucial votes on bills into the time frame when the president's power begins to grow weaker. Perhaps the classic case of such delay proving costly was the comprehensive healthcare plan developed by the Clinton administration. Efforts at putting together a proposal during the transition proved unproductive. Once in office, the president turned the effort over to his spouse, Hillary Rodham Clinton. She favored a comprehensive effort, rather than piecemeal legislation, and organized a large task force to explore options. They operated in secret and took their time. On September 22, 1993, Clinton made a special address to a joint session of Congress in which he outlined the broad contours of the plan. However, it was not until late November 1993 that a bill was presented to Congress; it was over one thousand pages in length. Unfortunately, the delay in getting it to Congress—however well intentioned—allowed opponents to organize and mobilize. Television ads opposing the Clinton plan appeared. Even stalwart Democrats, such as Sen. Daniel Patrick Moynihan (D-NY), had major reservations. Over the summer of 1994, Senate Democrats attempted to craft an acceptable compromise, but it failed to garner sufficient Senate support. By that point in time, however, the plan was politically toxic as the 1994 midterm elections loomed.

If there is one major lesson that newly elected presidents should absorb it is that they must act swiftly and smartly in advancing their policy agendas, beginning this process during the transition period, even before they are in office.

Campaign proposals must be cut and pruned into just a handful of initiatives and quickly rolled out before Congress. Presidents need to be realistic about what Congress is willing to do as well as understand the realities of congressional politics. Administrations must be flexible and willing to bargain and build alliances in efforts to influence Congress. Most importantly, they must recognize that time is working against them. Year one in office affords the best opportunities in making legislative progress; year two is soon clouded by the distracting politics of the midterm elections.

ACHIEVING SUCCESS AFTER THE FIRST MIDTERM ELECTIONS

In theory, midterm elections should reaffirm the agenda of a popular president, thereby bolstering his or her position of power. But in reality they almost never do. Since Lincoln's presidency, on only three occasions has a president's party gained seats in the House in an initial midterm: 1902 under Theodore Roosevelt, 1934 under FDR, and 2002 under George W. Bush. But all three involved special circumstances: then vice president Roosevelt had assumed office just over a year before, following the assassination of President William McKinley; FDR was dealing with the Great Depression; and G. W. Bush had a commanding and popular position in the aftermath of 9/11. In fact, to say that Roosevelt's party made gains is a bit misleading: the size of the House expanded in the 1902 election following the 1900 census, and the Democrats actually won more House seats than the Republicans. In addition, he was a vice president who had recently assumed office. So, really, only two *elected* presidents since the Civil War have gained seats in the House in the first midterm.

Table 6.2 illustrates just how bad the first midterms are for sitting presidents. Their party's control of the House almost certainly declines, with an average loss of about twenty-four seats. With the exception of George W. Bush in 2002, each of these presidents going back to Eisenhower suffered a loss in their party's representation in the House. The Senate is a little bit more of a toss-up, but the president's party is still likely to lose seats, with an average loss of two seats (but note that only one-third of the Senate is up for election in any midterm). Kennedy, Nixon, and Reagan achieved some minor gains in the Senate. The first midterm elections likely mattered most—but certainly not for the best—for Eisenhower, Clinton, and Obama: seat losses in both the House and the Senate shifted party

TABLE 6.2. Presidential Party's Gains/Losses in First Midterm

Year	President (Party)	House	Senate
1954	Eisenhower (R)	(–18)	(–1)
1962	Kennedy (D)	(–4)	3
1966	Johnson (D)	(–47)	(–4)
1970	Nixon (R)	(–12)	2
1978	Carter (D)	(–15)	(–3)
1982	Reagan (R)	(–26)	1
1990	G. H. W Bush (R)	(–8)	(–1)
1994	Clinton (D)	(–52)	(–8)
2002	G. W. Bush (R)	8	2
2010	Obama (D)	(–63)	(–6)
Average Gain/Loss		(–23.7)	(–1.7)

SOURCES: Gerhard Peters, "Seats in Congress Gained or Lost by the President's Party in Presidential Election Years," in *The American Presidency Project,* ed. John T. Woolley and Gerhard Peters (Santa Barbara: University of California, Santa Barbara, 1999–2013), http://www .presidency.ucsb.edu/data/presidential_elections_seats.php; History, Art and Archives, US House of Representatives, "Election Statistics, 1920 to Present" http://history.house.gov /Institution/Election-Statistics/Election-Statistics/.

control of Congress to the opposition. Although some scholars, David Mayhew most notably, have argued that divided government has little effect upon a president's legislative success, these shifts in party control surely make things more difficult for a sitting president.

The implication and logical conclusion are that presidents must take advantage of their first two years in office. After the first midterm, presidents' power most likely weakens, not only because presidents have less partisan support in Congress but also because attention begins to shift to the next presidential election. However, this is not to say that nothing occurs; some major legislation does pass, especially if it is well along in the legislative pipeline. Some presidents have adapted to the situation to their benefit. We discuss below several successful strategies and examples that might prove useful to a future president.

Courting the Opposition

One strategy that might be useful is to cultivate positive relationships with members of Congress, especially those in the opposition party, beginning even before the midterms. This is strategically useful not just for the purpose of bargaining but also in setting the conditions and context under which a variety of exercises of presidential influence might prove effective. Eisenhower's situation is of particular interest here, because he faced opposition in Congress from both more conservative, "old guard" members of his own party as well as Democrats. Unlike his successors, he actually met with difficulty from his own party, especially in the Senate, during his first two years in office. Sen. Robert Taft (R-OH), the son of former president and chief justice William Howard Taft, was the initial Republican majority leader in the Senate. The catch was that he was Eisenhower's chief opponent for the 1952 GOP nomination. Eisenhower recognized the difficulty and sought to develop a good relationship with Taft, including appointing a key Taft supporter as his secretary of the treasury. Unfortunately, Taft's tenure was short-lived, and he succumbed to cancer later in 1953.

From the start of his presidency, Eisenhower also sought to cultivate congressional Democrats for support. When the Democrats took control of the Senate and the House after the 1954 midterms, Eisenhower was able to use his connections and his "hidden-hand" style of presidency to continue to court the new majority leader, Sen. Lyndon B. Johnson (D-TX), as well as Rep. Sam Rayburn (D-TX), who once again returned as Speaker of the House. As noted in Chapter 2, Eisenhower had close relationships with key figures in the Texas oil and gas industry, who were also benefactors of LBJ and Rayburn, and a comment from Eisenhower during a golf game to his friends was often useful in bringing the two Democrats around to his side.[13] But Eisenhower also developed a personal relationship with LBJ and Rayburn, hosting informal meetings with them about every six weeks. According to one account, "The three enjoyed a friendly relationship, with the only thing the Democratic leaders disliking about the President was the he had chosen to be a Republican."[14]

Eisenhower's efforts were bolstered by his decision to replace the previous haphazard White House efforts to lobby members of Congress with an official and properly organized congressional affairs staff, a unit that continues to this day. Eisenhower also had the smarts to appoint former Major Gen. Wilton Persons, who had been one of his military aides, as the head of that unit. Persons was a genial and conservative southerner who had also been the War Department's (today's Department of Defense) chief liaison with Congress during World War II. Persons quickly developed strong and productive ties with the Democratic leadership, many of whom were fellow conservative southerners. Persons was as much an effective "courter" of Congress as Eisenhower was.

These efforts paid off for Eisenhower. The most important victory was final passage of the act creating the interstate highway system in 1956. Although a costly endeavor, Eisenhower was especially shrewd in emphasizing its use for national defense—something likely to resonate in the immediate years after World War II and in the midst of the Cold War with the Soviet Union. In fact, the legislation was formally titled the "National Interstate and Defense Highway Act of 1956." Eisenhower also gained congressional approval of his efforts to protect Taiwan from military actions by the People's Republic of China. And there was little serious congressional opposition to his handling of the Suez Canal crisis in 1956. Eisenhower achieved more successes during his second term as a result of the relationships he had built with Congress, most notably working with LBJ to pass civil rights legislation.

Adjusting to Circumstances by Making Compromises or Threatening to Veto

Another potential strategy presidents have used is to simply adjust to the circumstances and find ways within that new reality to advance their agenda, whether by compromising or by using their veto powers or the threat of the veto to block legislation. This is the strategy Bill Clinton embraced after his party's unexpected loss to the Republicans in the 1994 midterms. The GOP, under the leadership of the new Speaker of the House Newt Gingrich (R-GA), came on like gangbusters, proposing a new "Contract with America," a document that outlined the wide array of policies the Republicans wanted to enact into law when they became the majority party in the House. Clinton accepted and signed into law a few of its key elements, especially those regarding welfare reform. At the same time, he opposed many others, using a more defensive approach. According to one account, Clinton "depended on veto threats as an alternative mode of influence to win concessions from intransigent opposition leaders, temper the opposition majority's agenda, and occasionally re-frame the public debate by placing boundaries on the range of acceptable outcomes."[15] One of Clinton's most notable victories came when he called Gingrich's bluff to force a shutdown of the federal government over their differences in the federal budget. Here, Clinton played his cards wisely. A shutdown did occur for a time, but it was Gingrich and the GOP who bore the blame. Despite the setback of the 1994 midterms, Clinton largely coasted to reelection in 1996.

For Barack Obama, the final two years of his first term did not yield major legislative achievements in the domestic arena, and what he did achieve was also done by working within his circumstances and finding small areas for compromise with the Republicans. Foreign policy issues loomed especially large: disengagement from the war in Afghanistan and Iraq, the Arab uprisings and its fallout in many Middle East countries, Iran's quest for nuclear weapons, and the latest antics of North Korea. The White House also faced major losses in the House after the 2010 midterms; Democrats lost sixty-three seats in the House (the largest loss of any post–World War II president to that date, and enough to shift the House to GOP control) and six seats in the Senate. Although the Senate remained under Democratic control, given the ideological polarization of Congress, there were few moderate Republicans in the House to appeal to for support. The administration also stuck to its guns. Accounts in the press criticized the Obama administration for failing to reach out and build bridges. Was the White House too insular, too sure of its own correct policy course? Or, did it correctly gauge that outreach to the congressional GOP was likely a futile exercise?

George C. Edwards posits that presidents are not likely to alter the broader political landscape; instead, "successful presidents facilitate change by recognizing opportunities," and then by "fashioning strategies and tactics to exploit them."[16] Edwards argues that this is important in understanding both the strengths and weaknesses of the Obama presidency. During his first two years in office, Obama attempted to enact great changes along the lines of his campaign promises through public appeals and attempts at bipartisan persuasion. Unfortunately, the public remained divided about his presidency and agenda, and Obama was most successful when he mobilized his preexisting supporters and rallied the Democratic congressional majority.[17] Edwards's argument is insightful, particularly because it draws our attention not just to the limits of going public and persuasion but also to opportunities that the internal rhythms of a presidential term present. In this case, some promise at the start, but increasing constraint as time wears on.

After the 2010 midterms, bipartisan appeals were even further doomed for the most part. However, in the lame duck session of the 111th Congress after the 2010 midterms, a compromise was reached with Republican leaders. A budget bill passed that extended the Bush-era tax cuts for another two years as well as reduced federal payroll taxes and further continuing extensions in unemployment benefits. Although the Democrats still retained control of both the House and the Senate, sufficient Republican support was needed, and achieved, to enable the bill's passage: 138 Republicans voted in favor along with 139 Democrats. Finding a compromise was essential for both parties. The sunset provisions in the Bush tax-cut legislation meant that if nothing happened the tax cuts would expire—an outcome Republicans wanted to avoid. Democrats also wanted to prevent the tax cuts from expiring because that might have negative consequences for the economy in the ongoing Great Recession. Moreover, there were positive outcomes for Democrats, such as the extension of unemployment benefits, which had also been set to expire. This lame duck session also saw a process put in place for the repeal of the "Don't Ask, Don't Tell" policy on gays in the military as well as Senate ratification of a new strategic arms reduction treaty. Here, Obama took advantage of the soon-to-disappear Democratic majorities in Congress, which were crucial to these victories.

Obama did achieve reelection in 2012, perhaps indicating that he had done enough in the eyes of the public. Interestingly, during the lame duck session of the 112th Congress right before the start of Obama's second term, a similar situation unfolded as had occurred in 2010. The Bush tax cuts were again set to expire, and several budget bills and other legislation mandated the start of automatic cuts in domestic spending (budget "sequestration"). Taken together, the country was headed for what was termed the "fiscal cliff": simultaneous increase in taxes and mandated reductions in spending. At the last minute, however, Congress passed the American Tax Relief Act of 2012, and Obama signed it into law on January 2, 2013. This made permanent most of the tax cuts (a Republican goal), but taxes on capital gains and dividends also increased (a Democratic goal). Just as it did two years prior, unique circumstances brought both sides to the bargaining table and eventually led to an agreed-upon outcome. To track back to earlier chapters, these examples show that Neustadt's bargaining still remains a relevant and effective tool for exercising presidential power.

Changing the Agenda

Presidents might also consider shifting their political agenda in the aftermath of losses during the first midterm and as a way to better position themselves for the upcoming reelection campaign. Clinton's shift toward more piecemeal legislation after the Republicans took control over Congress is an example of this. After 1994, grand proposals were abandoned and the White House pursued smaller, more incremental legislation that would be more palatable to Congress. These included the telecommunications act establishing more competition in the assignment of broadcasting licenses as well as laws creating new tax credits for small businesses, protecting the portability of healthcare coverage when employees change jobs, creating new safe drinking water standards, and regulating pesticide residues in food.

Nixon provides the most radical example: he made foreign policy the clear centerpiece of his efforts prior to his reelection bid. Improving relations with the Soviet Union and the People's Republic of China and ending the Vietnam War were the cornerstones of his agenda. On two out of the three he succeeded; the third occurred later, and with mixed results. In February 1972, Nixon undertook an historic visit to China, which served to dramatically alter prior frosty relations. Nixon and his National Security Council (NSC) adviser Henry Kissinger also sought to play the card of a China "opening" as part of US strategy in dealing with the Soviet Union. In May 1972, Nixon traveled to Russia to negotiate with Soviet leader Leonid Brezhnev on a nuclear arms reduction treaty. Both of these efforts with China and the Soviet Union were regarded as significant achievements, although some conservatives viewed them as unneeded concessions, especially because of the declining power of the USSR.

Vietnam was another matter. Weeks before the 1972 election, Kissinger secured an agreement with North Vietnam to end the war. Kissinger may have been too eager to secure a settlement; in fact, Nixon's view was that their bargaining position might be greater after a strong showing in the November election.[18] South Vietnam balked at the terms, scuttling the talks, so the Nixon administration was forced to resume extensive bombing of North Vietnam to bring them back to the bargaining table. Secret agreements were subsequently established with the government of South Vietnam, including the promise of US intervention should North Vietnam violate any of the terms. In January 1973, an agreement was eventually signed and the war ended. However, North Vietnam's offensives resumed during Gerald Ford's presidency, and the United States did not uphold its agreement to intervene.

Pushing Forward with the Original Agenda

The final strategy to note is one that George W. Bush employed: simply pushing forward with the agenda as planned. Of course, Bush was able to use this strategy to some success in large part because his first midterm elections brought good news. Republicans added eight seats to their majority in the House and two seats in the Senate. These two seats shifted the Senate back to GOP control, albeit narrowly.

The Republican majority in Congress emboldened the administration to seek a second round of tax cuts. In 2003, the Bush administration was successful in gaining additional cuts in the tax rates for individuals as well as further reductions in rates for dividends, capital gains, and estates. However, it was almost a pure partisan vote with just a handful of members defecting to either side. In the Senate, the vote was particularly close: a 50–50 tie, with Vice President Cheney casting the tie-breaking vote.

Under the rules of the Senate, as part of the annual budget process, this revenue bill was not subject to Senate filibuster. This made the administration's task easier in the sense that it could adopt a highly partisan strategy of simply keeping its congressional base intact with the addition of a few more conservative Democrats to balance off any GOP defectors. However, as a more general strategy to achieve other domestic legislation, it might not work. Democrats, if they all toed the party line, could use the filibuster to block legislation in the Senate. One major piece of domestic legislation did pass with at least some Democratic votes—a ban on partial-birth abortion. Public opinion polls were divided on this controversial issue but with stronger margins supporting the ban. In the end, sixty-three Democrats in the House and seventeen in the Senate supported the legislation.

In my view, the Bush White House and its efforts to secure its agenda largely by pressing ahead is a bit of an outlier. Bush is one of the few whose party gained seats in the first term (notably in the House of Representatives), and he benefited at the time from strong public support. In March 2003, at the start of the war in Iraq, 72 percent of the public approved of Bush's actions. It was not until May 2004 that the percentage of those who disapproved of Bush began to grow larger than the percentage of those who approved.[19]

All of these examples of different presidential strategies post-midterms suggest that presidents cannot simply stick to one method of exercising power throughout their first term. Presidents must carefully reassess what they *had* been doing and how they should adjust to this now more negative context—whether it be by making more compromises or threatening to veto or by changing the agenda entirely. This is crucial, because presidents' difficulties are compounded by the third year when reelection quickly looms.

THE NEXT ELECTION:
SOWING THE SEEDS FOR A SECOND TERM

After the first midterms are over, attention in the media soon begins to focus on the next presidential election, in large part because of changes in the party nomination process starting in the 1970s. This, naturally, has made the legislative efforts of recent presidents even more difficult—it's hard to get people to focus on the bills to pass when they are already talking about who might challenge or even replace the president! Prior to the 1970s, presidential primaries were fewer in number, and the party usually elected a presidential candidate at the summer convention in an election year. In some instances, that decision was the product of deals and "understandings" that transpired in the smoke-filled rooms of convention hotels: a cabinet position offered here, legislation promised there, and perhaps even a running mate guarantee.

Moreover, candidates generally did not announce their quest for the presidency or begin campaigning until January of the election year, at the earliest. It was a custom then not to seem to be too eager to aspire to the presidency. For example, although there was an active "draft Eisenhower" movement that secured victories in a number of primaries, Ike did not declare his candidacy or resign his army command at North Atlantic Treaty Organization (NATO) until June 2, 1952. He gave his first campaign speech in his hometown of Abilene, Kansas, on June 4, 1952. In early July, just weeks later at the GOP national convention, he became his party's nominee. JFK did not announce his bid for office until January 2, 1960. This would be unthinkable today. Back then, incumbent presidents seeking reelection had a bit more breathing room than they do today.

The 1968 Democratic convention, held in Chicago that year, was politically divisive and proved to be the turning point in the presidential nomination process. Antiwar demonstrators flocked to the city to protest the Johnson administration's Vietnam policies. Demonstrations broke out, and the Chicago police responded with great force, all of which were played out on national television. It did not help that the party's eventual nominee, Vice President Hubert Humphrey, had not run in any of the primaries that year and that the principal primary contenders had been antiwar candidates Sen. Eugene McCarthy (D-MN) and then Sen. Robert Kennedy (D-NY), who was assassinated in June on the evening of his victory in the California primary.

After the convention, the Democratic Party undertook a major effort to reform and democratize the nomination process. Candidates needed to accumulate delegates in primaries and "open" caucuses. The prior political practice of "favorite sons" automatically winning their home state delegates' votes or party bosses controlling the votes of their state's delegates disappeared. The Republicans followed suit, though their rules regarding primary votes and delegates differed somewhat. Competing for votes in primaries and open caucuses—and the allocation of delegates determined by them—became necessary to securing a party's nomination for president. Presidential candidates must actually *campaign* for the nomination, not just be available to accept it, as was often the case previously.

Equally important, the timing of campaigns changed. To secure their party's nomination, presidential candidates must organize, staff, and finance their campaigns well before the actual election year. Supporters must be lined up in each state, especially political notables and potential donors. Indeed, the media often speaks of an "invisible" primary well before election year. Gauging potential candidate support and reading the "tea leaves" by visiting key states such as New Hampshire and Iowa start even earlier—sometimes even in year two of a president's administration. During year three of the president's term, actual campaigning begins. In 2011, for example, the Republican presidential candidates challenging Obama appeared in about a dozen debates; more debates followed during the primaries in 2012. In 2015, both parties sought to limit the number of debates, viewing them as divisive and contentious. However, those that were held attracted record-breaking audiences. The first GOP debate on August 7, 2015, attracted an estimated audience of 24 million, the largest of any primary debate in history, while the second GOP debate on September 17 captured 23.1 million viewers and was the largest audience for any program in CNN's history.[20]

The result, for sitting presidents, is that earlier and earlier media attention shifts away from White House efforts at securing legislative achievements to the upcoming presidential election. This is not good news for the White House. While it tries to focus on continued governance, the media focuses on the opposition party's upcoming challenge, and the administration's messages on policy and legislation get drowned out and lost. This is not just a matter of ceding news "space" to electoral politics; the sitting president and the administration's record become targets much earlier than in the past. Moreover, the media's attention focuses not on the substance of policy difference but more on the "horse race" of candidates' support and standing as well as what gaffes candidates might make.

For sitting presidents seeking reelection, one strategy to counter potential opposition is to go public and plant the seeds for their second-term policy efforts.

These seeds may not bloom or ripen by the time of the presidential election, but they might be useful in jump-starting legislative efforts if reelection is successful. Herbert Brownell, Eisenhower's attorney general, began cultivating public support in 1956 for a civil rights act. Although he realized that it would not pass that year, he recognized that an early start would give it a better chance. He was right: his efforts would attain fruition in the Civil Rights Act of 1957.[21] Another example is Reagan's second major effort at tax reform, which he started planning for, and talking about, in 1984. No one in the White House thought it would pass then. However, their early efforts culminated in a major tax-reform bill that passed in 1986, perhaps one of the most significant legislative achievements of a recent president's second term.

Presidents who don't sow the seeds for their second-term agenda early can see that agenda fail to pass. This was the case for George W. Bush. Social Security reform was one of his early policy initiatives upon taking office in 2001. It encountered immediate opposition, so the Bush White House put it on the back burner. At the start of his second term, Social Security was moved forward and it became Bush's signature agenda. However, despite a major public appeals effort, it encountered opposition and ultimately failed to get congressional approval. Had Bush planned more carefully and perhaps devised a strategy later in his *first* term to build public support, he might have paved the way to possible success. We cannot know for sure, of course. However, planning key initiatives and getting the public on board early are likely central to success. Whereas going public cannot simply be used as a meat axe to beat Congress into submission, failing to bring the public along can make matters more difficult.

CONCLUSION: IMPLICATIONS AND QUESTIONS

The internal rhythms of a president's first term matter. Political forces and a president's own influence and energy vary across the first four years, and they can foster legislative achievements or make them more difficult. To maximize the success of their first term, presidents must be adept at understanding the opportunities presented to them and recognizing the best strategies to use in exercising presidential power to accomplish goals in each year.

Given that these opportunities change with each passing year, generally at the president's expense, it is important for presidential candidates to get a head start and ensure a smooth and strong transition to office even before Election Day.

I would argue that the more traditional efforts of going public and persuasion matter most during this early period. Key to a smooth transition is reintroducing the candidate to the American public as its president. The president-elect also needs to start establishing ties to the Washington community, through publicized events, meetings, and even "get-to-know-you" social occasions. These efforts are not just about getting socially acquainted; they are part of the foundation of presidential power.

However, the more important task is preparing to *govern* as a new president. This involves selecting and organizing a postelection transition team, most notably settling on the appointment of key White House figures such as the chief of staff, who is instrumental in planning the administration's initial policy efforts. Those policy efforts, in turn, need paring down. Although much is promised during the campaign, political realities dictate that the new White House think strategically about what is most important. A lean and focused agenda, for which presidents can find at least some common ground and bargaining leverage with Congress, is one that will be most successful. Power wanes over time. This is why new presidents need to hit the ground running and present their agenda to Congress early.

The first midterm does not generally present good news. For some presidents— Clinton, Obama, and Eisenhower, most notably—midterms brought decidedly bad news: major losses in congressional seats and a shift in congressional control to the other party. However, even for other presidents, the congressional midterms do not generally help the perception of presidential power, although some policy initiatives that are already in the pipeline may come to fruition. By year three, attention shifts to the politics of the next election. This further diminishes a president's ability to be perceived as powerful and to successfully exercise what elements of power remain; legislative gains are even less likely to occur. However, presidents who are running for reelection can get a jump start on their second term by sowing the seeds for new policies, which can help them succeed down the line.

Essentially, what matters are the first two years of a presidency. The biggest window of opportunity for setting things in motion opens in the early months of the new presidency, when prospects are most favorable for a new president. Ideally, key provisions of a president's agenda come to fruition during the first year or early in the second. After that, a president's power and situation worsen considerably, though some presidents have been able to adapt admirably to changed circumstances. Power wanes over the course of the first term, and I don't see this changing in the future, unless the dynamics of midterm elections change or a new system for nominating presidential candidates is devised that replicates earlier times when campaigning began only during the election year. Both scenarios seem unlikely, so all future presidents need to be attuned to the varying opportunities and challenges presented by the internal rhythms of the first term and assess the best strategies for exercising power accordingly.

NOTES

1. For a good introduction and critique of the notion of a presidential mandate, see Robert A. Dahl, "Myth of the Presidential Mandate," *Political Science Quarterly* 105, no. 3 (1990): 355–372.

2. Norman J. Ornstein, Thomas E. Mann, Michael J. Malbin, Andrew Rugg, and Raffaela Wakeman, *Vital Statistics on Congress* (Washington, DC: Brookings Institution, 2013), 5, 7, http://www.brookings.edu/-/media/Research/Files/Reports/2013/07/vital%20statistics%20 congress%20mann%20ornstein/Vital%20Statistics%20Chapter%203%20%20Campaign %20Finance%20in%20Congressional%20Elections.pdf.

3. On FDR's transition to office and the first one hundred days, see Adam Cohen, *Nothing to Fear: FDR's Inner Circle and the Hundred Days That Created Modern America* (New York: Penguin Press, 2009).

4. On Carter's efforts, as well as other presidents through Clinton, see John P. Burke, *Presidential Transitions: From Politics to Practice* (Boulder, CO: Lynne Rienner, 2009), 17–94.

5. On the role of the NSC adviser and its historical development, see John P. Burke, *Honest Broker? The National Security Advisor and Presidential Decision Making* (College Station: Texas A&M University Press, 2009). The staff of the NSC has been a particularly important addition: starting in the Kennedy administration, it has grown in size and has become the primary in-house source of foreign and national security advice to the president, often eclipsing the counsel provided by the Departments of State and Defense. Its principal, the NSC adviser, generally serves as the most important source of daily counsel to the president on foreign policy and defense issues.

6. Prior to FDR's administration, the number of staff working directly for a president was negligible. In the very late nineteenth and early twentieth centuries, this began to change. FDR, facing the challenge of the Great Depression, attempted to "muddle through": he formed a policy "brain trust," many of whom had their salaries paid through vacant departmental positions even though they worked at the White House and reported directly to FDR. In 1936, he created the Brownlow Committee to provide recommendations on how to strengthen presidential management and decision making. Only three of its proposals survived congressional scrutiny: the creation of an Executive Office of the President (EOP), a slight increase in White House staff support, and the transfer of the Bureau of the Budget to the new EOP. Although the changes brought about by the Brownlow Committee might seem minimal, they actually served as the foundation for the creation of a large White House staff. The White House Office

(WHO), the central core of the EOP and what we normally think of as the White House staff, increased dramatically from fewer than 10 members in 1939 to about 250 during the Eisenhower administration, and to around 500–600 today. In addition to the WHO, other units were created as part of the EOP. The Council of Economic Advisers was added in 1946 and the National Security Council was created in 1947. Other units were added in subsequent administrations, including an Office of Science and Technology Policy, Council on Environmental Quality, Office of the US Trade Representative, Office of National Drug Control Policy, and, during Carter's presidency, an Office of Administration to manage all of these other White House offices. Eisenhower established the first formal congressional liaison and lobbying unit as part of the White House staff. FDR created the position of White House legal counsel in 1943. Carter created a variety of White House positions to liaise with state and local governments and a variety of public groups. The one-person press secretary in the days of FDR and his predecessors has evolved into a complex White House Office of Communications. Recent presidents have designated key aides as "policy czars," with extensive authority in the development of policy initiatives. Budgets are sometimes an indicator of resources. In 1857, Congress appropriated $2,500 for the president to hire one clerk. By Calvin Coolidge's presidency, the budget for all of the White House staff was $80,000—the equivalent of slightly over $1 million today. For fiscal year 2015, the Obama administration requested $692.4 million from Congress (http://www.whitehouse.gov/sites/default/files/docs/2015-eop-budget_03132014.pdf). On the development and challenges of these resources, what might be termed an "institutional presidency," see John P. Burke, *The Institutional Presidency: Organizing and Managing the White House from FDR to Clinton,* 2nd ed. (Baltimore: Johns Hopkins University Press, 2000).

7. Thomas P. O'Neill with William Novak, *Man of the House: The Life and Political Memoirs of Speaker Tip O'Neill* (New York: St. Martin's Press, 1987), 368.

8. Burke, *Presidential Transitions,* 75–80.

9. Perhaps Carter's most important miscalculation was in dealing with energy policy. Carter achieved some goals, such as the creation of a new department of energy. However, policy-wise, White House efforts were again strategically flawed. What might have been an historically important, comprehensive energy plan, if handled properly and the focal point of a presidential agenda, was diminished to limited, piecemeal legislation. All of this, taken together, was not an auspicious beginning to the Carter presidency. In fact, it may have doomed his presidency from the start.

10. Steven E. Schier, *Panorama of a Presidency: How George W. Bush Acquired and Spent His Political Capital* (Armonk, NY: M. E. Sharpe, 2009), 18.

11. On the G. W. Bush transition and early presidency, see John P. Burke, *Becoming President: The Bush Transition, 2000–2003* (Boulder, CO: Lynne Rienner, 2004).

12. Paul C. Light, *The President's Agenda: Domestic Policy Choice from Kennedy to Reagan,* rev. ed. (Baltimore: Johns Hopkins University Press, 1991), 36–37.

13. Fred I. Greenstein, *The Hidden-Hand Presidency: Eisenhower as Leader* (New York: Basic Books, 1982), 59–60.

14. Ken Collier, "Eisenhower and Congress: The Autopilot Presidency," *Presidential Studies Quarterly* 24, no. 2 (Spring 1994): 317.

15. Richard S. Conley, "President Clinton and the Republican Congress, 1995–2000: Vetoes, Veto Threats, and Legislative Strategy" (paper presented at the annual meeting of the American Political Science Association, San Francisco, CA, August 30–September 2, 2001), 8.

16. George C. Edwards III, "Strategic Assessments: Evaluating Opportunities and Strategies in the Obama Presidency," in *The Obama Presidency: Appraisals and Prospects,* ed. Bert A. Rockman, Andrew Rudalevige, and Colin Campbell (Washington, DC: CQ Press), 37.

17. Edwards, "Strategic Assessments," 61.

18. See Burke, *Honest Broker,* 141–143.

19. An interesting and movable week-by-week average of Bush's approval ratings can be found at http://www.gallup.com/poll/124922/Presidential-Job-Approval-Center.aspx?utm _source=WWWV7HP&utm_medium=topic&utm_campaign=tileshttp://www.realclear politics.com/epolls/other/president_bush_job_approval-904.html.

20. Brian Stelter, "23 Million Watched GOP Debate, a Record for CNN," CNN Money, September 17, 2015, http://money.cnn.com/2015/09/17/media/cnn-republican-debate-ratings/. The first debate was held on August 7, 2015, and the second on September 17, 2015; three more debates were held in October, November, and December.

21. Herbert Brownell with John P. Burke, *Advising Ike: The Memoirs of Attorney General Herbert Brownell* (Lawrence: University Press of Kansas), 217–220.

7

The Second Term: Internal Time and Presidential Power

Conventional wisdom suggests that second terms have generally proved disappointing. There is a long history here. Franklin D. Roosevelt's overwhelming electoral victory in 1936 did not yield the legislative successes of his first four years in office. His plan to pack the Supreme Court by expanding its membership ended in failure, conservative opposition developed within his own party, and his efforts to defeat a number of anti–New Deal, conservative Senate Democrats in the 1938 midterm elections proved largely futile. The successes of Woodrow Wilson's progressive policy agenda were largely confined to his first term. His reelection victory in 1916 was a narrow one, and by April 1917 the nation was drawn into World War I, despite his campaign platform to keep the country out of war. And despite victory in World War I, Wilson's efforts to secure a lasting peace through Senate ratification of the Versailles Treaty and US participation in the League of Nations ended in failure. Since the adoption of the Twenty-Second Amendment in 1951, establishing a two-term limit, the situation has become even worse. Presidents have not managed to build a second-term record more impressive than their first term's—and they don't have the prospect of a third term. The "lame duck" problem further diminishes a second-term president's power and legislative achievements, particularly in the final two years.

Scholarly analysis of second terms, unfortunately, has been quite limited, especially from a comparative perspective. However, a few do offer some insight. Grossman, Kumar, and O'Rourke note a presidential tendency to overinterpret reelection results, especially in claiming political mandates that are not really there. They also note that there is a general failure to use the reelection campaign to articulate and build public support for a second-term agenda, that the quality of appointments decreases, and that a sense of overconfidence develops.[1] On the other hand, King and Riddlesperger argue that some presidents view second terms as a new beginning.[2] For example, Nixon felt Eisenhower had missed an opportunity for change after his reelection, and wanting to avoid that, Nixon dramatically shook up his personnel. Of course, Nixon did suffer from the over-confidence problem that Grossman and his colleagues pointed out. Nixon and some of his White House associates became mired in the Watergate scandal, and he was forced to resign only a year and a half into his second term.

Fortier and Ornstein capture the general consensus: "Second terms have not been good to American presidents. They often are characterized by hubris, burn-out, a paucity of new or bold ideas and are plagued by scandal, party infighting, lack of legislative success, and loss of seats in the midterm election."[3] In short, successful reelection is often not matched by successful second-term governing. Presidential power is at a lower ebb than in the first term. In this chapter we examine the reasons why, including the lack of a mandate even with reelection, the issues of second-term staff, the challenges in developing and achieving a second-term agenda, the disappointment of midterm elections, the lack of traction post-midterms, and the hubris and scandal that seem to plague second terms. Given the overwhelming odds facing second termers, what presidential strategies and tactics might bolster success?

REELECTION: A PERSONAL TRIUMPH, BUT NOT A MANDATE

Reelection is certainly a major achievement for a sitting president, but it rarely translates into a policy mandate for a second term. On the surface, things do seem to get better compared to first-term election results. With the exception of Obama, each reelected president post–Twenty-Second Amendment achieved gains in the popular vote. The net average improved performance is a gain of almost 6 percent (see Table 7.1).

Still, the evidence for a mandate is unclear, if not nonexistent. Although all of Obama's five predecessors increased their percentage of the popular vote, nobody except for Nixon received the 60-plus percent that typically indicates a mandate.

TABLE 7.1. Electoral Performance by Term

Year	President	Party	Vote (%)	Gain/Loss (from First Term, %)
1952	Eisenhower	R	55.2	
1956	Eisenhower	R	57.4	2.2
1968	Nixon	R	43.4	
1972	Nixon	R	60.7	17.3
1980	Reagan	R	50.7	
1984	Reagan	R	58.8	8.1
1992	Clinton	D	43.0	
1996	Clinton	D	49.2	6.2
2000	G. W. Bush	R	47.9	
2004	G. W. Bush	R	50.7	2.8
2008	Obama	D	52.9	
2012	Obama	D	51.1	−1.8
Average				5.8

SOURCES: Gerhard Peters, "Seats in Congress Gained or Lost by the President's Party in Presidential Election Years," in *American Presidency Project,* ed. John T. Woolley and Gerhard Peters (Santa Barbara: University of California, Santa Barbara, 1999–2013), http://www.presidency.ucsb.edu/data/presidential_elections_seats.php; History, Art and Archives, US House of Representatives, "Election Statistics, 1920 to Present," 2015, http://history.house.gov/Institution/Election-Statistics/Election-Statistics/.

Clinton and George W. Bush are on even more tenuous grounds. Clinton didn't even hit the 50 percent mark, though he did have an 8.5 percent margin over his Republican opponent, and Bush received 50.7 percent in 2004, which was better—but only a little—than his first election results. At least Bush managed to win the popular vote, which eluded him four years earlier.

In addition, with the exception of Nixon in 1972 and Reagan in 1984, the net gains of the others are not particularly impressive. In 1956, Eisenhower managed a 2.2 percent gain from 1952, once again beating former governor Adlai Stevenson. However, we might argue that it was an election less about policy differences and once again more about the personal qualities and appeal of the candidates. As for Obama, the results are even more dismal. Of the six second-term presidents, he is the only one to have his percentage of the popular vote decline: from 52.9 percent in 2008 to 51.1 percent in 2012. His Electoral College vote, although a solid victory, also declined from 365 in 2008 to 332 in 2012. Here, too, he stands out from his predecessors, all of whom increased their electoral vote totals the second time around.

Recall also that another important feature of an electoral mandate for a president is that it is not just a personal victory but also sweeps members of the president's party into Congress. Calculating the coattail effect, as we saw in the previous chapter, is almost impossible to determine with any accuracy. However, a surrogate indicator is to look at the simple gain or loss of seats in Congress by the president's party (significant gains probably indicate at least some coattail effect). Moreover, we could take it a step further and compare the shift in seats in the reelection year to the previous midterm election.

As Table 7.2 indicates, losses can be significant, as they were for Clinton in 1996, following upon an even more significant decline in his first midterm in 1994. Only Bush and Obama managed to gain in both the House and the Senate in reelection. But for Obama, the net gains since his first election remained in negative territory because of the major losses in his first midterm in 2010. Note especially that in two of the three major electoral triumphs—Nixon in 1972 and Reagan in 1984—House shifts are only in the low double digits. For Eisenhower, there was a loss of two seats in 1956. None of the three made positive headway in the Senate; all lost seats despite impressive reelection majorities. These numbers do not suggest a substantial coattail effect at the start of the second term. Few make significant progress in reversing the negative trends of the first midterm. Even if some make up some lost ground, it is rarely of significant numbers.

Third, as we discussed in the previous chapter, for a *policy* mandate to be believably claimed, the candidates must articulate issue and policy differences during the campaign and the presidential incumbent must lay out a clear policy agenda for the second term. This, unfortunately, has not been the case for most recent second-term elections. Although presidential challengers have sought to emphasize policy differences and engage in retrospective attacks on the president's first-term record, presidential incumbents have generally focused on the weaknesses of their rivals or broad generalities about their own leadership rather than specify their own policies for a second term. The classic case is Reagan in 1984. On the one hand, his campaign sought to link his opponent, former vice president Walter Mondale, to the presumably failed Carter presidency while also

TABLE 7.2. Presidential Party's Gains/Losses in First Midterms and Reelection Years

Year	House	Senate	Year	House	Senate
EISENHOWER (R)			NIXON (R)		
1952	22	1	1968	5	6
1954	(–18)	(–1)	1970	(–12)	2
1956	(–2)	(–1)	1972	12	(–1)
REAGAN (R)			CLINTON (D)		
1980	34	12	1992	(–10)	0
1982	(–26)	1	1994	(–52)	(–8)
1984	14	(–2)	1996	(–9)	(–2)
G. W. BUSH (R)			OBAMA (D)		
2000	(–3)	(–4)	2008	23	8
2002	8	2	2010	(–63)	(–6)
2004	3	4	2012	8	1

SOURCES: Gerhard Peters, "Seats in Congress Gained or Lost by the President's Party in Presidential Election Years," in *The American Presidency Project,* ed. John T. Woolley and Gerhard Peters (Santa Barbara: University of California, Santa Barbara, 1999–2013), http://www.presidency .ucsb.edu/data/presidential_elections_seats.php; History, Art and Archives, US House of Representatives, "Election Statistics, 1920 to Present," 2015, http://history.house.gov/Institution /Election-Statistics/Election-Statistics/; and History, Art and Archives, US House of Representatives, "Party Divisions of the House of Representatives," 2015, http://history.house.gov /Institution/Party-Divisions/Party-Divisions/.

running ads that showed gauzy images of a now happy and contented nation under Reagan in contrast to the long, dark nights under Carter *and* Mondale.[4] In 2004, the Bush campaign paired Kerry's "flip-flops" on the Iraq war with images of Kerry tacking back and forth while windsurfing.[5] The theme was Kerry's vacillation and lack of leadership, not a future Bush agenda.

In 2012, Obama campaign ads attacked Romney as a heartless "job destroyer" while he was in private business, a user of offshore banks to evade taxes, and someone who would say anything to get elected, among other themes.[6] It was a "strategic calculation" by the Obama camp, according to George C. Edwards III. "Romney wanted a referendum on Obama's performance, but Obama made it a choice between two people."[7] Budget and tax issues did emerge in the debates and in the candidates' speeches, but other issues that would come to prominence early in Obama's second term, such as immigration reform, were mostly on the back burner. Gun control did not figure at all in political discourse, yet it emerged postelection with a vengeance following the carnage at the Sandy Hook Elementary School in Newtown, Connecticut, in December 2012. For the most part, the prospective agenda of a second Obama presidency was not front and center during the campaign.

Looking at these three indicators, a presidential mandate for a second term seems elusive. All in all, reelection appears to be largely a personal achievement, not a foundation for policy change. Still, that doesn't stop presidents from claiming a mandate. Although Obama had a weak claim to a mandate, that did not prevent him from announcing at his first press conference after Election Day that his reelection sent a clear message in support of his plans to increase taxes on wealthier Americans. Although he was able to secure expiration of some of the Bush-era tax cuts at the end of the year, that was largely the result of prior legislative mechanics because they were automatically scheduled to expire if no congressional action was taken.

CHANGES TO CABINET AND WHITE HOUSE STAFF IN THE SECOND TERM

Even if mandates are elusive, preparation for a second term is still required. Just as presidential candidates begin selecting key personnel before Election Day, so too do sitting presidents. A second term provides presidents with the opportunity for a fresh start or at least the opportunity to take stock of their team. It is also a natural time for staffers to reconsider their jobs or their roles within the administration. Some may be eager to return to the private sector, but the president may wish to persuade those most loyal and effective to stay on. For those who wish to remain, there is the challenge of evaluating their service. Some members may be interested in other jobs in the administration. Which moves are appropriate, who will they replace, and who will replace them? For those who are deemed less than successful, this is an opportunity for a graceful exit, at a lower political cost because change is expected. In terms of filling vacancies, decisions must be made about whether to promote from within or to seek new talent from outside. The start of a second term also serves as an occasion for reassessing what a president needs from his or her team. The pressure to hire and organize staffers and key officials is not as great as four years earlier, because at least part of the team remains in place. Still, the sooner needed personnel changes are made, the better positioned the administration is to hit the ground running on its second-term agenda.

Second-term presidents differ in terms of the degree of changes they make in cabinet and White House staff positions. Dwight D. Eisenhower largely kept the same team because he wanted continuity. In early 1956, Eisenhower told his assembled cabinet, "If I find myself here next January, you will have to stay here too."[8] He got what he wanted: the White House staff largely remained intact, and there were no cabinet changes through the early months of 1957. Three members—his secretaries of treasury and defense and the attorney general—were interested in leaving government for a variety of reasons, but Eisenhower persuaded them to stay a bit longer until key goals under their purviews were completed.

By contrast, following Nixon's reelection, change in the cabinet was significant. Although Nixon did not intend to change personnel wholesale, he asked everyone to submit resignation letters because he wanted free choice in making any changes. This ended up being a ham-handed decision. Nixon himself concedes in his memoirs that the request for wholesale resignations was a mistake, noting that he "did not take into account the chilling effect this action would have on the morale of people who had worked so hard during the election and who were . . . suddenly having to worry about keeping their jobs."[9] Out of the eleven cabinet slots, eight were filled with new members. By the end of the year, two more were replaced. This much change within the cabinet undermined the morale of those who remained, and the new members had a lot of catching up to do, reducing the Nixon administration's ability to quickly launch into the second term's agenda. On the other hand, key players on the White House staff remained in place. Henry Kissinger, his national security adviser, remained. Chief of Staff H. R. Haldeman and domestic adviser John Ehrlichman were kept on until Watergate caught up with them. Both Haldeman and Ehrlichman were key figures in the Watergate cover-up—it is interesting to speculate what might have happened had Nixon made changes in his White House staff earlier.

For George W. Bush, although there was the normal attrition in White House staff through the first term, several of the major staff members remained in place: Chief of Staff Andrew Card Jr., communications chief Dan Bartlett, Office of Management and Budget Director Josh Bolten, and senior adviser Karl Rove. In the cabinet, nine (out of fifteen) new appointments were made. For Bush, as Shirley Anne Warshaw notes, this lack of change may have led to "a narrower focus in the decision maker structure" and "reduced the number of differing opinions in the policy-making process."[10] Also notable is *who* was kept on: Donald Rumsfeld, the most controversial of cabinet members, continued as secretary of defense until the midterm elections of 2006. This may have been another missed opportunity for change. We can wonder what the administration's strategies—and fortune—in Iraq might have been had Rumsfeld been replaced two years earlier.

For Obama, change was also significant but followed the pattern of his predecessors. Nine of fifteen cabinet members were replaced during 2013. Initial White House staff changes included a new chief of staff and a new NSC adviser. For Obama, these were largely internal promotions. Denis McDonough, the deputy NSC adviser, was tapped to become the new chief of staff, while Susan Rice, who had been US ambassador to the United Nations, became the new NSC adviser in July 2013. Both were longtime members of the Obama inner circle. Many press reports noted an insular White House, one lacking fresh faces. One other important change was the September 25, 2014, resignation of Attorney General Eric Holder, pending the appointment of a successor. It took until April 2015, almost seven months later, for Loretta Lynch to finally be sworn in to succeed him. The Senate confirmation process moves slowly, a further hindrance to personnel changes and to getting a quick start on second-term agenda items.

How do these personnel opportunities affect presidential power? Sitting presidents face a number of similar challenges as they consider who will serve them during a second term:

- Many of the best appointees of the first term may be ready to move on; work in either the White House or at the highest levels of cabinet departments can be grueling, and, for many, government service is a financial handicap.
- The pool of new prospects may be less talented or less willing to serve.
- Those continuing in office or promoted to higher positions may have become more allegiant to their department's interests and needs rather than the president's agenda.
- Political pressure on appointments from constituency groups may be greater and more organized the second time around.
- For White House staff members, a measure of insularity may emerge: those who stay on may be prone to thinking of themselves as the most loyal, the "true believers."

All in all, the quality of presidential personnel in the second term tends to suffer. The degree of honest and fair advice offered to a president may be compromised as a result. For presidents, the challenge is not simply to clean house and get a fresh start or adopt the "steady as she goes" mentality and promote from within. Rather, after four years in office, presidents must take stock of how their administration is doing and figure out what is working and what requires change. Unlike for the initial transition to office, second-term presidents have firsthand knowledge and experience of how a presidency works. They need to draw upon this familiarity and move forward. They need to analyze why first-term failures occurred and what changes in personnel are needed as a result. They must examine first-term victories to find who played a role and where the best place is for these players in the administration's future.

THE CHALLENGES OF A SECOND-TERM AGENDA

Just as they did four years earlier during the initial transition to office and the early months of the new administration, presidents must plan a policy agenda for the second term. Now the challenges are even greater. There is likely to be little in the way of a "second honeymoon" period. Also, as noted above, they are very likely to have fewer fellow partisans in the House and Senate. Although presidents often claim a mandate, few Washington insiders are likely to pay it much heed. In short, presidents' "power stakes," to use Neustadt's term, are lessened. Second-term presidents, therefore, must choose their legislative agenda carefully: opposition is likely to be greater, more political compromise and concessions will be needed, and the lame duck president will be perceived as ever lamer as time moves on. The probability of new and ambitious proposals being enacted is not high.

Failing to Plan for a Second Term Dooms Some Presidents

Some recent presidents, however, have further compromised their situation by failing to plan adequately for a second term. Nixon, although cognizant of the policy difficulties of a second term—having, as vice president, witnessed Eisenhower's firsthand—kept delaying policy planning. Shortly after Election Day, Nixon acknowledged to reporters that second terms "usually coast downhill,"[11] and later in his memoirs, Nixon noted that he was determined not to fall into the "lethargy that had characterized Eisenhower's second term."[12] But even with this insight, Nixon spent most of his time before Inauguration Day on personnel, often at Camp David or at his presidential retreats in Key Biscayne, Florida, and San Clemente, California. He spent no full, nontravel days at the White House in November, only seven in December, and nine in January. To be fair, part of the problem was the ongoing Vietnam War. In his diaries, then chief of staff Haldeman noted that Nixon "still hasn't clearly focused on getting down to work on the second term, he's using the Inaugural as an excuse for not scheduling things, but he's not working on the Inaugural. I think until he gets Vietnam settled, everything else is going to pretty much stay in the background, and there won't be much concentration on anything."[13]

Nixon had hoped his landslide victory would improve his relationship with Congress, but the "Christmas bombing" of North Vietnam caused it to deteriorate further. Nixon didn't help matters with his limited efforts to build congressional support after Election Day 1972. According to aide John Ehrlichman, Nixon "virtually disappeared behind the fences of Camp David."[14] Several formal events were held with some members of Congress, but these were not attempts to reach out and build policy support. Although Watergate was what ultimately doomed Nixon's second term, we can imagine that even without the scandal, Nixon would not have had an easy go of it, what with the lack of planning and strained relations with Congress.

For Reagan, troubles in his personnel changes and policy agenda were linked. At the start of his second term, his treasury secretary, Donald Regan, and his chief of staff, James Baker, privately agreed to swap jobs. What is most notable is that Reagan was a passive bystander to the swap. His diary entry for January 7, 1985, is revealing: "Biggest event today was a meeting with Don Regan and then with Jim Baker. They want to trade jobs. I've agreed."[15] This change, and Reagan's lackadaisical attitude about it, had a significant negative impact on the Reagan presidency. Whereas Baker proved a skilled secretary of the treasury, Regan was largely a disaster as chief of staff. He put a number of his lieutenants at Treasury in key White House positions; they were quickly dubbed "Regan's mice." Regan publicly touted himself as the president's "prime minister," which did not sit well with the old Reagan hands and especially not with the First Lady, with whom he began to clash. Regan also sought to have a greater role in foreign policy, which alienated the NSC staff as well as State and Defense. Finally, he was a contributing factor to President Reagan's later difficulties with Iran-Contra.[16] Regan poorly advised the president on the steps needed when news of Iran-Contra was made public. Although Reagan's second-term difficulties might not have been entirely avoided even if he had been more methodical and thoughtful in his personnel changes, they certainly did not help matters.

Political Landscape Works Against Other Presidents

For Bill Clinton, George W. Bush, and Barack Obama, the political landscape largely worked against them. Clinton was organized and methodical in the run-up to Inauguration Day, holding events to highlight everything that he had achieved in his first term and gathering staffers for strategy meetings. In Clinton's mind, his first term had yielded a number of important accomplishments that gave him a solid foundation for launching his second-term agenda, but he also recognized the political situation he faced and the difficulties it posed for an expansive agenda of new initiatives. As he noted in his memoirs, "Because the Republicans were in control of Congress and because it is more difficult to enact large reforms when times are good, I wasn't sure how much we could achieve in my second term."[17] Still, Clinton was determined to keep trying, but given an aggressive, Republican-controlled Congress, his hands were largely tied. His most significant achievement was expansion of healthcare coverage for children; it was a legacy of his failed healthcare proposal of the first term. Clinton's greatest benefit was the booming economy during his second term. Extra revenues permitted an important budget agreement with Congress in 1997, one that soon led to budget surpluses for the first time since the early 1960s.

For George W. Bush, his situation at the beginning of his second term with respect to Congress was the reverse of Clinton's. Republicans added seats in both the House and the Senate in 2004. But he underperformed in terms of his own second-term gains, receiving only 50.7 percent of the popular vote. Yet, that did not stop him from making claims about a mandate, telling reporters in his first postelection news conference: "I've earned capital in this election, and I'm going to spend it on . . . the agenda: Social security and tax reform, moving this economy forward, education, fighting and winning the war on terror."[18] It was great political bravado, and it resembled his attempts to seize the agenda as he had done in 2001 despite losing the popular vote to Al Gore.

However, the nation was more politically divided than it had been four years earlier. As Gary C. Jacobson has noted, he was "president of half the people."[19]

Whereas 92 percent of Republicans approved of his presidency in the first post-election Gallup survey, only 16 percent of Democrats did. The latter was the lowest rating of all second termers in terms of opposition support. Even Clinton did better at 20 percent among Republicans.[20] Despite the fact that Bush's party held control of the House and the Senate, Republicans did not have a superma-jority in the Senate and the Democrats could still filibuster. Bush could not get the hallmark of his second-term agenda—privatizing Social Security—enacted. The administration was not able to build bipartisan support with Congress or the public for Social Security reform in the first year of his second term. As Jacobson notes, in one December 2004 poll, only 33 percent of respondents believed that Bush had a mandate to change Social Security.[21] Bush also did not help himself during his reelection campaign: he spent most of it demonizing his Democratic opponent, Senator John Kerry, and emphasizing his commitment to the war on terror. He exerted little effort promoting his domestic initiatives going forward.

Indeed, in his memoirs, Bush especially acknowledges his error in pushing for change in Social Security first: "I may have misread the electoral mandate by pushing for an issue on which there had been little bipartisan agreement in the first place." He also notes that he should have pushed for immigration reform instead, because it had more bipartisan support, and its success could have given him the momentum he needed to tackle Social Security reform. Unfortunately, "the reverse happened. When Social Security failed, it widened the partisan divide and made immigration reform tougher."[22] This failure plus two other major missteps effectively weakened his presidency by the end of the first year of his second term: one was his bungled response to Hurricane Katrina, which signaled slippage in his abilities as a leader and manager in the wake of national crises.[23] The second was his ill-advised nomination of Harriet Miers, a longtime friend from Texas who was serving as White House legal counsel, to a Supreme Court vacancy. Miers's lack of judicial experience and her unclear record on abortion rights roused opposition from both liberals and conservatives; her nomination was eventually withdrawn. Many saw this pick as a sign of the insularity of the Bush White House.

For Obama, the political situation was even worse. Although the Democrats scored gains in both the House (+8) and the Senate (+1) in 2012, Republicans still maintained control of the former. The Democrats' massive 63-seat loss in the 2010 midterms, two years earlier, presented a near-impossible electoral barrier to overcome. In addition, unlike those of his predecessors going back to Eisenhower, Obama's share of the popular and Electoral College votes was less than it had been four years earlier. Like Bush, Obama was president of half the people—except it was the other half. On Inauguration Day 2013, his approval rating stood at only 52.1 percent while disapproval was at 43 percent, and by early June 2013, his disapproval rating was greater than his approval rating. The decline in his approval rating continued; by late December 2015, it stood at 45 percent, with disapproval at 50 percent.[24] Public support was tenuous, so, just as for Bush, Obama faced a strong barrier to making successful public appeals for support on major initiatives.

In his 2013 inaugural address, Obama emphasized three major domestic initiatives: immigration reform, climate change, and new tax policies. The latter largely disappeared from political view, at least as a major legislative initiative. Obama fought hard for immigration reform, but by July 2014 any hope of a compromise bill was dead. Not surprisingly, the White House fought a continuous battle with congressional Republicans on budget and appropriation bills. In October 2013, the federal government shut down for two weeks when neither side could reach an agreement to even permit temporary funding. Earlier, following shootings at an elementary school in Newtown, Connecticut, in December 2012, the administration had attempted to seize the policy moment by proposing further gun control legislation. It seemed this would have been an opportune time to act, but there too Congress failed. By the time the 2014 midterms rolled around, in terms of domestic legislation, Obama had little to show for his efforts. The botched rollout of his healthcare plan and a major scandal in treatment patterns and long waits at veterans' hospitals did not help either. Although the economy had largely rebounded from the Great Recession, the public remained cautious. In close races in the 2014 midterms, Democratic candidates distanced themselves from the president, and he made few public campaign appearances. One bright spot did emerge in December 2015, as a result of an international conference sponsored by the United Nations. The United States joined with 195 other nations in forging the Paris Agreement on climate change. It was a diplomatic victory for the Obama administration and a major step forward, but it was nonbinding and largely aspirational. Time will tell whether the agreement has any practical effect on global warming.

A Glimmer of Hope: Strategies for Second-Term Success

Although it seems that the deck is stacked against second termers, it is not as if presidents never achieve anything. Presidents can use certain strategies to exercise power and attain some of their goals in their second terms. For example, Clinton strategically used budget agreements to expand and enhance some programs such as college scholarship tax credits and changes in Medicare benefits. He also built on existing regulatory authority to make further changes, including enacting stronger air quality rules and expanding the Head Start program, and he made some strides in areas where there might have been broader support such as legislation dealing with the quality of nursing homes or cutting the time for approval of new drugs.

The first two years of Bush's second term were also not without some achievements. Legislation passed limiting class-action law suits, which the administration backed. An act making it more difficult to declare personal bankruptcy passed. An administration energy bill passed in 2005. A new Central American Free Trade Agreement also gained assent. Bush received congressional support, as we discussed in Chapter 3, to deal with the legal and due process issues of alleged terrorist detainees and a series of Supreme Court decisions. (Ultimately, the court had the final say in this matter, restricting the president's power and granting broader habeas corpus rights to detainees.) Although these were not the major initiatives, such as Social Security and immigration reform, that he had hoped for, they were areas in which broader congressional support could be selectively assembled. As with Clinton, the lesson here is that more modest proposals might still have a chance for success even if the major ones prove beyond grasp. And, as we discussed at length in Chapter 3, executive orders and related actions could sometimes be useful tools in achieving what cannot be legislatively accomplished—tools that both Bush and Obama made good use of.

THE MIDTERM DEBACLE
AND THE FINAL TWO YEARS

Midterm elections bring more political bad news, making the exercise of presidential power in the final two years even more difficult. As a number of scholars have noted, the numerical strength of the president's party members in Congress is very likely to decline as a result of the midterm elections—a result of the so-called sixth-year itch.[25] Since 1906, no second-term president has had his party gain seats in either the House or the Senate during a midterm, with one exception—in 1998, under Clinton, Democrats gained five House seats, but no Senate seats (see Table 7.3). But 1998 was an interesting midterm, and likely an outlier in its effect. Although Republicans in Congress were conducting impeachment hearings

TABLE 7.3. Presidential Party's Gains/Losses Across Two Terms

Year	House	Senate	Year	House	Senate
EISENHOWER (R)			**NIXON (R)**		
1952	22	1	1968	5	6
1954	(–18)	(–1)	1970	(–12)	2
1956	(–2)	(–1)	1972	12	(–1)
1958	(–48)	(–13)	1974	N/A resigned 8/9/74	
REAGAN (R)			**CLINTON (D)**		
1980	34	12	1992	–10	0
1982	(–26)	1	1994	(–52)	(–8)
1984	14	(–2)	1996	(–9)	(–2)
1986	(–5)	(–8)	1998	5	0
G. W. BUSH (R)			**OBAMA (D)**		
2000	(–3)	(–4)	2008	23	8
2002	8	2	2010	(–63)	(–6)
2004	3	4	2012	8	1
2006	(–30)	(–6)	2014	(–13)	(–9)

SOURCES: Gerhard Peters, "Seats in Congress Gained or Lost by the President's Party in Presidential Election Years," in *The American Presidency Project,* ed. John T. Woolley and Gerhard Peters (Santa Barbara: University of California, Santa Barbara, 1999–2013), http://www.presidency.ucsb.edu/data/presidential_elections_seats.php; History, Art and Archives, US House of Representatives, "Election Statistics, 1920 to Present," 2015, http://history.house.gov/Institution/Election-Statistics/Election-Statistics/; and History, Art and Archives, US House of Representatives, "Party Divisions of the House of Representatives," 2015, http://history.house.gov/Institution/Party-Divisions/Party-Divisions/.

over the Monica Lewinsky scandal in an attempt to remove the president from office during this time, Clinton's approval ratings remained high.

For most of the other presidents, the results were devastating. The GOP never held the House during the Reagan years, and it lost control of the Senate in the 1986 midterms. George W. Bush and the Republicans lost control of both the House and the Senate in 2006. For Obama, Republicans already controlled the House, but the 2014 midterms gave them control of the Senate as well, by a substantial 54–46 margin. These results were particularly devastating for the last two years of the Obama presidency, because the GOP attained its largest majority in the House since the start of the Seventy-First Congress in 1929.

Sitting presidents are in a particularly weak position for attaining domestic and economic goals in the final two years because of these midterm losses. In addition, after the second midterms, attention begins to turn to the *next* president. Finally, starting in the seventh year, longtime White House and administration officials begin to leave their positions. According to one account, "The seventh year of any administration is the traditional time for senior officials to start preparing to head for the Golden Revolving Door (GRD) to lucrative private-sector jobs."[26] As highly qualified personnel begin to drift out of the administration in search of future career opportunities, they are replaced by lower-level staff or the positions are left vacant, meaning that the president is left with a dwindling cast of experienced operatives. This can be detrimental to the White House and other executive branch departments and agencies, serving to further weaken the president's power position in the final two years.

Measures of Presidential Success

In his study on the effects of divided government, which we examined in Chapter 5, David Mayhew also provides some general insight on legislative achievements during a president's final two years in office. In his analysis of legislation passed by Congress from 1946 to 1990, Mayhew notes that "enactment of a sizable White House domestic agenda never happens beyond any president's sixth year in office. The seventh and eight years (and beyond) are always fallow." Moreover, he notes, "By the seventh year, a president no doubts runs out of programs, will, or skill, or else Congress settles into an attitude of boredom, hostility, or simply unforthcomingness towards a president now perceived as a lame duck."[27] In the second edition of his book, Mayhew takes the analysis up through 2002, and he has posted results through 2012 on his personal website.[28] Although Mayhew's data measure *passage* of major legislation by Congress, some key nuances are missing from his analysis as it relates to presidential power. It does not distinguish which pieces of legislation stem from *presidential* policy proposals, nor does it take into consideration how strongly the White House favors a particular piece of legislation or the degree of compromise needed to get it passed.

That said, let us consider his results for Clinton and George W. Bush. By Mayhew's count, there were 41 major bills throughout Clinton's presidency, only 6 of which passed during his last two years in office (spread evenly, there would have been 10.25 per each two-year session of each Congress).[29] For George W.

Bush, the differences between the first and second terms are less clear, with a more even distribution across his eight years in office.[30] However, let us keep in mind the depressing reality of the last months of the Bush presidency. The beginning of an economic decline unseen since the Great Depression—it would, indeed, earn the label of the "Great Recession"—required quick remedial action, including three major pieces of legislation directed at economic relief (a $700 billion bank bailout bill, a $168 billion stimulus package, and a $300-plus billion mortgage-relief measure).

Mayhew provides further insight by taking his analysis one step further, narrowing it to only *significant* legislation for each president, acts that "reach beyond being important to being historically important."[31] Their number is small, but they support the claim that less gets done in the second term. Of the 17 total pieces of legislation for all two-term presidents from Eisenhower through George W. Bush, 12 (70.6 percent) occurred in the first term, while only 5 (29.4 percent) occurred in the second term.[32] Some of the second-term bills could also be considered "term-straddlers," meaning that although the legislation passed during a second term, the ground was really laid during the president's first term. For example, Eisenhower had only one significant piece of legislation—the Civil Rights Act of 1957—and it occurred in his second rather than first term. But this bill had been percolating in the House in 1956 and was enacted by the fall of 1957, so it does not quite count as a wholly *second-term* initiative. Reagan's tax-reform act in 1986 could also be considered a term-straddler because the preparations for the legislation began in late 1984. For Clinton, his 1997 budget proposal was the one piece of legislation during his second term. But, like Reagan's tax reform, much ground had been laid in the fall prior to his reelection, when preparations for the next fiscal year had begun, hard budget decisions were made, and drafting the president's annual economic and budget address in February commenced. Notably, all of these bills occurred within the first two years of reelection. None of these second-term presidents, with the exception of George W. Bush, as noted earlier, scored *any* significant legislation in the final two years.

Another way of potentially ascertaining presidential success over time is *Congressional Quarterly Weekly*'s annual measure of important votes issued each year starting in 1953. The data measure floor votes in the House and the Senate on which the president has taken a position on "major issues of the year."[33] Unlike Mayhew's data, the *CQ* measure factors in presidential support. However, it is still somewhat limited: it does not reflect which bills clearly stem from the president's

TABLE 7.4. *Congressional Quarterly* Support Scores by Term/Ranking

Rank	President	Term	% Support	Total Average (%)
1	G. W. Bush	I	81.6	
2	Eisenhower	I	76.75	
3	Reagan	I	71.9	
4	Clinton	I	66	
				74
5	Eisenhower	II	63.25 (−13.5)	
6	G. W. Bush	II	61.2 (−20.4)	
7	Reagan	II	51.8 (−20.1)	
8	Clinton	II	49.25 (−16.75)	
				56.4 (−17.6)

SOURCES: Norman J. Ornstein, Thomas E. Mann, and Michael Malbin, *Vital Statistics on Congress 2008* (Washington, DC: Brookings Institution Press, 2008), 144–145; *Congressional Roll Call 2009* (Washington, DC: CQ Press, 2010).

agenda, nor does it distinguish between major and minor legislation (all bills are weighted equally).[34] Still, it is one gauge of presidential success (or failure) that may be helpful in determining the legislative records of second terms.

As Table 7.4 indicates, there are significant differences between first and second terms. The four highest four-year averages all occur in the first term, ranging from Bush's 81.6 percent to Clinton's 66 percent. The four lowest four-year averages occur in the second term, ranging from Eisenhower's 62 percent to Clinton's 49 percent. The first-term average for all four presidents is 74 percent, the second-term average stands at 56.4 percent, a net average decline of 17.6 percent. This is yet another indication that presidents have a much more difficult time achieving legislative success in their second term than in the first.

Pressing Power Until the End in the Domestic Arena

As noted in Chapter 6, it is essential for presidents to hit the ground running when they are first elected, and this is the case after reelection as well, because chances of passing legislation decrease significantly after the midterms. Still, even though prospects might seem bleak post-midterms, presidents can still employ *some* strategies to achieve a measure of success. For example, presidents are sometimes able to expand policies and protections on the basis of prior legislation. The Eisenhower administration was able to pass the Civil Rights Act of 1960, which provided a bit more federal power than the 1957 act to ensure protection of voting rights. Reagan was able to secure further housing and community development legislation and to gain passage of the Family Support Act of 1988, which made changes in a number of federal programs. For Clinton, his last two years in office saw expanded federal investment in after-school programs, expanded Medicaid coverage for women with breast and cervical cancer, and a bill requiring further disclosure of the names of campaign donors. In 2008, George W. Bush was able to successfully expand education benefits for recent veterans. In 2015, Obama secured changes in how physicians were reimbursed under Medicare and extensions in the Children's Health Insurance Program. These may not seem like much compared to first-term achievements, but they are advances nonetheless.

Passing new legislation is possible, but the legislation tends to be more limited in scope, and bipartisan and broad appeal is key. Reagan was able to secure anti-drug-abuse legislation and backed bipartisan legislation providing support for homeless shelters—who could be against these efforts if fiscally feasible? Clinton continued on his course of proposing and passing incremental legislation that would attract some Republican support, such as a banking reform bill, legislation that gave states greater flexibility in using federal education funds, and changes in how earnings affect Social Security benefits.

Adept bargaining and use of other presidential power tools, namely, executive action, during annual budget negotiations is another strategy lame duck presidents can and have used. In the last two years, presidents have less leverage than they did earlier in their presidencies, but they can still attempt to bargain with Congress, and they can certainly threaten to veto. This is a bit of a riskier prospect, because presidents do risk a government shutdown if a new annual budget (or a "continuing resolution" of the current one) is not passed. Through this political give-and-take, in his final budgets Clinton was able to secure funding for additional police officers and emergency school repairs as well as provisions allowing persons with disabilities to maintain federal health benefits (Medicare or Medicaid) when they entered the workforce. Bush, however, was less successful in dealing with the Democrat-controlled Congress in his last two years. His final months in office were funded by a continuing resolution to keep the federal government from shutting its doors rather than a formal budget agreement for fiscal year 2009 (the federal fiscal year starts on October 1). It is also worth noting that three out of the four congressional overrides of his vetoes occurred during the last year of his presidency.

Responding to crises presents yet another opportunity for end-of-term presidents to flex their muscles. Here, Bush stands out. As the Great Recession and the financial crises that produced it suddenly deepened in 2008, the Bush administration secured a number of pieces of legislation in response. These included a major federal bailout effort for financial institutions threatened with insolvency, a mortgage-relief program for homeowners facing foreclosure, and an economic stimulus package. By contrast, the Obama administration was stymied in its attempts to parlay the rash of school and other public mass shootings into stricter gun control legislation.

In short, the final two years in office are not great times for launching major initiatives. But presidents need not be complacent. They remain in office, and they still possess its powers. Treading carefully and strategically, they can move forward. It is more by inches and feet than the greater distances they might have achieved earlier in their tenure.

Turning to Foreign Policy

Presidents often sense that not much can be achieved in the domestic arena, so they look toward foreign policy as a realm of possible achievement. This makes sense because presidents have much greater domain over foreign affairs, and they do not require the same level of cooperation from Congress as they do with domestic policy. The practical results are mixed, however. Eisenhower embarked on a successful world tour in 1960, but that was also the year of US political estrangement with Cuba, a deteriorating situation in Laos, and continued difficulty in South Vietnam. Clinton made strides in dealing with Northern Ireland but little progress in dealing with the Palestinians and the Israelis. George W. Bush made the choice in favor of a further "surge" in troops in Iraq, which brought some stabilization, but then his administration ended.

As for Obama, significant military disengagement in Afghanistan occurred and diplomatic relations were reestablished with Cuba. However, the great efforts made in dealing with the Arab uprisings, the Syrian civil war, ISIS, Russia, and North Korea bore little success. Negotiations with Iran over its nuclear weapons capability proved productive, but details over the treaty were highly controversial. By the end of his presidency, Afghanistan remained politically and militarily destabilized, and ISIS controlled large swaths of Iraq, despite resumption of US airstrikes. In fact, the foreign and national security situation was more uncertain at the end of his presidency than at the start of it. All in all, exercises of presidential power in foreign policy are attractive to many presidents, but success stories are still just as, if not more, elusive as those in the domestic arena.

HUBRIS AND SCANDAL
PLAGUE SECOND-TERM PRESIDENTS

One final observation about second terms: presidents tend to overreach and claim mandates—and power—that are likely nonexistent, which is a key reason for why they pursue failed policy courses. As we discussed at the beginning of the chapter, reelected presidents read too much into the election results. Sabato notes that Bush and his staff "were deceived by the election returns. The President naturally reveled in his arduous triumph. . . . A euphoric chief executive spoke of 'capital earned' in the election, which he intended to spend on big goals such as Social Security and tax reform."[35] We now know what happened with Bush's Social Security reform. Had Bush perhaps "reality-tested" this proposal, rather than pursuing it blindly because he wanted to, he might have seen earlier on that the nation simply was not ready for change and he could have avoided expending resources where success was unlikely. Another example of presidents overreaching is FDR's "court-packing" plan during his second term, when he attempted to change the anti–New Deal composition of the Supreme Court by getting Congress to pass legislation allowing him to appoint a new member for each justice older than the age of seventy. It generated national controversy that could have been avoided: the aging of the Supreme Court was likely to produce vacancies. Indeed, it soon did. He should have let it play out naturally rather than forcing the issue because he (falsely) believed in the power reelection gave him.

Perhaps in part because of the hubris and inflated egos of reelected presidents and their top aides, scandals seem to arise largely in the second term, although their roots may have been planted earlier. Eisenhower faced problems with his highly valued chief of staff, Sherman Adams, the former governor of New Hampshire. Adams was accused of receiving a variety of gifts from a prominent New England businessman with matters before the federal government. Eisenhower was loath to let him resign, but because the facts came out eventually, Adams was forced to do so. Nixon, of course, had to deal with the Watergate scandal. The problem here was not so much the break-in at headquarters of the Democratic Party at the Watergate complex as it was the cover-up and obstruction of justice by the White House afterward. For Reagan, it was Iran-Contra. The whole affair could have brought down the Reagan presidency had there been credible evidence that Reagan knew about the diversion of funds from the sale of arms to Iran to the Nicaraguan Contras, which was illegal, at least according to some interpretations.

For Clinton, his affair with Monica Lewinsky cast a pall over his presidency from January 1998, when details first came to light, until the end of his second term. The issue was not his sexual activities with Lewinsky; they were both consenting adults. The legal issue was whether Clinton had lied under oath during a deposition in the lawsuit Paula Jones, a state of Arkansas employee, had filed in federal court alleging sexual harassment by him when he was governor of Arkansas. Clinton denied any sexual contact with Jones. Moreover, he also denied any subsequent affairs with other government employees, which brought into question his relationship with Monica Lewinsky. Once the Lewinsky affair was uncovered, the issue became whether Clinton had lied under oath and also attempted to obstruct justice in his cover-up of the affair. He was impeached by the House in December 1998 but then acquitted by the Senate at his "trial" in January and February 1999. It was not a good start to Clinton's last two years, even though he was not removed from office.

How to avoid scandal? Eisenhower, Nixon, Reagan, and Clinton all faced major ones during their second terms. Truman did as well toward the end of his presidency. FDR is an exception, but perhaps dealing with the Great Depression and World War II kept everyone too preoccupied for major mischief. George W. Bush and Obama had their troubles, but not ones that engulfed the very heart of the Oval Office; perhaps they were wise to the difficulties of presidents serving before them.[36] Continued presidential vigilance is needed. But perhaps more important are efforts to make sure the presidential team is on target and does not stray. Remaining humble is another matter. Even the ever-skilled and strategic FDR erred in this regard. Time spent in office may simply build a false sense of power and even of personal pretense. Self-reflection is one antidote. But more important is a sitting president's own sense and appreciation of his predecessors' history. Unfortunately, these lessons of history are often lost or forgotten.

CONCLUSION: IMPLICATIONS AND QUESTIONS

Just as for the first term, the internal rhythms of the second term can have an impact on presidential power. There are some similarities between the internal time of a first term and that of a second term, but there are differences as well. At the start of both terms, presidents face the same two problems, which ultimately have bearing on their exercise of power and achievement of policy goals: selecting personnel, and establishing a policy agenda.

In the initial transition to office before the first term, the task of selecting personnel is especially daunting because newly elected presidents are likely succeeding an outgoing president of the opposing party, so there is probably very little carryover in terms of staff. In addition, the Twentieth Amendment in 1933 moved Inauguration Day from March to January 20, thus shortening the time available for a newly elected president to take office. It would seem that reelected presidents have more breathing room: they already have an administration in place, and they don't need to replace a full staff; they can selectively make changes and make them over a longer period of time. The problem here, however, is that some mismanage the process and misunderstand the stakes involved. Nixon ostensibly gave notice that all might be replaced; unfortunately, this led to demoralization among his team, especially in departments and agencies. At the same time, he had no intention, at that point in time, of replacing his top White House staff. Change in the latter, however, might have been beneficial. Reagan was a passive observer of the job swap between Baker and Regan; the latter proved a flop as chief of staff. A more searching examination of staff and cabinet members might have benefited both George W. Bush and Barack Obama.

In terms of coming up with a workable and winnable policy agenda, presidents have a tougher time in their second term. Presidents' reelection strategy likely focuses on the opponent's weaknesses, and who can blame them? It wins reelection. Yes, policy issues and differences may be featured, but not enough for reelected presidents to claim a policy mandate going forward. This is not to say that presidents cannot make a pitch for major policy proposals, only that they face a tougher time getting legislation passed during the second term. Second-term presidents need to do more. One possible tool to enhance the probability of success is to plant seeds and start growing major second-term initiatives during the latter part of the first term. This approach helped Eisenhower on civil rights in 1957, Reagan on his 1986 tax-reform proposal, and Clinton on his 1997 budget package.

Also, related to this theme, is factoring in the reality of the second term, the difficulty of creating and sustaining "actual" as opposed to "claimed" political capital, and the appropriate prioritization of a second-term agenda. Particularly notable here is George W. Bush's later realization that it might have been wiser to move first with immigration reform, which had larger bipartisan support, than with changes in Social Security. Success on the first, had it occurred, might have built support for the more difficult latter; this is something Bush himself acknowledges. Future presidents might draw important lessons from this.

These initial choices at the start of a second term are crucial because the president's power only becomes more constrained in the lead-up to and after the midterms. The "sixth-year itch" is likely to lead to further loss in congressional seats. Here, only Clinton has some marginal gains to brag about. Even FDR's party lost seats in 1938. In addition, the loss of staff, particularly experienced hands, comes in the seventh year and means even more destabilization. As examination of both the *Congressional Quarterly* support scores and Mayhew's analysis of major policy proposals indicates, legislative success in the last two years in office is likely to be slim, though not impossible to achieve. Likely, it is more incremental. Presidents can build upon prior legislation, especially when it comes up for reauthorization, take advantage of the opportunities in annual budget negotiations, strategically and adeptly use the powers of bargaining and executive action to achieve policy ends, and recognize that crises can present major opportunities for policy advancement. Presidents can also turn to foreign policy as a place to exert power and achieve their goals.

There is no sugarcoating the fact that presidents face greater difficulties exercising power in their second term than they did in their first term. Whereas, in many ways, the challenges presidents face in the second term are similar to those of the first, their resources of power are weaker overall. They do have opportunities, albeit limited ones, to exercise influence in the second term, especially in the first two years. Presidents must set themselves up to capitalize on these openings. At the start of the second term, presidents must be vigilant in deciding who will be retained on their staff and in making new appointments. Politically, times are more difficult, and the risk of scandal is greater during the last four years, so presidents need competent and experienced advisers to assist in navigating these tricky waters. In addition, second termers must be even more strategic in crafting their policy agenda than they were at the start of their presidency. What is politically feasible becomes more important than what is most desirable.

NOTES

1. Michael B. Grossman, Martha Joynt Kumar, and Francis E. Rourke, "Second Term Presidencies: The Aging of Administrations," in *Presidency and the Political System,* ed. Michael Nelson (Washington, DC: CQ Press, 1990), 213–232.

2. James D. King and James W. Riddlesperger Jr., "Getting Started in the White House: Variations in Modern Presidential Transitions," *White House Studies* 3, no. 2 (Spring 2003): 115–131.

3. John C. Fortier and Norman J. Ornstein, "Introduction," in *Second Term Blues: How George W. Bush Has Governed,* ed. John C. Fortier and Norman J. Ornstein (Washington, DC: Brookings/AEI, 2007), 1–15.

4. See the Reagan campaign ads on this website: http://www.livingroomcandidate.org /commercials/1984.

5. See the Bush campaign ads on this website: http://www.livingroomcandidate.org /commercials/2004.

6. Devin Dwyer, "Obama Ad Attacks Romney Bain Capital Record," ABC News, May 14, 2012, http://abcnews.go.com/blogs/politics/2012/05/obama-ad-attacks-romney-bain-capital -record/; Tim Hanrahan, "Obama, Romney Attack Ads Top Charts," Washington Wire (blog), *Wall Street Journal,* July 23, 2012, http://blogs.wsj.com/washwire/2012/07/23/obama-wins -attack-ad-battle-online/. See the Obama campaign ads on this website: http://www.livingroom candidate.org/commercials/2012.

7. Thomas DeFrank, "Obama Campaign Attack Ads Appeared Effective in Defeating Mitt Romney," *New York Daily News,* November 7, 2012, http://www.nydailynews.com/news /election-2012/obama-campaign-attack-ads-appeared-effective-article-1.1198517.

8. Sherman Adams, *Firsthand Report: The Story of the Eisenhower Administration* (New Yorker: Harper, 1961), 225.

9. Richard Nixon, *RN: The Memoirs of Richard Nixon,* vol. 2 (New York: Warner Books, 1979), 285.

10. Shirley Anne Warshaw, "Choices for the President: Structuring the Second Term Cabinet of President George W. Bush," in *The Second Term of George W. Bush: Prospects and Perils,* ed. Robert Maranto, Douglas Brattelbo, and Tom Lansford (New York: Palgrave Macmillan, 2006), 77.

11. "Remarks on Plans for the Second Term, November 27, 1972," in *Public Papers of the Presidents of the United States: Richard Nixon* (Washington, DC: US Government Printing Office, 1974), 1151.

12. Nixon, *RN,* 284.

13. H. R. Haldeman, "January 3, 1973," in *The Haldeman Diaries: Inside the Nixon White House* (New York: G. P. Putnam's Sons, 1994), 561–562.

14. John Ehrlichman, *Witness to Power: The Nixon Years* (New York: Simon & Schuster, 1982), 204. White House records indicate that Nixon met with Senate Majority Leader Mike Mansfield (D-MT) on January 2 for a 44-minute meeting, and then the next morning met with Speaker of the House Carl Albert (D-OK) for a meeting that lasted 65 minutes. The topic of both was listed as "discuss the 93rd Congress." On January 5, there was a bipartisan

breakfast meeting with congressional leaders and select committee chairs. That evening there was a reception for newly elected members of Congress and congressional leaders.

15. Ronald Reagan, *The Reagan Diaries,* ed. Douglas Brinkley (New York: HarperCollins, 2007), 292.

16. Regan quickly moved to put some of his subordinates in place in key White House positions. On January 30, the White House announced the appointment of Alfred Kingon as cabinet secretary and deputy assistant to the president. Kingon had been assistant secretary of the treasury for policy planning and communications since March 1984. Prior to that, he served as assistant secretary of commerce for international economic policy. Christopher Hicks was tapped as deputy assistant to the president for administration; Hicks had been executive assistant to the secretary of the treasury and executive secretary for the Treasury Department. Thomas C. Dawson was named as executive assistant to the chief of staff and deputy assistant to the president; Dawson had been assistant secretary of the treasury for business and consumer affairs. David L. Chew was appointed staff secretary and deputy assistant to the president; Chew had been senior deputy comptroller of the currency for policy and planning. They came to be known as Regan's "mice" by many of the continuing Reagan staffers.

17. Bill Clinton, *My Life* (New York: Alfred A. Knopf, 2004), 742–743.

18. "The President's News Conference of November 4, 2004," *Public Papers of the Presidents of the United States: George W. Bush, Book III—October 1 to December 31, 2004* (Washington, DC: US Government Printing Office, 2007), 2943.

19. Gary C. Jacobson, *A Divider, Not a Uniter: George W. Bush and the American People* (New York: Pearson Longman, 2007), 203.

20. Ibid., 202.

21. Ibid., 205–206. Support for further tax reform was only slightly higher at 38 percent.

22. George W. Bush, *Decision Points* (New York: Crown, 2010), 300, 306.

23. For further analysis of Bush's errors during the Katrina disaster, see James P. Pfiffner, "The First MBA President: George W. Bush as Public Administrator," *Public Administration Review* 67, no. 1 (January 2007): 15–17. According to Pfiffner, Bush's "public image as a competent, MBA-type manager of the executive branch probably suffered most from the disaster" (15).

24. "Presidential Approval Ratings—Barack Obama," Gallup Poll, http://www.gallup.com /poll/116479/barack-obama-presidential-job-approval.aspx.

25. See, for example, Grossman, Kumar, and Rourke, "Second Term Presidencies," and Larry Sabato, "Historical Imperative," in *The Sixth Year Itch: The Rise and Fall of the George W. Bush Presidency,* ed. Larry Sabato (New York: Pearson/Longman, 2008), 1–46.

26. Al Kamen and Colby Itkowitz, "Meet the Presidents who would like to be president," *Washington Post,* January 14, 2015, https://www.washingtonpost.com/politics/meet-the -presidents-who-would-like-to-be-president/2015/01/14/2bc17ba2-9c31-11e4-a7ee-526210 d665b4_story.html.

27. David Mayhew, *Divided We Govern: Party Control, Lawmaking, and Investigations, 1946–1990,* 1st ed. (New Haven, CT: Yale University Press, 1991), 118–119. Note that Reagan stands out as the anomaly in Mayhew's data, although Mayhew does not make reference to it: 9 major bills in 1981–1982, 7 in 1983–1984, 8 in 1985–1986, and 9 in 1987–1988. Of the four major laws passed on a veto override, three were in his final two years in office.

28. David Mayhew, *Divided We Govern: Party Control, Lawmaking, and Investigations, 1946–2002,* 2nd ed. (New Haven, CT: Yale University Press, 2005). All of his data from 1991 through 2012 can be found on his personal website: http://campuspress.yale.edu/davidmayhew/files/2014/01/datasets-laws-1991-2012-arnold.pdf.

29. I exclude veto overrides, which Mayhew includes, so the number is slightly reduced from Mayhew's count. For Clinton, there were 12 major bills passed in his first two years (1993–1994), 14 passed in the next two years (1995–1996), 9 passed in the first two years of his second term (1997–1998), and 6 in his last two years in office (1999–2000). Also note the difference between the first term—26 major bills—and the second term—15 bills.

30. For Bush, the results are 16 major bills in 2001–2002, 10 in 2003–2004, 14 in 2005–2006, and 12 plus one major veto override in 2007–2008. The 52 total bills throughout his presidency are evenly split 26–26 between his first and second terms.

31. Mayhew, *Divided We Govern,* 2nd ed., 74.

32. Data from Eisenhower through the first year of the Bush presidency come from Mayhew, *Divided We Govern,* 2nd ed., 52–73, 208–213; data for the remainder of the Bush presidency come from Mayhew's personal website, http://campuspress.yale.edu/davidmayhew/files/2014/01/datasets-laws-1991-2012-arnold.pdf.

33. According to *CQ Weekly,* a major issue of the year is "judged by the extent to which it represents: a matter of major controversy; a matter of presidential or political power; a matter of potentially great impact on the nation and lives of Americans." In addition, if there are "related votes on an issue, one key vote is usually chosen—one that, in the opinion of CQ editors, was most important in determining the outcome" (Lori Nitschke, "Key Votes: Members Made the Deals, but Scandal Made the News," *CQ Weekly,* December 19, 1998, 33–43).

34. The "score" reflects roll-call votes and thus does not include legislation that may have passed on voice vote. The score does not measure presidential agenda items that failed to make it to floor vote (not an unsubstantial problem; e.g., the Clinton 1993 healthcare reform package). It does not distinguish between initiatives that are presidential versus those that are congressional in origin but that have elicited White House support at some point; as well, votes include legislation on which the administration may have taken a *negative* stand. It does not measure the degree of compromise and change that might have occurred through the legislative process even if the initial proposal was presidential in origin (e.g., Carter's energy conservation bill). Most problematic: each vote is weighted equally; major agenda items (e.g., Reagan's 1981 tax-cut legislation; G. W. Bush's in 2001) count the same as other legislation. Finally, the ultimate number is based on the sum of House and Senate roll calls that is deemed important for each chamber, not roll calls that eventuated in final passage or defeat of legislation.

35. Sabato, "Historical Imperative," 1–46.

36. Obama had to deal in his second term with lengthy investigations of delays in treatment, sometimes resulting in deaths, at hospitals for military veterans. For Bush, the scandals came earlier, especially with the treatment of military detainees and other prisoners in the war on terror and during the war in Iraq.

Conclusion

Lessons for Presidential Power, Today and Beyond

Perhaps the clearest and most important point that emerges from the preceding chapters is that there are, indeed, dilemmas of presidential power, stemming from the way our Constitution structures power and from the historical, political, and internal forces with which presidents must contend. It is also clear that those dilemmas have only gotten more complex over time. Expectations upon the president have decidedly increased. The nation now expects a president to ably fill a number of roles—not only to provide policy solutions for a variety of problems, domestic, economic, and international, but also to fulfill a broader yearning for effective leadership. Presidents now need to accomplish a mind-boggling number of tasks to be considered a successful leader, including prepare for a transition to assume office, assemble an achievable policy agenda that encompasses what the public needs and wants in the present and even in the future, see to its legislative adoption, persuasively communicate their goals to the public, effectively manage crises both foreign and domestic, and be a strong moral and compassionate presence for the country and the world. And this, by the way, is an incomplete list.

The ability of modern presidents to take measure of, and to fulfill, the ever-growing demands of the office has lagged. Neustadt clearly recognized this decades ago, when he first conceived of bargaining as a way for presidents to exercise power, as have other scholars, many of whose analyses and arguments we have explored in this book. As we advance further into the twenty-first century, the dilemmas and exercise of presidential power have become even more complex. A new, comprehensive theory of presidential power may be elusive and perhaps even impossible to spell out, but we can begin to map out the terrain a bit. What is clear is that presidents must utilize all the tools and strategies of exercising influence available to them, all of which we discussed in this book. What lessons have we learned about these tools and strategies, and how might they inform future presidents who must maneuver through the dilemmas of presidential power?

LESSON ONE: NAVIGATING THE FRAMERS' PERSPECTIVE TODAY

The demands upon presidential leadership have grown tremendously. The Framers of the Constitution surely made a very bold move in creating a presidency that, at the time, invested significant executive power in a single person. However, they also feared returning to some type of unlimited monarchy and the problems posed by excessive executive power, a fear that can be seen throughout Madison's notes of the Constitutional Convention of 1787. The question was how to achieve a middle ground: the establishment of a reasonably strong executive, but one whose powers might be constrained or otherwise checked. Madison's solution was a system of shared powers: each branch possessed some degree of participation in the exercise of the powers of the others. It seemed a neat solution at the time. However, would it pass the test of political change and development? Would it stand the test of time?

The answer to these questions forms the central dilemma of presidential power that presidents face today and into the future. The modern presidency has called not for constraint upon the president but for more executive empowerment, and the federal government and president's policy responsibilities have rightfully expanded. Taking that into consideration, the Framers' system begins to unravel a bit. However, they could not anticipate the shifts that were to occur: ever-increasing governmental authority, activity, policy expectations, and results, especially at the federal level. Nor could they have anticipated how presidents, not just Congress, would come to play a major role in setting and then politically advancing this agenda.

The expansion of the powers of the federal government began, albeit slowly, during the nineteenth century. Jefferson's role in the Louisiana Purchase and his military efforts to deal with the Barbary pirates off the coast of North Africa, Andrew Jackson's battle over a national bank, James K. Polk's efforts to expand the nation further westward that led to the Mexican-American War, and Lincoln's Emancipation Proclamation are important examples. The dawn of the twentieth century saw further developments in the growth of presidential power. Presidents Theodore Roosevelt and Woodrow Wilson, despite their party differences, both advanced agendas that sought more robust federal action, and each achieved a measure of it. Roosevelt embraced an expansive view of a president's constitutional powers that likely would have left the Framers worried, if not appalled. Starting with FDR's New Deal in the 1930s through Lyndon B. Johnson's Great Society in the 1960s and up to the present, the expansion in governmental programs has been enormous and clearly beyond anything the Framers might have thought appropriate for government to do back in 1787. In the twenty-first century, and particularly post-9/11, the power of government at the federal level has grown even further.

Still, the Framers were right—Madison, in particular—that executive power needs to be checked. With today's expanded presidential purview, how can presidential power be appropriately controlled and constrained? What are the proper bounds for the exercise of presidential power? We are still in a representative democracy after all, not one designed for executive dictate, a subservient legislative branch, and a passive public. The dilemma for contemporary and future presidents is that they must still operate within the constitutional framework crafted back in 1787, albeit one that maintains some flexibility for interpretation and contestation. Their challenge is how to be allegiant to it while still exercising legitimate presidential power. Presidents pushing for power, by the way, would not be foreign to the Framers. As Madison famously noted in *Federalist No. 51,* the way to ensure a balance between executive and congressional powers and to protect individual rights is to pit ambition against ambition. This is a path that contemporary and future presidents still need to pursue. As members of the public, we will likely find all of this frustrating. Especially in periods of divided government, depending on which branch aligns with our political views, we might think: Why doesn't the president get to prevail? Or, why doesn't Congress have a greater say in things? The answer, of course, is that that is how our constitutional democracy works, for better or for worse. It is a system of checks and balances not wholesale dominance of one branch over the other. For presidents, the task is to figure out how to tip the balance a little their way without damaging this broader constitutional framework.

LESSON TWO: RELYING ON
CONSTITUTIONAL POWER IS NOT ENOUGH

In looking at how the executive branch's responsibilities have expanded in the nineteenth and twentieth centuries, it is obvious that presidents' reliance on power as *strictly* defined by the Constitution is insufficient. Such a narrow reading would create a gulf between what we expect of our presidents and their abilities to successfully meet those expectations—creating, as Neustadt well pointed out, fundamentally weak presidencies.

Neustadt's response, as we saw in Chapter 2, was to pull together a mid-twentieth-century theory for exercising power. He posits that presidents need to bargain and persuade to achieve their presidential ends. Yet, Neustadt's formulation may be too restrictive and time bound. There are other arrows in the presidential quiver. One example we explored is Eisenhower's hidden-hand presidency. Here, more indirect means might also secure presidential ends. Although its more oblique methods may not be applicable to all presidents or in all situations, it or some variation remains an alternative to Neustadt's emphasis on direct bargaining as the primary power resource for presidents.

Still, bargaining and influence continue to be important parts of the power equation, and Neustadt's crucial insight on the need to recognize power stakes is one that all presidents, present and future, must consider and deal with. Legislation is still fundamentally grounded in the negotiation back and forth between the White House and Capitol Hill. Presidents surely have added tools to aid them such as going public and strategic assessment of their place in the historical and internal time of a presidency, as we have explored. However, successful bargaining remains a foundation of presidential power, so presidents must continue to be adept in its exercise.

Yet bargaining has become a more difficult foundation upon which to build for legislative success. Members of Congress have become increasingly polarized along ideological lines, and the crucial middle—those most amenable to a reasonable bargain—has lessened in numbers. Speaker of the House John Boehner's (R-OH) resignation in October 2015 is real testimony to how congressional leaders can become frustrated and disillusioned with the demands of their more extreme fellow partisans. His exit also made an already rough relationship between House Republicans and the Obama administration even more difficult. Boehner was a tough negotiator, but he was willing to compromise and make deals if an acceptable deal could be made. That Boehner's resignation occurred toward the end of his presidency was problematic for Obama, because bargaining power becomes weaker as the end of a presidency approaches. This suggests that presidents must recognize and be prepared to use a variety of strategies and resources to exercise power.

LESSON THREE: INHERENT POWERS GIVE PRESIDENTS GREATER REACH

Simply relying on the words and expressly stated powers of the Constitution may not be enough for a president, but the Constitution still remains relevant as a resource in the exercise of presidential power. As we saw in Chapter 3, presidents can benefit from the interpretation of presidential powers that might be implied or assumed to exist within it. This impact of the document especially comes to the fore in times of great crisis: the Civil War, the Great Depression, and the aftermath of September 11. Since September 11, there has been an expansion of the exercise of presidential power through inherent powers of the presidency, such as through executive orders and other unilateral actions. However, the use of such resources has been contested domain—and will likely continue to be. In some cases, the Supreme Court has even stepped in and provided constitutional guidance on the use of inherent powers: it has allowed presidents claims to such powers, but on other occasions it has restricted their use.

One of the most striking recent developments is how the Obama presidency's view was not all that far from George W. Bush's understanding of the great reach of the office's inherent powers. Although Obama pledged to be a different kind of president from Bush, the reality is that he soon largely adhered to his predecessor's broad and expansive constitutional understanding of presidential power. Following legislative failure, the Obama administration turned to executive actions to attain domestic policy goals. This pattern of presidential action, by the way, is likely to continue for Bush's and Obama's successors. Ideological polarization in Congress not only makes bargaining more difficult to achieve but also encourages presidents to turn inward toward their own powers to secure desired outcomes. Divided government further fuels a reliance on executive actions.

But executive actions do not necessarily endure; they can end with a mere stroke of a pen by a presidential successor. There is also the risk that they can backfire. Recall Clinton's initial hope to end discrimination against gays in the military by executive order and the opposition that then forced him into accepting the "Don't Ask, Don't Tell" policy. It was a painful defeat. Congress can always counter any presidential order with legislation that imposes alternative policies if there are enough votes to override a presidential veto. And let us not forget that the Supreme Court can step in as well. Asserting executive power can be an attractive option, but it is not a trump card that presidents can always play to their advantage. Presidents need to be just as strategic in relying upon executive actions as they must be in using other instruments of presidential power and influence.

LESSON FOUR: GOING PUBLIC IS NECESSARY BUT INCREASINGLY CHALLENGING

Both Teddy Roosevelt and Woodrow Wilson are informative in moving our thinking forward about how presidents might exercise power. Not only did both have expansive views of the presidency and a robust presidential agenda but also they began to utilize strategies for attaining political and policy goals that did not rely on just bargaining and legislative persuasion. Both presidents appealed to the public and used that support to pressure Congress into doing what they wanted. My view is that this would have left the Framers aghast. Washington's gentlemanly tour of the states might have been one thing. Rallying public support to put pressure on Congress is quite another.

Today, "going public" is commonplace; indeed, the public expects it to occur. As Kernell rightly observes, the "institutionalized pluralism" of bargaining and persuasion has been augmented by the "individualized pluralism" of appealing for public support. For Kernell, this has opened an entirely new vista of presidential power. Public support is not just some ancillary factor that bolsters the ability to strike a bargain, as Neustadt would have it. Rather, it is a direct resource of power in its own right. In theory, a mobilized public can pressure Congress to do the president's bidding. Reagan used this resource of power to great positive effect, especially in the early years of his presidency.

However, the proliferation of media and other information sources since the 1990s has complicated the process of appealing to the public. Presidents no longer command the airwaves. Key events such as the State of the Union addresses and other important presidential speeches at times of national crises might still be broadcast on the television networks, but smaller and smaller audiences are tuning in to these, with many preferring to watch clips later or to watch or read a political reporter's take on the speech. Some simply tune out.

Even when people do pay attention, modern media sources, such as cable news and Internet news, are more politically polarizing in their coverage: MSNBC versus Fox News, or ThinkProgress and Daily Kos versus RedState and Breitbart, for example. Furthermore, information compartmentalization occurs. The public has a tendency to pay attention to news sources—whether from the old or new media—that reinforce their existing views. Both polarization and compartmentalization make it more difficult for presidents to directly reach a broad audience—they are likely reaching only the audiences that already agree with them. The recent advent of social media does further expand the avenues of communication presidents can use to get their message across, but social media also presents new challenges in going public, as we saw in Chapter 4. And given the media's evolution from the 1980s to the present, further change will undoubtedly occur. The challenge of exercising presidential power through public communication will likely become even more complex in the future.

Still, challenging or not, presidents need to engage in extensive public communication. The public now assumes that presidents will be skilled communicators and effectively "go public" as circumstances demand. There is no dialing back to an earlier era. One way of mitigating the limitations and challenges of going public is to meld the tools of bargaining and persuasion with public appeal and support. Reagan is a good example. His early efforts to rally the public to his tax-cut and other proposals were an inspirational source, prompting Kernell to write the first edition of *Going Public*. Reagan, however, did not rely on just public appeals; he and his White House team also engaged in bargaining and persuasion. Although Reagan's particular effort at combining a very strong dose of going public with bargaining may be a bit outdated, a similar method of blending the various tools of presidential power, depending on the specific situation, can help future presidents exercise influence and achieve their goals.

Some scholars have warned of the dangers of a presidency too strongly grounded in public appeals. Too heavy a reliance on popular appeal may move the nation beyond the framework of representative government set out in the Constitution. Taken to extremes, it may upset the delicate arrangement of checks and balances among the branches of government. In addition, too much reliance on going public may actually weaken a presidency if there is no positive public response. Given the ever-changing and increasingly fragmented nature of the media, presidents cannot assume that their appeals will reach *both* an attentive *and* supportive public. As with all of the strategies for exercising influence that we have discussed, presidents need to factor in both the positive and negative consequences that might result.

LESSON FIVE: HISTORICAL TIME
AFFECTS OUR VIEW OF PRESIDENTIAL POWER

Changes in the media are not the only way history might influence the exercise of presidential power. The various patterns and cycles in historical time and a president's place within them affect not only a president's opportunities and strategies for exercising power but also our perception of a president's successes and failures. As we saw in Chapter 5, we can take a variety of approaches to determine how history factors in to the presidential power equation: Skowronek's theory of political time and regime cycles and Hargrove and Nelson's theory of policy cycles are the most grounded and promising; the theories based on swings in ideology and changes in public mood, less so. Historical context can aid presidential scholars and historians in assessing presidential performance, but how can sitting presidents determine their place in historical time? Further complicating the issue, presidents can occupy different points in a cycle, depending on the historical construct used. Recall that Jimmy Carter is categorized as a disjunctive president, a "regime ender," in Skowronek's theory. Yet he changed policy discourse and introduced new policy ideas, and Hargrove and Nelson put him at the start of their policy cycle, classifying him as a preparation president.

For past presidents the task of determining their point in history and its implications was difficult enough. Moving forward, history's bearing on a president's vision for the time in office becomes much more problematic. As Skowronek notes, the nation may be entering a postregime period, an era in which partisan ties are weaker and have less relevance. As a result, presidents are more politically alone, which could make it even harder to marshal support for a legislative agenda. In addition, cycles of policy ideas are increasingly constrained by budgetary limits and opposition as a result of a more polarized Congress. Finally, domestic issues are increasingly overshadowed by changing international forces. Although the Cold War was surely a weighty factor from Truman's presidency to Reagan's time in office, the country now faces greater foreign policy challenges with the proliferation of nonstate rogue actors and global terrorism.

This globalization of politics has meant that the historical patterns of presidential power are less predictable. During the Cold War, Truman, Eisenhower, Kennedy, Johnson, and Nixon faced a somewhat predictable and rational actor in the Soviet Union; contemporary and future presidents face quite different foes.

However imperfect or incomplete, each of the theories of historical time give us some insight on how political and historical context can affect a president's opportunities for, and challenges in, exercising power. A president's place in history does matter, and it has bearing on how the chief executive exercises power, what resources the president might draw upon to do so, and what ends the administration might reasonably and strategically pursue and achieve.

LESSON SIX: PLAN WELL FOR THE INTERNAL TIME OF A PRESIDENCY

Broader historical time is not the only frame of reference with bearing on presidential power. The internal time of a presidency also matters: each stage of a presidency has its own dynamics, and these very much affect a president's ability to exercise power and influence. The dynamics of a first term and of a second term are different, though both terms have key periods—election or reelection, midterms, and post-midterms—with specific opportunities and challenges in the exercise of presidential power. Although electoral mandates rarely exist, presidents can take steps to maximize their success at each stage.

Planning for a successful presidency must begin early, even before Election Day. Most important is ensuring a successful transition to office, the first step of which is to set an administration in place as soon as possible. The president should settle on key personnel such as White House chief of staff, a national security adviser, and a director of White House personnel operations early. Their quick selection directly influences getting the rest of the large White House staff in place, and hopefully at their desks right after Inauguration Day. Presidents are challenged in how to organize and manage these resources. Although they have a degree of freedom in choosing their staff because many of these positions are not subject to Senate confirmation, they are often ill-prepared for the task. Staff members brought in from a new president's previous position are usually loyal and "true believers," but often they lack Washington knowledge and "inside the Beltway" street smarts. On the other hand, those steeped in Washington experience may lack a deep commitment to the presidential agenda. Another challenge, particularly for second-term presidents, is the development of a "White House bubble" that promotes detachment from challenge, change, honest advice, and "reality testing." The bubble mentality can be particularly damaging in a president's relations with Congress.

Outreach to the Washington community is a must. The president-elect must be redefined not as a candidate but as the president. Equally important is to have a finely tuned, limited, and strategically planned political agenda in place: a myriad of campaign proposals must be whittled to a lean and strategic agenda, one that is best positioned to achieve congressional assent. Over a possible eight years in office, the first two years are the president's most opportune time for legislative success. Note that an effective transition to office is crucial for the administration to hit the ground running and take advantage of this relatively narrow window of opportunity.

As we saw in Chapters 6 and 7, for most presidents, the first midterm is likely to bring bad news, and presidents typically see their party support in Congress wane and attention shift to reelection in the last two years of their first term. Although reelection rarely brings a popular mandate, it does offer the reelected president the chance to reevaluate and shake things up. Yet, the track record of presidents taking advantage of this opportunity is not great. Opportunities for replacing personnel clearly occur, yet they are often missed or squandered. Hubris sometimes clouds assessments of presidential opportunity, leading presidents to overreach in agenda choices. History and conventional wisdom suggest that presidential opportunity and presidential power decline in the second term. Yet presidents can influence the degree of decline and its trajectory by planting seeds for their second term at the end of the first term and by making their second-term agenda a part of their reelection campaign.

The final two years of a presidency are especially problematic. Very few presidential initiatives are likely to achieve fruition. Among recent presidents, none have achieved significant success on major new domestic initiatives. Presidents often turn to their foreign policy objectives as they look to secure and bolster their legacies, but even this area tends to be more of a miss than a hit, especially in today's complex global political situations. But still, some hope exists. Presidents can achieve progress by building upon incremental change to past initiatives, by skillfully using the annual budget bills to fund presidential initiatives, by leveraging crises to presidential advantage, and by using executive action adeptly but appropriately to attain policy ends. Past presidencies have included bits and pieces of these strategies, but no one presidency has made a complete and effective effort. Future presidents must clearly understand the difficulties, opportunities, and historical records of their predecessors. Most importantly, they must ask themselves: What did they do, and how can I do better?

A FINAL NOTE

All of these challenges and lessons suggest that the exercise of presidential power is demanding and complex because the nation continually wants presidents to do more and because presidents must increasingly rely on multiple strategies for exercising power. The Framers sought to create a more powerful chief executive. Yet they were mindful—perhaps at times *too* mindful—of seeking ways to constrain governmental power, and presidential power, in light of their own historical experience. Since the Framers created the Constitution, the political and historical context has clearly changed and continues to change. Consider just the shifts in our politics since September 11, 2001. But our presidency still operates within the bounds of the Constitution, so the central dilemma for contemporary presidents remains one that has been present since 1787: How should presidents exert power to achieve their legislative agendas within the limits of our system of shared powers? Finally, much like the Framers, we cannot know what the future holds, but we do know that because of our changing nation and world, new and still unknown challenges and lessons of presidential power lie ahead.

Index

CPSIA information can be obtained
at www.ICGtesting.com
Printed in the USA
LVOW04s1122230216

476342LV00002B/2/P